LIFE IN A
MEDIEVAL
VILLAGE

LIFE IN A MEDIEVAL VILLAGE

Frances and Joseph Gies

1817

HARPER & ROW, PUBLISHERS, New York
Grand Rapids, Philadelphia, St. Louis, San Francisco
London, Singapore, Sydney, Tokyo, Toronto

FIRST EDITION

Designed by Karen Savary

Library of Congress Cataloging-in-Publication Data

Gies, Frances.
  Life in a medieval village/Frances and Joseph Gies.—1st ed.
    p. cm.
  Bibliography: p.
  Includes index.
  ISBN 0-06-016215-5
  1. Elton (Cambridgeshire, England)—Social conditions. 2. Elton
(Cambridgeshire, England)—Rural conditions. 3. Peasantry—England—
Elton (Cambridgeshire)—History. 4. England—Social life and
customs—Medieval period, 1066–1485. I. Gies, Joseph. II. Title.
HN398.E45G54   1989
306′.09426′5—dc20   89-33759

90 91 92 93 94 CC/MPC 10 9 8 7 6 5 4 3 2 1

To Dorothy, Nathan, and Rosie

CONTENTS

ACKNOWLEDGMENTS

This book was researched at the Harlan Hatcher Graduate Library of the University of Michigan.

The authors gratefully acknowledge the assistance of Professor J. A. Raftis of the Pontifical Institute of Mediaeval Studies in Toronto, who read the manuscript and made valuable suggestions. We also wish to express thanks to Mr. Alan Clark of Elton and to Miss Kate Chantry of the Cambridgeshire Public Record Office in Huntingdon.

PROLOGUE: ELTON

I N THE DISTRICT OF HUNTINGDON THERE IS A CER-
tain village to which far-distant antiquity gave the name of
Aethelintone," wrote the twelfth-century monk who chronicled
the history of Ramsey Abbey, "on a most beautiful site, provided with a course of waters, in a pleasant plain of meadows
with abundant grazing for cattle, and rich in fertile fields."[1]

The village that the Anglo-Saxons called Aethelintone (or
Aethelington, or Adelintune), known in the thirteenth century,
with further spelling variations, as Aylington, and today as
Elton, was one of the thousands of peasant communities scattered over the face of Europe and the British Isles in the high
Middle Ages, sheltering more than 90 percent of the total population, the ancestors of most Europeans and North Americans
alive today.

Many of these peasant settlements were mere hamlets or scattered homesteads, but in certain large areas of England and
Continental Europe people lived in true villages, where they
practiced a distinctive system of agriculture. Because England
has preserved the earliest and most complete documentation of
the medieval village, in the form of surveys, accounts, and the

*The River Nene at Elton.**

rolls of manorial courts, this book will focus on an English village.

Medieval villages varied in population, area, configuration, and social and economic details. But Elton, a dependency of wealthy Ramsey Abbey, located in the East Midlands, in the region of England where villages abounded and the "open field" agriculture associated with them flourished, illustrates many of the characteristics common to villages at the high point of their development.

Elton stands today, a village of about six hundred people, in northwest Cambridgeshire,† seventy miles north of London, where it has stood for more than a thousand years. Its present-day gray stone houses cluster along two axes: one the main road from Peterborough to the old market town of Oundle; the other, at right angles to it, a street that ends in a triangular village green, beyond which stands an eighteenth-century mill

---

*Photographs are the authors' unless otherwise credited.
†Formerly Huntingdonshire, until the redrawing of county lines in 1974.

on the banks of the River Nene. Smaller streets and lanes inter-
sect these two thoroughfares. The two sections have long been
known as Overend and Nether End. Nether End contains the
green, with a Methodist chapel adjoining. Near the river here
the construction of a floodbank in 1977 uncovered the foundations of the medieval manor house. Overend centers around the
church, with its school and rectory nearby. At the southern
limit of Overend stands the village's tourist attraction, Elton
Hall, a stately home whose gatehouse and chapel alone date as
far back as the fifteenth century, the rest from much later.

Two pubs, a post office/general store, and a garage comprise
Elton's business center. Buses and cars speed along the Peter-
borough-Oundle road. Some of the cottages, nestling in their
neat gardens, are picturesquely thatched. Off beyond the streets,
sheep graze in the meadows. Yet Elton, like many other English
villages, is no longer a farming community. Most of its inhabitants work in nearby Peterborough, or commute to London.
The family that owns Elton Hall operates an agricultural enterprise, and one independent farmer lives in the village; two have
farms outside, in the parish. A few descendants of farm laborers
live in subsidized housing on a Council estate.

Except perhaps for the sheep, almost nothing medieval survives in twentieth-century Elton. In the northwest corner of the
churchyard, inconspicuous in the shadow of the great square
tower, stand the oldest identifiable objects in Elton, a pair of
Anglo-Saxon crosses found during a nineteenth-century restora-
tion of the church.* The present building is mainly the product
of the fourteenth and fifteenth centuries; only the stones of the
chancel arch date from the thirteenth.

The oldest house surviving in Elton today was built in 1690.
Medieval Elton, its houses, yards, sheds, and gardens, the
smithy, the community ovens, the cultivated fields, even the
meadows, marsh, and woods have vanished. Not only were
medieval villages constantly rebuilt, but as forms of agriculture
changed and new kinds of landholding were adopted, the very

*One expert dates them later, c. 1100.

fields and meadows were transformed. We know how villages like Elton looked in the Middle Ages not so much from modern survivals as from the recent investigation of England's extraordinary archeological trove of deserted villages, victims of dwindling population, agricultural depression, and the historic enclosure movement that turned them from busy crop-raising communities to nearly empty sheep pastures. More than two thousand such sites have been identified. Their investigation, based on a technique introduced into England during World War II by German refugee Gerhard Bersu, was pioneered in the 1950s by archeologist John Hurst and historian Maurice Beresford in the now famous Yorkshire deserted village of Wharram Percy. Excavation and aerial photography have since recovered

Two crosses in the churchyard, dating from the eleventh century or the beginning of the twelfth, are the oldest monuments in Elton.

The deserted village of Wharram Percy. Only the ruins of St. Martin's church still rise above ground, but street plan and layout of houses have been recovered.

the medieval shape of many villages, the sites of their houses and enclosures, and the disposition of fields, streets, paths, and embankments.[2]

The deserted villages, however, left few written records. These are rich, on the other hand, for many of the surviving villages. They document not merely details of the houses and holdings, but the names of the villagers themselves, their work arrangements, and their diet, recreation, quarrels, and transgressions. Much can be learned from the records of the Ramsey Abbey villages, of which Elton was one, and those of contemporary estates, lay as well as ecclesiastical. The documents are often tantalizing, sometimes frustrating, but supplemented by the archeological record, they afford an illuminating picture of the open field village, a community that originated in the central Middle Ages, achieved its highest stage in the late thirteenth century, and left its mark on the European landscape and on Western and world civilization.

1

THE VILLAGE
EMERGES

IN THE MODERN WORLD THE VILLAGE IS MERELY A
very small town, often a metropolitan suburb, always very
much a part of the world outside. The "old-fashioned village"
of the American nineteenth century was more distinctive in
function, supplying services of merchants and craftsmen to a
circle of farm homesteads surrounding it.

The medieval village was something different from either.
Only incidentally was it the dwelling place of merchants or
craftsmen. Rather, its population consisted of the farmers themselves, the people who tilled the soil and herded the animals.
Their houses, barns, and sheds clustered at its center, while their
plowed fields and grazing pastures and meadows surrounded it.
Socially, economically, and politically, it was a community.

In modern Europe and America the village is home to only
a fraction of the population. In medieval Europe, as in most
Third World countries today, the village sheltered the over-
whelming majority of people. The modern village is a place
where its inhabitants live, but not necessarily or even probably

where they work. The medieval village, in contrast, was the primary community to which its people belonged for all life's purposes. There they lived, there they labored, there they socialized, loved, married, brewed and drank ale, sinned, went to church, paid fines, had children in and out of wedlock, borrowed and lent money, tools, and grain, quarreled and fought, and got sick and died. Together they formed an integrated whole, a permanent community organized for agricultural production. Their sense of common enterprise was expressed in their records by special terms: *communitas villae*, the community of the vill or village, or *tota villata*, the body of all the villagers. The terminology was new. The English words "vill" and "village" derive from the Roman *villa*, the estate that was often the center of settlement in early medieval Europe. The closest Latin equivalent to "village" is *vicus*, used to designate a rural district or area.

A distinctive and in its time an advanced form of community, the medieval village represented a new stage of the world's oldest civilized society, the peasant economy. The first Neolithic agriculturists formed a peasant economy, as did their successors of the Bronze and Iron Ages and of the classical civilizations, but none of their societies was based so uniquely on the village. Individual homesteads, temporary camps, slave-manned plantations, hamlets of a few (probably related) families, fortresses, walled cities—people lived in all of these, but rarely in what might be defined as a village.

True, the village has not proved easy to define. Historians, archeologists, and sociologists have had trouble separating it satisfactorily from hamlet or settlement. Edward Miller and John Hatcher (*Medieval England: Rural Society and Economic Change, 1086–1343*) acknowledge that "as soon as we ask what a village is we run into difficulties." They conclude by asserting that the village differs from the mere hamlet in that "hamlets were often simply pioneering settlements established in the course of agricultural expansion," their organization "simpler and more embryonic" than that of the true village.[1] Trevor Rowley and John Wood (*Deserted Villages*) offer a "broad definition" of the village as "a group of families living in a collection of houses and having a sense of community."[2] Jean Chapelot and Robert Fossier (*The Village and House in the Middle Ages*) identify the "characteristics that define village settlement" as "concentration of population, organization of land settlement within a confined area, communal buildings such as the church and the castle, permanent settlement based on buildings that continue in use, and . . . the presence of craftsmen."[3] Permanence, diversification, organization, and community—these are key words and ideas that distinguish the village from more fleeting and less purposeful agricultural settlements.

Archeology has uncovered the sites of many prehistoric settlements in Northern Europe and the British Isles. Relics of the Bronze Age (roughly 3000 B.C. to 600 B.C.) include the remains of stone-walled enclosures surrounding clusters of huts. From the Iron Age (600 B.C. to the first century A.D.), circles of postholes mark the places where stood houses and sheds. Stones and

Circle of megaliths at Avebury (Wiltshire), relic of Neolithic Britain.

Reconstruction of Iron Age house on site of settlement of c. 300 B.C., Butser Ancient Farm Project, Petersfield (Hampshire).

ditches define the fields. Here we can first detect the presence of a "field system," a historic advance over the old "slash and burn" agriculture that cleared, cultivated, then abandoned and moved on. The fields, delineated by their borders or barriers, were cultivated in a recognized pattern of crops and possibly fallow.[4] The so-called Celtic fields, irregular squares of often less than an acre, were cultivated with the ard, a sharpened bough of wood with an iron tip, drawn by one or two oxen, which scratched the surface of light soil enough to allow sowing. Other Iron Age tools included hoes, small sickles, and spades. The rotary quern or hand mill (a disklike upper stone turning around a central spindle over a stationary lower stone) was used to grind grain. Crops included different kinds of wheat (spelt, emmer), barley, rye, oats, vetch, hay, flax, and dye-stuffs. Livestock were cattle, pigs, sheep, horses, domestic fowl, and honeybees.[5]

A rare glimpse of Iron Age agriculture comes from the Roman

Scratch plow, without coulter or mouldboard, from the Utrecht Psalter (c. A.D. 830). British Library, Harley Ms. 603, f. 54v.

historian Tacitus, who in his *Germania* (A.D. 98) describes a farming society primitive by Roman standards:

> Land [is divided] among them according to rank; the division is facilitated by the wide tracts of fields available. These plowlands are changed yearly and still there is more than enough. . . . Although their land is fertile and extensive, they fail to take full advantage of it by planting orchards, fencing off meadows, or irrigating gardens; the only demand they make upon the soil is to produce a grain crop. Hence even the year itself is not divided by them into as many seasons as with us: winter, spring, and summer they understand and have names for; the name of autumn is as completely unknown to them as are the good things that it can bring.

Tacitus seems to be describing a kind of field system with communal control by a tribe or clan. The context, however, makes it clear that he is not talking about a system centered on a permanent village:

The peoples of Germany never live in cities and will not even have their houses adjoining. They dwell apart, scattered here and there, wherever a spring, field, or grove takes their fancy. Their settlements (*vici*) are not laid out in our style, with buildings adjacent and connected. . . . They do not . . . make use of masonry or tiles; for all purposes they employ rough-hewn timber. . . . Some parts, however, they carefully smear over with clay. . . . They also dig underground caves, which they cover with piles of manure and use both as refuges from the winter and as storehouses for produce.[6]

Tacitus here is referring to the two main house types that dominated the landscape into the early Middle Ages. The first was the timber-framed building, which might, as in his account, be covered with clay, usually smeared over a framework of branches (wattle and daub), its most frequent design type the longhouse or byre-house, with animals at one end and people at the other, often with no separation but a manure trench. The second was the sunken hut or *grubenhaus*, dug into the soil to the depth of half a yard to a yard, with an area of five to ten square yards, and used alternatively for people, animals, storage, or workshop.

The Roman occupation of Gaul, beginning in the first century B.C., and of Britain, starting a century later, introduced two types of rural community to northwest Europe. The first was the slave-manned villa, a plantation of 450 to 600 acres centered on a lord's residence built in stone. The second was similar, but worked by peasants, or serfs, who cultivated their own plots of land and also that of their lord.[7] To the native Iron Age crops of wheat, barley, flax, and vetch, the Romans added peas, turnips, parsnips, cabbages, and other vegetables, along with fruits and the grape.[8] Plows were improved by the addition of iron coulters (vertical knife-blades in front of the plowshare), and wooden mouldboards, which turned the soil and made superfluous the cross-plowing (crisscrossing at right angles) formerly

Reconstruction of Iron Age longhouse (c. A.D. 60) at Iceni Village, Cockley Cley (Norfolk).

practiced. Large sickles and scythes were added to the Iron Age stock of tools.[9]

The Romans introduced not only a craftsman's but an engineer's approach to farming: wells, irrigation systems, the scientific application of fertilizer, even consideration of the effect of prevailing winds on structures. The number of sheep and horses increased significantly.[10] The Romans did not, however, work any revolution in basic agricultural methods, and the true village remained conspicuous by its absence. In Britain, in Gaul, and indeed throughout the Empire, the population dwelt in cities, on plantations, or dispersed in tiny hamlets and isolated homesteads.

Sometimes small pioneering groups of settlers entered an area, exploited it for a time, then moved on, whether because of deficient farming techniques, a fall in population, military insecurity, or a combination of the three. Archeology has explored a settlement at Wijster, in the Netherlands, dating from about A.D. 150, the site of four isolated farmsteads, with seven buildings, four large houses and three smaller ones. In another century, it grew to nineteen large and seven small buildings; by the middle of the fifth century, to thirty-five large and fourteen small buildings in an organized plan defined by a network of roads. Wijster had, in fact, many of the qualifications of a true village, but not permanence. At the end of the fifth century, it was abandoned. Another site was Feddersen Wierde, on the North Sea, in the first century B.C., the setting of a small group of farms. In the first century A.D. the inhabitants built an artificial mound to protect themselves against a rise in water; by the third century there were thirty-nine houses, one of them possibly that of a lord. In the fifth century it was abandoned. Similar proto-villages have been unearthed in England and on the Continent dating on into the ninth century.[11]

The countryside of Western Europe remained, in the words of Chapelot and Fossier, "ill-defined, full of shadows and contrasts, isolated and unorganized islands of cultivation, patches of uncertain authority, scattered family groupings around a patriarch, a chieftain, or a rich man . . . a landscape still in a state of anarchy, in short, the picture of a world that man seemed unable to control or dominate."[12] Population density was only

Foundation lines of walled Roman villa at Ditchley (Oxfordshire), with field boundaries and cropmarks. Ashmolean Museum.

two to five persons per square kilometer in Britain, as in Germany, somewhat higher in France.[13] Land was plentiful, people scarce.

In the tenth century the first villages destined to endure appeared in Europe. They were "nucleated"—that is, they were clusters of dwellings surrounded by areas of cultivation. Their appearance coincided with the developing seigneurial system, the establishment of estates held by powerful local lords.

In the Mediterranean area the village typically clustered around a castle, on a hilltop, surrounded by its own wall, with fields, vineyards, and animal enclosures in the plain below. In contrast, the prototype of the village of northwest Europe and England centered around the church and the manor house, and was sited where water was available from springs or streams.[14] The houses, straggling in all directions, were dominated by the two ancient types described by Tacitus, the longhouse and the sunken hut. Each occupied a small plot bounded by hedges, fences, or ditches. Most of the village land lay outside, however, including not only the cultivated fields but the meadow, marsh, and forest. In the organization of cropping and grazing of these surrounding fields, and in the relations that consequently developed among the villagers and between the villagers and their lord, lay a major historical development.

Crop rotation and the use of fallow were well known to the Romans, but how the application of these techniques evolved into the complex open field village is far from clear. The theory that the mature system developed in Germany in the early Middle Ages, diffused to France, and was brought to England by the Anglo-Saxons has been exploded without a satisfactory new interpretation gaining consensus. In Anglo-Saxon England a law of King Ine of Wessex (late seventh century) refers to "common meadow and other land divided into strips," and words associated with open-field agriculture turn up in many other laws and charters of the Saxon period. Recent research has revealed common pasturing on the post-harvest stubble as early as the tenth century. Possible contributory factors in the evolution can be discerned. The custom of partible inheritance—dividing the family lands among children, or among male children—may have fragmented tenements into numerous small holdings that made pasturing difficult without a cooperative arrangement. A rising population may have promoted cooperation. The increasing need for land encouraged "assarting," in which a number of peasant neighbors banded together to fell trees, haul out stumps, and cut brush to create new arable land, which was then divided among its creators. An assart, cultivated in strips, usually became a new "furlong" in the village field system. A strong and enlightened lord may often have contributed leadership in the enterprise.[15]

What is clear is that a unique form of agrarian organization gradually developed in certain large regions. "On most of the plain of Northern Europe, and in England in a band running southwest from the North Sea through the Midlands to the English Channel, the land lay in great open stretches of field broken here and there by stands of trees and the clustered houses of villages."[16] This was the "champion" country of open field cultivation and the nucleated village, in contrast to the "woodland" country of west and southeast England and of Brittany and Normandy. In woodland country, farming was typically carried on in compact fields by families living on individual homesteads or in small hamlets. Neither kind of landscape was exclusive; hamlets and isolated farmsteads were found in champion country, and some nucleated villages in woodland country.

In champion (from *champagne*, meaning "open field") country an intricate system evolved whose distinctive feature was the combination of individual landholding with a strictly enforced, unanimous-consent cooperation in decisions respecting plowing, planting, weeding, harvesting, and pasturing.[17]

Scholarly controversy over the beginnings of the system has a little of the chicken-and-egg futility about it. Somehow, through the operation of such natural forces as population growth and inheritance customs on traditional farming methods, the community organized its arable land into two (later often three) great fields, one of which was left fallow every year. Within each field the individual villager held several plots lying in long strips, which he plowed and planted in concert with his fellow villagers.

Common agreement was needed on which large field to leave fallow, which to plant in fall, which in spring. To pasture animals on the stubble after the harvest, an agreed-on harvest procedure was needed. Exploitation of the scarce meadow available for grazing was at least smoothed by cooperative agreement, while fencing and hedging were minimized.

By the year 1200, the open field system had achieved a state of advanced if still incomplete development. Some degree of cooperation in cultivation and pasturage governed farming in thousands of villages, in England and on the Continent.

The broad surge, economic and demographic, that marked the eleventh century continued fairly steadily through the twelfth and thirteenth. Settlements—homesteads, hamlets, villages—were planted everywhere. The peasant villagers who formed the vast majority of the population cultivated wheat above all other crops, followed by rye, barley, oats, beans, peas, and a few other vegetables. Low and precarious crop yields meant that most available land had to be consigned to cereal, the indispensable staff-of-life crop. The value of manure as fertilizer was well understood, but so few animals could be maintained on the available pasture that a vicious circle of reciprocal scarcity plagued agriculture.

Yet there were notable improvements in technology. The heavy, often wet soils of Northern Europe demanded a heavier plow and more traction than the sandier soils of the Mediterranean region. The large plow that evolved, fitted with coulter and mouldboard and requiring several plow animals, represented "one of the most important agricultural developments in pre-industrial Europe."[18] It favored the open field system by strengthening the bias toward long strips.

The Romans had never solved the problem of harnessing the horse for traction. The padded horse collar, invented in Asia and diffusing slowly westward, was joined to other improve-ments—horseshoes, whippletrees, and traces—to convert the horse into a farm animal. Faster-gaited and longer-working, the horse challenged the strong, docile, but ponderous ox as a plow beast and surpassed it as a cart animal. One of the earliest representations of a working horse is in the Bayeux Tapestry (c. 1087). The ox also profited from technical innovation in the form of an improved yoke,[19] and refused to disappear from agriculture; his slow, steady pull offered advantages in heavy going. Indeed, the debate over the merits of the two traction animals enlivened rustic conversation in the England of Queen Victoria, though the horse slowly won ascendancy. The horse's needs for fodder stimulated cultivation of oats, a spring crop that together with barley, peas, beans, and vetches fitted ideally into open field rotation. Stall-feeding became more prevalent, permitting more use of fertilizer, while the leguminous fodder crops restored nitrogen content to the soil.[20]

The cooperative relationships of the peasants belonged to what might be called the village aspect of their existence; that existence also had a manorial aspect. In Northern Europe and in England following the Norman Conquest, the countryside came to be organized into land-management units called man-ors. The manor is usually defined as an estate held by a lord, comprising a demesne directly exploited by the lord, and peas-ant holdings from which he collected rents and fees. The village might coincide with the manor, or it might not. It might be divided into two or more manors, or it might form only part of a manor.

The combination of demesne and tenants, a version of which dates back to the late Roman Empire, is first specifically men-tioned in documents of the ninth century in northern France, and in the tenth century in central Italy and England. By the eleventh century it was well established everywhere.[21]

It fitted comfortably into the contemporary political-military order known as feudalism. Evolving in medieval Europe over a lengthy period and imported to England by the Normans, feu-dalism united the European elite in a mutual-aid society. A lord granted land to a vassal in return for military and other services;

lord and vassal swore reciprocal oaths, of protection by the lord, loyalty by the vassal; the vassal received as fief or fee a conditional gift of land, to "hold" and draw revenue from. Older historians, including Marx, used the term feudalism for the whole medieval social order, a peasant society dominated by a military, land-owning aristocracy. Modern usage generally restricts the word to the network of vassal-lord relations among the aristocracy. The system governing the peasant's relation to the lord, the economic foundation of medieval society, is usually designated the "manorial system." Feudalism meant much to the lord, little to the peasant.

The relationships embodied in the feudal and manorial systems were simple enough in theory: In the manorial system, peasant labored for lord in return for land of his own; in the feudal system, lord held lands from king or overlord in return for supplying soldiers on demand. In practice the relationships were never so simple and grew more complicated over time. All kinds of local variations developed, and both peasant labor service and knightly military service were increasingly converted into money payments.

Whatever the effects of the two overlapping systems, they did not prevent villages from flourishing, until everywhere villages began to crowd up against each other. Where once the silent European wilderness had belonged to the wolf and the deer, villagers now ranged—with their lord's permission—in search of firewood, nuts, and berries, while their pigs rooted and their cattle and sheep grazed. Villages all over Europe parleyed with their neighbors to fix boundaries, which they spelled out in charters and committed to memory with a picturesque annual ceremony. Every spring, in what were known in England as the "gang-days," the whole population went "a-ganging" around the village perimeter. Small boys were ducked in boundary brooks and bumped against boundary trees and rocks by way of helping them learn this important lore.[22]

A thirteenth-century European might be hazy about the boundaries of his country, but he was well aware of those of his village.

2

THE ENGLISH VILLAGE: ELTON

B Y THE THIRTEENTH CENTURY, THE FERTILE RIVER valleys of Huntingdonshire, along with most of the best farmlands of England, had been continuously inhabited for at least five thousand years. The story of their occupation over these five millennia is the story of a series of incursions of migrating or invading peoples, in varying numbers, affecting the population at different levels and in different degrees.[1]

Native Paleolithic hunting communities were displaced in about 2000 B.C. by newcomers from the Continent who planted crops, founding the first British agricultural communities. Immigrants in the Bronze and Iron Ages expanded the area of settlement, making inroads into the poorer soils of the uplands and forested areas.

By the first century A.D. a modest agricultural surplus created a trickle of export trade with Roman Gaul, possibly contributing to the somewhat undermotivated Roman decision (A.D. 43) to send an army across the Channel to annex Britain. The network of symmetrical, square-cornered fortifications built by the legionaries provided local security and stimulated economic life, which was further assisted by newly built Roman roads, canals, and towns.

One road, later named Ermine Street, ran north from London to York. At the point where it crossed the River Nene a city called Durobrivae was built. Many kilns from the Roman period found in the area indicate a flourishing pottery industry. Villas dotting the neighboring countryside marketed their produce in the city. At one time it was thought that such villas belonged to Roman officials; now it is established that most belonged to a native class of Romanized nobles. Far more numerous were the farmsteads, mostly isolated, some huddled in small, probably kinship, groupings.[2]

Further traces of Roman agriculture have been found in Huntingdonshire along the edge of the fens as well as on the River Ouse. Across the border in Bedfordshire, on the River Ivel, aerial photographs show patterns of Roman field systems. The rich farmlands that bordered the fens became chief providers of grain for the legions in the north of England, transported through the fenland rivers and Roman-built canals.[3]

As multiple problems began to overwhelm the Roman Em-

Reconstruction of houses on site of Anglo-Saxon settlement (c. A.D. 500) at West Stow (Suffolk). Left background, sunken hut.

West Stow reconstruction. Round structure in foreground is poultry house.

pire, the legions were withdrawn from Britain (A.D. 410). Trade and the towns fostered by it declined, the roads fell into disuse, and the new cities shrank or, like Durobrivae, disappeared.

Later in the fifth century a new set of uninvited foreigners came to stay. In the violent early phase of the invasion, in the south of England, the Anglo-Saxons wiped out native populations and replaced them with their own settlements, creating a complete break with the past, and leaving the old Romano-British sites, as in Wessex and Sussex, "a maze of grass-covered mounds."[4] In the later stages, as the Anglo-Saxons advanced to the north and west, the occupation was more peaceful, with the newcomers tilling the soil alongside their British neighbors.[5] Scholars believe that some of the Romano-British agricultural patterns survived into the Middle Ages, particularly in the north of England, where groups of estates administered as a single unit, the "multiple estate," flourished.[6]

West Stow reconstruction.

In the seventh century the newly melded "English" population converted to Christianity. In what historians have entitled England's "Saxon" period, little other change occurred except perhaps a partial loss of Roman technology. The English agriculturalists cultivated the cereal grains and herded the animals that their Roman, Iron Age, and Neolithic forebears had known. Pigs, which could largely support themselves by foraging in the woods, were the most numerous livestock. Cows were kept mainly to breed oxen for the plow team; sheep and goats were the milk and cheese producers. Barley was the favored crop, ground up for baking or boiling or converted to malt—"the Anglo-Saxons consumed beer on an oceanic scale," notes H. P. R. Finberg.[7]

A new wave of invasion was heralded by a piratical Danish raid in 793. In the following century the Danes came to stay. The contemporary Anglo-Saxon Chronicle recorded the landing in

East Anglia in 865 of a "great heathen army" which the follow-ing year advanced north and west, to Nottingham and York. In 876, Viking leader Healdene "shared out the land of the Northumbrians, and [the Danes] proceeded to plow land to support themselves." In 877, "the Danish army went away into Mercia, and shared out some of it, and gave some to Ceowulf," a native thegn, or lord.[8] The territory the Danes occupied in-cluded the future Huntingdonshire. At first few in numbers, the Danish warriors were supplemented by relatives from Denmark and also by contingents from Norway and Frisia.

Late in the tenth century Alfred the Great of Wessex (849–

Saxon church of St. Laurence, Bradford-on-Avon (Wiltshire), founded by St. Aldhelm (d. A.D. 709).

899) organized a successful resistance to the Danes but was forced to conclude a peace which left them in possession of most of eastern England.

The Danes having converted to Christianity, a number of monasteries were founded in Danish England. In about 970, St. Oswald, archbishop of York, and Aethelwin, ealdorman (royal official) of East Anglia, donated the land on which Ramsey Abbey was built, a wooded island in Ramsey Mere on which Aethelwin had a hunting lodge.

Between the founding and their deaths in 992, Oswald and Aethelwin donated their own hereditary holdings to the abbey, added land obtained by purchase and exchange, and solicited donations from others, until the abbey held a large block of territory fanning out from the island of Ramsey through Huntingdonshire and three adjacent counties.[9]

A property that was given to the abbey a few years after the death of the founders was the manor and village of Elton. The origin of the name of the settlement that had grown up near the site of vanished Durobrivae is conjectural. The suffix *tun* or *ton* (fence or enclosure in Anglo-Saxon) had broadened its meaning to become "homestead" and finally "collection of homesteads," or "village"; the suffix *inga*, combined with a personal name, indicated the followers or kinsmen of a leader. Originally spelled "Aethelington" or "Ailington," Elton's name has been explained as either "Ella's village," or "the village of the Aethelings," or "the village of Aethelheah's people."[10]

The benefactor who donated Elton to the abbey was a prelate named Aetheric, who was among the first students educated at Ramsey. During his school days, Aetheric and three other boys as a prank tried to ring the great bell in the west tower and broke its rim. The monks angrily urged punishment, but the abbot declared that since the boys were well-born, they would probably repay the abbey a hundred times when they "arrived at the age of maturity."[11]

The Ramsey Abbey chronicler then relates Aetheric's fulfillment of the prophecy. Elton was by now (early eleventh century) a flourishing village with an Anglo-Saxon lord; when he died,

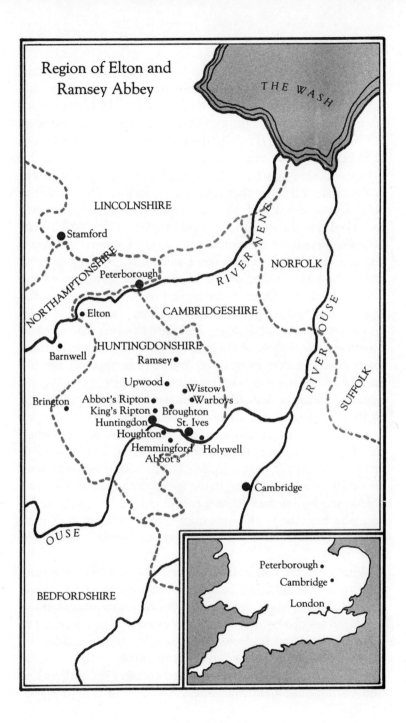

Region of Elton and Ramsey Abbey

his widow married a Danish noble named Dacus. In 1017 Aetheric, now bishop of Dorchester, joined an escort traveling with King Cnut "to the ends of the kingdom." When the party stopped to spend the night in Nassington, a few miles northwest of Elton, Aetheric and four of the king's secretaries were lodged at Elton in Dacus's manor house.

In the course of a festive evening, Dacus talked expansively of the cattle and sheep that grazed his meadows, the plows that cultivated his fields, and the rents the village paid him. Aetheric remarked that he would like to buy such a manor. Dacus had no intention of selling, but told his guest, "If tomorrow at dawn you give me fifty golden marks, I will turn the village over to you." The bishop called on the king's secretaries to witness the offer and asked if Dacus's wife agreed to it. The wife gave her assent. Host and guests retired, but Aetheric mounted a horse and rode to Nassington, where he found the king playing chess "to relieve the tedium of the long night." Cnut listened sympathetically and ordered a quantity of gold to be sent to Elton. At dawn Aetheric wakened Dacus and triumphantly presented him with the money. Dacus tried to renege, on the grounds that a contract damaging to an heir—his wife—was invalid. But the witnesses swore that the woman had ratified the pact, and when the dispute was submitted to the king, Cnut pronounced in favor of Aetheric. The wife made a last protest, that the village's two mills were not included in the sale and merited another two golden marks, but her claim was rejected. Packing their furniture and belongings, the outwitted couple departed with their household and their animals, leaving "bare walls" to the new lord.

What Aetheric had initially intended to do with his acquisition we are not told, but he soon found a use for it. Obtaining the king's permission, he left the retinue and visited Ramsey. There, to his dismay, he found the monastery in a turmoil. The current abbot had neglected the discipline of the monks and allowed them to fall into "error" (the chronicler gives no details). Aetheric entered the chapter "threatening and roaring and brandishing anathema unless they amended their ways."

The monks "threw themselves at his feet with tearful prayers." In reward for their repentance, Aetheric assigned them the village of Elton "in perpetuity for their sustenance."[12] Thus Elton came to belong to Ramsey Abbey as one of its "conventual" or "home" manors, designed for the monks' support.

Danish political power ceased in England in 1042, but the Danish presence survived in many details of language and custom. Danish suffixes—*thorpe* (hamlet), *toft* (homestead), *holm* (water meadow)—were common in the Elton neighborhood, including the names of Elton's own meadows and field divisions. The local administrative area was Norman (Northman) Cross Hundred, after a cross that stood on Ermine Street in the center of the hundred (district), probably marking the site where the hundred court met in the open air. The hundred was a division of the shire or county, part of a system of administration that had developed in the ninth and tenth centuries. Theoretically containing 100 hides, tax units each of about 120 acres, the hundreds were made up of "vills"—villages or townships. The village represented a physical reality alongside the institutional reality of the manor, the lord's estate. The two did not necessarily coincide, as they did in Elton. Throughout Huntingdonshire only 29 of 56 villages were identical with manors.[13] The village remained a permanent political entity, a territorial unit of the kingdom, subject to the royal government for military and police purposes.

The Anglo-Saxon and Scandinavian invasions had involved mass movements of peoples. The Norman Conquest of 1066 was more like the Roman conquest, the intrusion of a small power group. Where the Anglo-Saxons and Danes had displaced whole regional populations, the Normans at first scarcely disturbed the life of the peasants. Ultimately, however, they wrought an alteration in the social and political system that affected nearly everybody.

Both the feudal and manorial systems were present in some degree and in some regions of England at the time of the Conquest; what the Normans did amounted to performing a shot-gun marriage of the two and imposing them on all parts of the country. William the Conqueror appointed himself landlord of England and deputized a number of his principal followers as tenants-in-chief to hold most of it for him, supplanting the Anglo-Saxon nobles who formed the pre-Conquest elite.

The great ecclesiastical estates, such as Ramsey Abbey, re-mained relatively untouched unless they had aided the Anglo-Saxon resistance, as in the case of the neighboring abbeys of Ely and Peterborough. Ramsey was explicitly confirmed in its hold-ings:

> William, King of the English, to Archbishop Lanfranc and his bishops, and Abbot Baldwin, and the sheriffs, and certain of his faithful, French and English, greeting. Know that I concede to Herbert, Abbot of Ramsey, his sac, and tol and team, and infangenetheof [rights to tolls, fees, and certain judicial profits], in the town and outside, and all his customs, which his antecessor had in the time of King Edward. Witnesses: Robert, Count of Mortain, per Roger Bigod.[14]

William's tenants-in-chief in turn deputized followers of their own. Finding the manorial unit a convenient instrument, they used it where it was already at hand, imposed it where it was not, and effected whatever Procrustean alterations were needed with an unceremonious disregard for the affected locals. "Many a Norman newcomer did not find a manor equipped with a de-mesne [the lord's own arable land]," says Barbara Dodwell, or with "villein tenements owing week-work [a tenant's year-round labor obligation] . . . but rather a large number of petty tenants and cottagers, some free, some semi-free, some servile."[15] In such a case, the new lord arbitrarily appropriated land for a demesne and conscripted the needed labor. A fundamental Nor-man legal principle, "No land without a lord," was enunciated and given substance via the manorial system.

As William equipped his tenants-in-chief with collections of manors, and they in turn bestowed them on their vassals, a variety of lordships resulted, with a pyramid of military obligations. Ramsey Abbey's knight services were for unknown reasons light: although Ramsey was the fourth wealthiest ecclesiastical landholder in England, it owed only four knights. The burden of supporting the four, or of hiring substitutes, was shared among certain of the manors.[16]

As it turned out, the abbey might have done better immediately to endow knights with estates in return for military service—to create "knights' fees." The lack of clear-cut military tenures encouraged knights to settle illegally on abbey lands. Two sister villages of Elton, also bestowed on Ramsey Abbey by Bishop Aetheric, were seized by a knight named Pagan Peverel, a veteran of the First Crusade. The abbey protested and the suit was heard in Slepe, the village where St. Ives was buried and which soon after took his name. The biographer of St. Ives recorded with satisfaction that not only was justice rendered and the property returned to Ramsey Abbey, but that Pagan Peverel was further punished on his way home:

> On that same day, before Pagan arrived at his lodging, the horse on which he was riding had its feet slip from under it and fell three times to the ground . . . and a hawk which he was holding was shaken from his hand and made for the wood in swift flight, never to return. The horse of the priest who was traveling with him slipped and fell as well, and its neck being broken—although the priest was unharmed—it breathed its last. There was also Pagan's steward, called Robert, who came in for a more deserved punishment, because . . . most faithful to his master, he had given approval and assistance to the man's wickedness.

Robert succumbed to a serious illness but was cured after praying at St. Ives's shrine.[17]

Twenty years after the Conquest, to the inestimable profit of historians, was compiled the survey known as the Domesday

Book, which one historian has called "probably the most remarkable statistical document in the history of Europe."[18] Executed at the orders of William the Conqueror, the Domesday survey undertook to inventory all the wealth of England, to assure efficient tax collection. Consequently, after a long age of informational darkness, a floodlight of valuable data illuminates the English scene. After Domesday, the light dims once more, until almost as suddenly in the late twelfth century written manorial surveys make their appearance, and in the middle of the thirteenth manorial court records.

Domesday Book records about 275,000 heads of households, indicating a total English population of some one and a half to two million, much above early medieval times (though some scholars think that population was higher in late Roman times). Settlements—homesteads, hamlets, villages—already dotted the landscape. In Yorkshire, five out of six of all hamlets and villages had been founded by the time of Domesday.

The Domesday surveyors, proceeding from village to village and calling on lords and peasants to furnish them with information, confronted the difficulty that manor and village (*manerium* and *villa*, in Domesday's Latin) did not necessarily coincide. From the village's point of view, how it was listed in the survey made little difference, and the surveyors simply overrode the problem, focusing their data on the manor. Enough villages are named—some 13,000—to make clear their importance as population centers, however. Churches were given erratic notice, much in some counties, little in others, but enough to indicate that they were now common, if not yet universal, village features.

Under the abbot of Ramsey's holdings in Norman Cross Hundred, Elton was listed with a new spelling:

M. [Manor] In Adelintune the abbot of Ramsey had ten hides [assessed] to the geld [a tax]. There is land for four plows in the demesne apart from the aforesaid hides. There are now four plows on the demesne, and twenty-eight villeins having twenty plows. There is a

church and a priest, and two mills [rendering] forty
shillings, and 170 acres of meadow. T.R.E. [in the time of
King Edward, 1042–1066] it was worth fourteen *li.*
[pounds] now sixteen *li.* [19]

The "ten hides" credited to Elton tell us little about actual
acreage. Entries in Domesday were assessed in round numbers,
usually five, ten, or fifteen hides. Evidently each shire was assessed for a round number, the hides apportioned among the
villages, without strict attention to measurement. Furthermore,
though the hide usually comprised 120 acres, the acre varied.

No further information about Elton appears until a manorial
survey of about 1160; after that a gap follows until the middle
of the thirteenth century, when documentation begins to prolif-
erate.

Drawing on the collection of documents known as the Ramsey
Abbey cartulary, on a royal survey done in 1279, on the accounts and court records of the manor, and on what archeology
has ascertained from deserted villages, we can sketch a reason-
ably probable picture of Elton as it was in the last quarter of the
thirteenth century.

The royal survey of 1279 credited the "manor and vill" of
Elton with a total of 13 hides of arable land of 6 virgates each.
Originally designed as the amount of land needed to support a
family, the virgate had come to vary considerably. In Elton it
consisted of 24 acres; thus the total of village arable was 1,872
acres. The abbot's demesne share amounted to three hides of
arable, besides which he had 16 acres of meadow and three of
pasture. Two water mills and a fulling mill, for finishing cloth,
successors of the two mills that Dacus's wife had claimed in
1017, also belonged to the abbot. [20]

The village scarcely presented the tidy appearance of a modern English village. Houses did not necessarily face the street,
but might stand at odd angles, with a fence or embankment
fronting on the street. [21] The nexus of a working agricultural

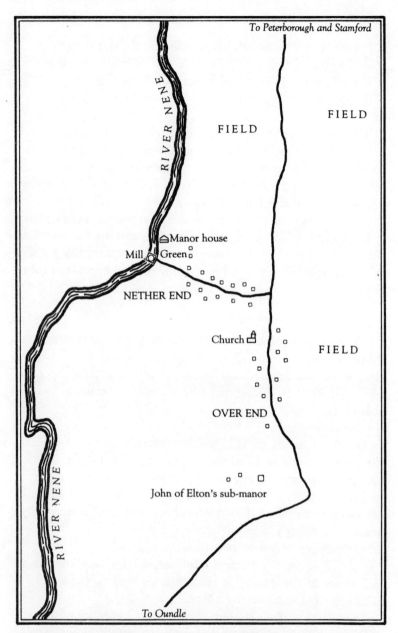

To Peterborough and Stamford

RIVER NENE

FIELD

FIELD

⌂ Manor house

Mill ⬠ Green

NETHER END

Church ⛪

FIELD

OVER END

RIVER NENE

John of Elton's sub-manor

To Oundle

Conjectural map of Elton, c. 1300. Exact location of tofts and crofts (house plots and gardens) and of lanes and secondary streets is unknown. The River Nene is now canalized at Elton; its course in the Middle Ages is uncertain.

system, the village was a place of bustle, clutter, smells, disrepair, and dust, or in much of the year mud. It was far from silent. Sermons mention many village sounds: the squeal of cartwheels, the crying of babies, the bawling of hogs being butchered, the shouts of peddler and tinker, the ringing of church bells, the hissing of geese, the thwack of the flail in threshing time. To these one might add the voices of the villagers, the rooster's crow, the dog's bark, and other animal sounds, the clop of cart horses, the ring of the smith's hammer, and the splash of the miller's great waterwheel.[22]

Stone construction was still rare in England, except in areas like the Cotswolds where stone was plentiful and timber scarce. Elton's houses in the thirteenth century were in all likelihood timber-framed with walls of wattle and daub (oak, willow, or hazel wands coated with clay). Timber-framing had been improved by the importation from the Continent of "cruck" construction, a system of roof support that added space to interiors. The cruck consisted of the split half of the trunk and main

Cruck construction supporting roof of early fourteenth-century tithe barn, Bradford-on-Avon.

branch of a tree. Two or three such pairs, sprung from the ground or from a foundation, could support a ridgepole, their curvature providing enough elevation to save the need for a sunken floor and to put an end to the long, murky history of the sunken hut. Progress in carpentry permitted the framing of walls with squared uprights planted in postholes or foundation trenches, making houses more weathertight.[23]

Roofs were thatched, as from ancient times, with straw, broom or heather, or in marsh country reeds or rushes (as at Elton). Thatched roofs had formidable drawbacks; they rotted from alternations of wet and dry, and harbored a menagerie of mice, rats, hornets, wasps, spiders, and birds; and above all they caught fire. Yet even in London they prevailed. Simon de Montfort, rebelling against the king, is said to have meditated setting fire to the city by releasing an air force of chickens with flaming brands attached.[24] Irresistibly cheap and easy to make, the thatched roof overwhelmingly predominated century after century atop the houses and cottages of medieval peasants and townsmen everywhere.[25]

Some village houses were fairly large, forty to fifty feet long by ten to fifteen wide, others were tiny cottages.[26] All were insubstantial. "House breaking" by burglars was literal. Coroners' records speak of intruders smashing their way through the walls of houses "with a plowshare" or "with a coulter."[27] In the Elton manorial court, a villager was accused of carrying away "the doorposts of the house" of a neighbor;[28] an angry heir, still a minor, "tore up and carried away" a house on his deceased father's property and was "commanded to restore it."[29]

Most village houses had a yard and a garden: a smaller "toft" fronting on the street and occupied by the house and its outbuildings, and a larger "croft" in the rear. The toft was usually surrounded by a fence or a ditch to keep in the animals whose pens it contained, along with barns or storage sheds for grain and fodder.[30] Missing was a privy. Sanitary arrangements seem to have consisted of a latrine trench or merely the tradition later recorded as retiring to "a bowshot from the house."[31]

Drainage was assisted by ditches running through the yards.

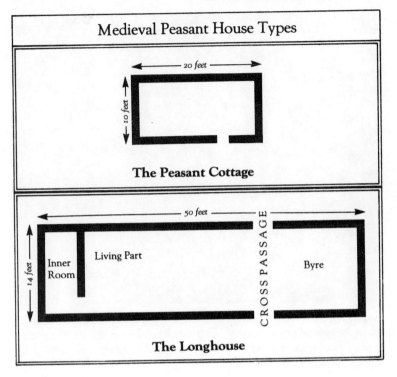

Medieval Peasant House Types

20 feet

10 feet

The Peasant Cottage

50 feet

14 feet

Inner Room

Living Part

CROSS PASSAGE

Byre

The Longhouse

Private wells existed in some villages, but a communal village well was more usual. That Elton had one is indicated by a family named "atte Well." Livestock grazed in the tofts—a cow or an ox, pigs, and chickens. Many villagers owned sheep, but they were not kept in the toft. In summer and fall, they were driven out into the marsh to graze, and in winter they were penned in the manor fold so that the lord could profit from their valuable manure. The richer villagers had manure piles, accumulated from their other animals; two villagers were fined when their dung heaps impinged "on the common highway, to the common harm," and another paid threepence for license to place his on the common next to his house. The croft, stretching back from the toft, was a large garden of half an acre or so, cultivated by spade—"by foot," as the villagers termed it.[32]

Snow highlights house sites, crofts behind them, and surrounding fields in aerial photograph of deserted village of Wharram Percy. Upper left, modern manor house, with ruined church behind it. Cambridge University Collection of Air Photographs.

Clustered at the end of the street in Nether End, near the river, were the small village green, the manor house, and the mill complex. An eighteenth-century mill today stands on the spot where in the thirteenth century "the dam mill," the "middle mill," and the "small mill" probably stood over the Nene, apparently under a single roof: "the house between the two mills" was repaired in 1296.[33] The foundations were of stone, the buildings themselves of timber, with a thatched roof, a courtyard, and a vegetable garden.[34] A millpond furnished power to the three oaken waterwheels.[35] Grass and willows grew all around the pond, the grass sold for fodder, the willow wands for building material.[36]

Back from the river stood the manor house and its "curia" (court), with outbuildings and installations. The curia occupied an acre and a half of land,[37] enclosed with a wall or possibly a fence of stakes and woven rods. Some manor houses had moats to keep livestock in and wild animals out; the excavations of 1977 at Elton revealed traces of such a moat on the side toward the river. An entry gate led to the house or hall *(aula)*, built of stone, with a slate roof.[38] Manor houses were sometimes constructed over a ground-level undercroft, used for storage. The Elton manorial accounts also mention a sleeping chamber, which had to be "pointed and mended" at the same time as the wooden, slate-roofed chapel adjacent to the hall.[39]

Kitchen and bakehouse were in separate buildings nearby, and a granary was built up against the hall.[40] The manorial accounts mention repairs to a "communal privy," probably restricted to the manorial personnel.[41] Elsewhere on the grounds, which accommodated a garden and an apple orchard, stood a stone dairy, equipped with cheese presses, settling pans, strainers, earthenware jars, and churns.[42] The "little barn" and the "big barn" were of timber, with thatched roofs; here mows of

Abbey barn, c. 1340, storehouse for the home manor of Glastonbury Abbey (Somerset).

Tithe barn, for tithes paid in grain, Bradford-on-Avon, with fourteen bays, two of them projecting into porches.

grain were stored. The big barn had a slate-roofed porch on one side protecting a great door that locked with a key, and a small door opposite. The door of the little barn was secured by a bolt.[43]

Under a thatched roof, the stone stable housed horses, oxen, and cows, as well as carts, tools, and harness.[44] A wooden sheep-fold, also thatched, large enough to accommodate the lord's sheep and those of the villagers, was lighted with candles and an oil lamp every spring at lambing time.[45] Still other buildings included a kiln for drying malt[46] and a pound—a "punfold" or "pinfold"—for stray animals.[47] Two large wooden thatched dovecotes sheltered several hundred doves, sold at market or forwarded to the abbot's table.[48] Among other resident poultry were chickens and geese, and, at least in one year's accounts, peacocks and swans.[49] On its waterfront, the manor possessed several boats, whose repairs were recorded at intervals.[50]

Across the street from the curia stood one of a pair of communal ovens to which the villagers were obliged to bring their bread; the other stood in Overend. The ovens were leased from the lord by a baker. A forge was leased by a smith who worked for both the lord and the tenants.[51] The green, whose presence is attested by the name of a village family, "atte Grene," could not have been large enough to serve as a pasture. Its only known use was as a location for the stocks, where village wrongdoers were sometimes held.

At the opposite end of the village, in Overend, stood the parish church, on the site of earlier structures dating at least to the tenth century. The records make no mention of the rectory, which the enclosure map of 1784 locates in Nether End.

South of the church in Overend lay the tract of land on which two hundred years later Elton Hall was built. In the thirteenth

Medieval dovecote, Avebury (Wiltshire).

Dovecote. Bodleian Library, Ms. Bodl. 764, f. 80.

century, this was a sub-manor of Elton, a hide of land held by a wealthy free man, John of Elton, who had tenants of his own.

A medieval village did not consist merely of its buildings. It

Man driving geese out of the grain with horn and stick. British Library, Luttrell Psalter, Ms. Add. 42130, f. 69v.

included the plowed fields, the meadows, and even the surrounding woods, moor, and marsh. Aerial photographs of deserted medieval villages show open fields with their characteristic pattern of ridge and furrow produced by the plowman. Elton's fields, under continuous and changing use, show few such traces. A survey of Elton at the beginning of the seventeenth century listed three fields—Ogerston, Middlefield, and Earnestfield—but whether they existed in the thirteenth century remains unknown.[52] None of the dozens of place names in the manorial records can be identified with an entire field. Many are names of furlongs, the subdivisions of fields (Holywellfurlong, Knolfurlong, Michelgrove), others of meadows (Gooseholm, Michelholm, Le Inmede, Butterflymead, Abbotsholm), or marsh (Oldmoor, Smallmoor, Newtonmoor, Broadmoor, Oldwychslade). Some are recorded as being leased on a regular basis—to the rector, a furlong called Le Brach, to others Milnespightle (Mill Close), and Clack. The village also had a vineyard, possibly connected with the curia.

Brian K. Roberts (The Making of the English Village) divides the elements of villages into three overlapping categories: public space, where everyone, including outsiders, has rights; communal space, where all inhabitants have rights, even when the lord holds the land; and private space, where access and use are open only to the proper individuals. The public elements are the church and churchyard, and the highways, streets, and lanes. The communal are the green, the punfold or pound, the oven, the pond, the wells, the stocks, and, most important, the open fields. The private are the manor house and its appurtenances, and the tofts and crofts of the peasants. Some elements are ambiguous: the entries and exits to the fields are both communal and public; the church is not only both public and communal but private, since it belongs to the lord; the smithy, the houses of the demesne servants (cowherd, shepherd), and the rector's house are both communal and private.[53]

Archeologists have classified village plans on the basis of major design elements: "green" villages, clustered around a green or common; street or row villages, built along a street or highway; polyfocal villages, with more than one hub; and composite villages combining several of these types. Elton would seem to be all of these, one of its two sections built around a central green, the other along a highway, each with a separate focus (the manor house, the church). The classification does not really seem very meaningful, and considering the difficulty in tracing the chronology of village plans, not very exact. R. H. Hilton comments that the main physical characteristic shared by medieval villages was their shapelessness. Village streets appear to have come into existence after the tofts and crofts were established, as the paths between the houses became worn down and sunken by the traffic of people, animals, and carts. The village network was in fact more paths than streets.[54]

Elton in the late thirteenth century was a large village, capable of summoning 327 residents to a harvest in 1287.[55] The royal survey of 1279 lists 113 tenants, heads of families.[56] Allowing for wives, children, and landless laborers, a figure of five to six hundred for the total population might be reasonable. This accords with Hilton's estimate that 45 percent of the villages of the West Midlands had a population of between 400 and 600, with 10 percent larger, the rest smaller.[57]

Villages like Elton were not cut off from the world around them. Many Elton surnames indicate family origins elsewhere, and the records sometimes explicitly speak of immigration: Richard Trune, a cotter (cottager), came to Elton from Fotheringhay, in Northamptonshire.[58] Many villagers paid an annual fee for license to live outside the manor (or were cited for failing to pay it). Elton village officials traveled to the fairs and markets to make purchases; so did ordinary villagers to sell their produce. Carrying services owed by villeins took them to Ramsey and "any market where the lord wishes inside the county [of Huntingdonshire]."[59] Other Ramsey Abbey villagers journeyed as far as London. Free tenants of Elton attended the abbot's honor (estate) court at Broughton twice a year, as well as the royal courts at Huntingdon and Norman Cross. The world came to Elton, too, in the guise of monks, churchmen, nobles, craftsmen, day laborers, and royal officials.

Thus the village of Elton, Norman Cross Hundred, Hunting-donshire, England, belonging to Ramsey Abbey, occupying some 1,800 acres of farmland, cultivated its crops and herded its animals in much the same fashion as thousands of other villages in England and on the Continent. By the standards of a later age, it was neither rich nor prepossessing. But in comparison with earlier times, it was a thriving social organism, and an important innovation in social and economic history.

3

THE LORD

EVERY VILLAGE HAD A LORD, BUT ONLY RARELY
was he in residence. A resident lord was usually a petty
knight who held only one manor, like Henry de Bray, lord of
Harlestone (Northamptonshire), whose account book has survived. Henry had twenty-four tenants sharing his five hundred
acres, contributing annually twelve pounds in cash rents, a
pound of pepper, and eight fowls, and performing harvest services.[1] At the other end of the spectrum was the earl, count,
abbot, or bishop, whose "honor" was composed of manors
scattered over a quarter of England.

On the Continent such a magnate—a count of Champagne
or Flanders—might rival kings in exercising political authority.
In Norman England, where William the Conqueror and his
successors monopolized political power, the great lords began as
generals in an army of occupation, their military role softening
over time into an economic one. A "tenant-in-chief" like the
earl of Warenne, lord of scores of villages in a dozen counties,
collected all kinds of rents and services at first- and second-hand
without ever setting eyes on most of his sixty-five knight-tenants,
hundreds of freeholders, and thousands of bondmen.[2] Between

the two extremes of Henry de Bray and the earl of Warenne were middling lords who held several manors and sometimes traveled around among them.

Besides great and small, lords divided more definably into lay and ecclesiastical. The abbot of Ramsey, whose twenty-three villages included Elton and who held parts of many others, is a good example of the ecclesiastical lord, whose numbers had steadily increased since the Conquest. The old feudal theory of lordship as a link in the legal chain of authority running from serf to monarch had lost much of its substance. The original basis of the feudal hierarchy—military service owed to the crown—had dissipated, owing partly to the objections of knights and barons to service abroad, and partly to the complexity wrought by the accidents of inheritance. It was easier to extract a money payment than to induce an unwilling knight to serve, and money fees, with which soldiers could be hired and equipped, were easier to divide into fractions when a property owed a third or half of a knight's service.

To the village, such legal complications hardly mattered, any more than whether the lord was great or small, lay or ecclesiastical (or male or female, since abbesses, prioresses, widows, and heiresses held many manors). A village might be comfortably shared by two or more lords. Tysoe (Warwickshire) was divided among five different manors, belonging to Baron Stafford, his son, two priories, and the local Knights Templar.[3] Often, however, as in the case of Elton, a village constituted a manor, and was one of several belonging to a single lord.

Whatever the technicalities, the lord was the lord, the consumer of the village surplus. The thirteenth-century manor was not a political or military enterprise but an economic one, with the lord its exploiter and beneficiary.

It already had a history. In the twelfth century, "farming," or leasing, the demesne or even the whole manor had been popular. An entrepreneur paid a fixed sum, assumed control of the day-to-day operation, and profited from the difference between the fee he paid and the revenues he collected. The farmer might be a local knight or rich peasant, or a businessman from a

nearby town. Sometimes the villagers themselves banded together in a consortium to farm their manor.[4] One lord might
farm another's land when geography made it more convenient.
The abbot of Ramsey farmed King's Ripton, a crown manor
lying next to Abbot's Ripton. The farm normally comprised
land, animals, implements, personnel, labor services of the villeins, and even the fines levied in the manorial court. The farmer
usually held the privilege of making land transfers to maintain
production, as when a tenant died without a direct heir.[5]

Beginning about 1200, the farming of manors went out of
style. The thirteenth century was an age of population expansion, and as town markets for agricultural products grew, more
and more lords decided to exploit their manors directly. Some
manors continued to be farmed (as was Elton at intervals), but
the trend was toward direct and active estate management. To
increase demesne production, villeins were often saddled with
new labor services, or resaddled with old ones from which they
had bought exemption. But the tenants, including the villeins,
also began selling in the market. The pendulum swung back,
with the lords accepting higher rents and other money payments
and using the cash to hire labor to work the demesne. It was an
era of prosperity for all, but especially for the lords, who saw
their incomes, especially their cash incomes, rise rapidly.

They had no trouble spending them. By his nature the feudal
lord was a dedicated consumer. His social status imposed a
life-style of conspicuous consumption, which in the Middle Ages
meant mainly consumption of food and drink. The lord was
"the man who could always eat as much as he wished," says
Georges Duby, and also "the man who provided others with
food," and was consequently admired for his openhandedness.
The very yardstick of his prestige was the number of people he
fed: staff, armed retainers, labor force, guests.[6]

The abbot of Ramsey's requirements from his manors included grain, beef, flour, bread, malt for ale, fodder, lard, beans,
butter, bacon, honey, lambs, poultry, eggs, herrings, and cheese.
Like other lords he also received cash to make the many purchases outside the estate that were needed to keep his household

going: horses, cloth, coverlets, hangings, robes, candlesticks, plate.

Thus as consumer the lord needed revenues both in kind and in cash. As a consumer, he also required services, especially carrying services, to bring the produce from his manors to his castle or monastery. He needed even more services in his other economic capacity, that of producer. Here disparity existed not only among greater and lesser lords, but among their manors. Some were large, some small, some contained much demesne land, some little (a few none). Elton's thirteen hides were proba-bly close to average, as was also its proportion of about one quarter demesne land. The precise size of the demesne was never regarded as of great moment. Extents for the Ramsey manors of Warboys and Holywell state disarmingly, "The demesne of this manor consists of many furlongs, but it is not known how many acres are contained in them."[7] The acre itself varied erratically even among manors of the same estate.* On Ramsey manors the hide ranged from four virgates to seven, the virgate from fifteen to thirty-two acres, and the size of the acre is uncertain.[8]

Demesne land might lie in a compact parcel, separate from the villagers' fields, or it might, as it evidently did in Elton, lie scattered in strips like those of the tenants with which it was intermingled.

Where the demesne was large, a large labor force was needed, usually meaning that a substantial proportion of the tenants were villeins owing week-work. Where the demesne was small, most of the tenants were likely to be free, or if unfree, paying a money rent rather than rendering work services.

To his economic roles as consumer, producer, and landlord, the lord added certain others. He had an important, centuries-old judicial function, his manor courts (hallmotes) dealing in a range of civil and criminal cases that provided him with fines,

---

*Conversion among variant acres was none too easy for medieval mathematics, which lacked plural fractions. The author of one treatise, attempting to express the quantity of one acre, three and nine sixteenths rods, gave it as "one acre and a half and a rod and a half and a sixteenth of a rod."

fees, and confiscations. In addition to dues exacted from his tenants on a variety of occasions—death, inheritance, marriage—the lord enjoyed the "ban," a monopoly on certain activities, most notoriously on grinding everybody's grain and baking everybody's bread. The ban was resented and sometimes evaded, though rigorously enforced by the manor court. So were the lord's other privileges, such as folding all the village sheep so that their manure could improve his demesne. In Elton in 1306 Richard Hubert and John Wrau were fined because they had "refused to allow [their] sheep to be in the lord's fold."[9] The same offense brought Geoffrey Shoemaker and Ralph Attwych penalties of sixpence each in 1312, and in 1331 nine villagers were fined for the infraction, in addition to Robert le Ward, who was penalized for harboring the flock of one of his neighbors "to the damage of the lord."[10] On the other hand, an animal that roamed too freely risked the lord's privilege of "waif and stray": "One female colt came an estray to the value of 18 pence, and it remains. Therefore let the reeve answer [let the reeve sell the colt and turn over the money]."[11] A villager who recovered his impounded animal without license was fined for "making a rescue," as were Thomas Dyer in 1294 and Isabel daughter of Allota of Langetoft in 1312.[12]

One of the lord's most valuable privileges aroused little resentment: his right to license markets and fairs, granted him by the king or sometimes by another overlord. The abbot of Ramsey's fair of St. Ives was internationally famous, patronized by merchants from Flanders, France, Italy, and Scandinavia.[13] Such fairs and markets enriched both lord and tenants, at least the luckier and more enterprising. (In 1279 the abbot of Ramsey contemplated a weekly market at Elton, and successfully negotiated an agreement for it with the abbot of Peterborough, but for some reason the project was never carried out.)[14]

Yet despite all his collections, enforcements, and impingements, perhaps the most arresting aspect of the lord's relations with the villagers is the extent to which he left them alone. The once popular picture of the lord as "an omnipotent village tyrant" was, in George Homans's words, "an unrealistic assumption."[15] The medieval village actually lived and worked in a state of near autonomy. The open field system exacted a concert of the community at every point of the agricultural cycle: plowing, planting, growing, and harvesting. It is now virtually certain that the village achieved this concert by itself, with little help or leadership from outside. To Marc Bloch's observation that there was never any "necessary opposition" between the lord's manor and the peasants' village, Homans added that "the manor could be strong only where the village was strong."[16] More recent scholarship has stressed the primacy of the village over the manor in historical development.

The lord could have little objection to village autonomy. What he wanted was the certainty of rents and dues from his tenants, the efficient operation of his demesne, and good prices for wool and grain. The popularity of treatises on estate management is an indicator of what occupied the minds of the great lords of the late thirteenth century. Walter of Henley's *Husbandry* advised its noble readers to "look into your affairs often, and cause them to be reviewed, for those who serve you will thereby avoid the more to do wrong."[17] It was prudent counsel because there was no way for an absentee lord to supervise his scattered manors except through appointed officials.

These officials, in fact, constituted the lord's material presence in the village. Three of them, the steward, the bailiff, and the reeve, were the key executives of the manorial system.

Originally a household servant or majordomo, the estate steward (sometimes called a seneschal) had in the twelfth and thirteenth centuries accomplished a progression paralleling that of Joseph, the Pharaoh's cupbearer who became chief administrator of Egypt. On estate after estate the steward became the lord's deputy, chief executive officer for the vast complex of lands, rights, and people. Bishop Robert Grosseteste (1175–1253), author of another widely read treatise, *Rules of St. Robert*, defined the steward's duty as to guard and increase the lord's property and stock "in an honest way," and to defend his rights and franchises.[18] A slightly later writer, the anonymous author of *Seneschaucie*, stipulated legal knowledge as a principal qualification, since the steward now represented the lord in court both on and off the estate. His main function, however, was supervision of all the manors of the estate, which he did primarily by periodic visitation.[19] It was hardly possible for a lord to be too careful in his choice, thought the author of *Seneschaucie*: "The seneschal of lands ought to be prudent and faithful and profitable, and he ought to know the law of the realm, to protect his lord's business and to instruct and give assurance to the bailiffs." It was useless to look for wisdom from "young men full of young blood and ready courage, who know little or nothing of business." Wiser to appoint from among those "ripe in years, who have seen much, and know much, and who . . . never were caught or convicted for treachery or any wrongdoing"[20]—something that often befell officials, according to many sermons and satires.

Typically the steward of a great lay lord was a knight, that of a great ecclesiastical lord was a cleric. In the latter case, he was sometimes known as the cellarer, the traditional title of the person in charge of a monastery's food and drink supply. At least two stewards of Ramsey Abbey in the late thirteenth century were monks.[21] Where a knight-steward received his compensation from his fee (land holding), a clerk-steward usually received his from his living, a parish church whose services were conducted by a vicar. Like most such officials, the steward of Ramsey Abbey, in company with his clerk, made periodic tours of the abbey's manors to review the management of the demesne. He did not, as many stewards did, himself audit the manorial accounts. This function was performed on Ramsey manors by a separate clerk of the account who made his own annual tour and who in a hand that reflected an excellent education recorded the details of the year's transactions. This clerk, who received a rather modest stipend of five shillings, thus provided an independent check for the abbot on the management of his estate.[22]

The steward appeared in each village only at intervals, usually no more than two or three times a year, for a stay of seldom

more than two days. The lord's deputy on each manor throughout the year was the bailiff. Typically appointed on the steward's
recommendation, the bailiff was socially a step nearer the villagers themselves, perhaps a younger son of the gentry or a member
of a better-off peasant family. He could read and write; seigneurial as well as royal officialdom reflected the spread of lay liter-
acy.[23]

The bailiff combined the personae of chief law officer and
business manager of the manor. He represented the lord both
to the villagers and to strangers, thus acting as a protector of the
village against men of another lord. His overriding concern,
however, was management of the demesne, seeing that crops
and stock were properly looked after and as little as possible
stolen. He made sure the manor was supplied with what it
needed from outside, at Elton a formidable list of purchases:
millstones, iron, building timber and stone, firewood, nails,
horseshoes, carts, cartwheels, axles, iron tires, salt, candles,
parchment, cloth, utensils for dairy and kitchen, slate, thatch,
quicklime, verdigris, quicksilver, tar, baskets, livestock, food.
These were bought principally at nearby market towns, Oundle,
Peterborough, St. Neots, and at the Stamford and St. Ives fairs.
The thirteenth-century manor was anything but self-sufficient.

Walter of Henley, himself a former bailiff, advised lords and
stewards against choosing from their circle of kindred and
friends, and to make the selection strictly on merit.[24] The bailiff
was paid an excellent cash salary plus perquisites, at Elton
twenty shillings a year plus room and board, a fur coat, fodder
for his horse, and twopence to make his Christmas oblation
(offering). Two other officials, subordinate to the bailiff, are
mentioned in the Elton accounts: the *claviger* or macebearer,
and the serjeant, but both offices seem to have disappeared
shortly after 1300.[25]

The bailiff's residence was the lord's manor house. Set clearly
apart from the village's collection of flimsy wattle-and-daub
dwellings, the solid-stone, buttressed manor house contrasted
with them in its ample interior space and at least comparative
comfort. The main room, the hall, was the setting for the
manorial court, but otherwise remained at the bailiff's disposal.

There he and his family took their meals along with such members of the manorial household as were entitled to board at the lord's table, either continuously or at certain times, plus occasional visitors. A stone bench at the southern end flanked a large rectangular limestone hearth. The room was furnished with a trestle table, wooden benches, and a "lavatorium," a metal washstand. A garderobe, or privy, adjoined. One end of the hall was partitioned off as a buttery and a larder. The sleeping chamber whose existence is attested by repairs to it and to its door may have been a room with a fireplace uncovered by the excavations of 1977. A chapel stood next to the manor house.[26] For the entertainment of guests "carrying the lord's writ," such as the steward or the clerk of the accounts, the bailiff kept track of his costs and submitted the expenses to Ramsey. Visitors included monks and officials on their way to the Stamford Fair, or to be ordained in Stamford; other ecclesiastics, among them the abbot's two brothers and the prior of St. Ives; and royal officials—the justice of the forest, the sheriff of Huntingdon,

Manor house, c. 1170, at Burton Agnes (Humberside): ground-floor undercroft.

Manor house, Burton Agnes: upper hall.

kings' messengers, and once "the twelve regarders," knights
who enforced the king's forest law.[27] The guests' horses and
dogs had to be lodged and fed, and sometimes their falcons,
including "the falcons of the lord abbot."[28] In 1298 when the
royal army was on its way to Scotland, a special expense was
incurred, a bribe of sixpence to "a certain man of the Exchequer
of the lord king . . . for sparing our horses."[29] On several later
occasions expenses are noted either for feeding military parties
or bribing them to go elsewhere.

Assisting the bailiff was a staff of subordinate officials chosen
annually from and usually (as in Elton) by the villagers themselves. Chief of these was the reeve. Always a villein, he was one
of the most prosperous—"the best husbandman," according to
Seneschaucie. [30] Normally the new reeve succeeded at Michaelmas
(September 29), the beginning of the agricultural year. His main
duty was seeing that the villagers who owed labor service rose
promptly and reported for work. He supervised the formation

Manor house at Boothby Pagnell (Lincolnshire), c. 1200, also built with an undercroft and an upper hall. Royal Commission on the Historic Monuments of England.

of the plow teams, saw to the penning and folding of the lord's livestock, ordered the mending of the lord's fences, and made sure sufficient forage was saved for the winter.[31] *Seneschaucie* admonished him to make sure no herdsman slipped off to fair, market, wrestling match, or tavern without obtaining leave and finding a substitute.[32] He might, as occasionally at Elton, be entrusted with the sale of demesne produce. On some manors the reeve collected the rents.

But of all his numerous functions, the most remarkable was his rendition of the demesne account. He produced this at the end of the agricultural year for the lord's steward or clerk of the accounts. Surviving reeves' accounts of Elton are divided into four parts: "arrears," or receipts; expenses and liveries (meaning deliveries); issue of the grange (grain and other stores on hand in the barns); and stock. The account of Alexander atte Cross, reeve in 1297, also appends an "account of works" performed by the tenants.

Each part is painstakingly detailed. Under "arrears" are given the rents collected on each of several feast days when they fell due, the rents that remained unpaid for whatever reason, and receipts from sales of grain, stock, poultry, and other products. Under "expenses and liveries" are listed all the bacon, beef, meal, and cheeses consigned to Ramsey Abbey throughout the year, and the mallards, larks, and kids sent to the abbot at Christmas and Easter. Numerous payments to individuals— carpenter, smith, itinerant workmen—are listed, and purchases set down: plows and parts, yokes and harness, hinges, wheels, grease, meat, herring, and many other items. The "issue of the grange" in 1297 lists 486 rings and 1 bushel of wheat totaled from the mows in the barn and elsewhere, and describes its disposal: to Ramsey, in sales, in payment of a debt to the rector, and for boon-works; then it does the same for rye, barley, and the other grains. In the stock account, the reeve lists all the animals—horses, cattle, sheep, pigs—inherited from the previous year, notes the advances in age category (lambs to ewes or wethers, young calves to yearlings), and those sold or dead (with hides accounted for).[33]

With no formal schooling to draw on, the unlettered reeve kept track of all these facts and figures by means of marks on a tally stick, which he read off to the clerk of the accounts. Written out on parchment about eight inches wide and in segments varying in length, sewed together end to end, the account makes two things clear: the medieval manor was a well-supervised business operation, and the reeve who played so central a role in it was not the dull-witted clod traditionally evoked by the words "peasant" and "villein."

The accounts often resulted in a small balance one way or the other. Henry Reeve, who served at Elton in 1286–1287, reported revenues of 36 pounds, ¼ penny, and expenditures of 36 pounds 15 ¾ pence, which he balanced with the conclusion: "Proved, and so the lord owes the reeve 15½ pence."[34] His successor, Philip of Elton, who took over in April 1287, reported on the following Michaelmas receipts of 26 pounds 6 shillings 7 pence, expenditures of 25 pounds 16 shillings ¼ penny: "Proved and thus the reeve owes the lord 10 shillings 6 ¾ pence."[35]

For his labors, physical and mental, the reeve received no cash stipend, but nevertheless quite substantial compensation. He was always exempted from his normal villein obligations (at Elton amounting to 117 days' week-work), and at Elton, though not everywhere, received at least some of his meals at the manor house table. He also received a penny for his Christmas obla-tion.[36] On some less favored manors, candidates for reeve de-clined the honor and even paid to avoid it, but most accepted readily enough. At Broughton the reeve was given the privilege of grazing eight animals in the lord's pasture.[37] That may have been the formal concession of a privilege already preempted. "It would be surprising," says Nigel Saul, "if the reeve had not folded his sheep on the lord's pastures or used the demesne stock to plow his own lands."[38] There were many other possibili-ties. Chaucer's reeve is a skillful thief of his lord's produce:

> Well could he keep a garner and a bin,
> There was no auditor could on him win.[39]

Walter of Henley considered it wise to check the reeve's bushel measure after he had rendered his account.[40]

Some business-minded lords assigned quotas to their man-ors—annual quantities of wheat, barley, and other produce, fixed numbers of calves, lambs, other stock, and eggs. The monkish board of auditors of St. Swithun's Abbey enforced their quotas by exactions from the reeve, forcing him to make up out of his pocket any shortfall. It might be supposed that St. Swithun's would experience difficulty in finding reeves. Not so, however. The monks were strict, but their quotas were moderate and attractively consistent, remaining exactly the same year after year for long stretches—60 piglets, 28 goslings, 60 chicks, and 300 eggs—making it entirely possible, or rather probable, that the reeve profited in most years, adding the surplus goslings and piglets to his own stock.[41]

The reeve in turn had an assistant, known variously as the beadle, hayward, or messor, who served partly as the reeve's deputy, partly in an independent role. As the reeve was tradi-tionally a villein virgater, his deputy was traditionally a villein half-virgater, one of the middle-level villagers.

The beadle or hayward usually had primary responsibility for the seed saved from last year's crop, its preservation and sowing, including the performances of the plowmen in their plowing and harrowing, and later, in cooperation with the reeve, for those of the villeins doing mowing and reaping. Walter of Henley warned that villeins owing week-work were prone to shirk: "If they do not [work] well, let them be reproved."[42] The hayward's job also included impounding cattle or sheep that strayed into the demesne crop and seeing that their owners were fined.[43]

Many manors also had a woodward to see that no one took from the lord's wood anything except what he was allowed by custom or payment; some also had a cart-reeve with specialized functions. One set of officials no village was ever without was the ale tasters, who assessed the quality and monitored the price of ale brewed for sale to the public. This last was the only village office ever filled by women, who did most of the brewing.

At Elton the titles "beadle" and "hayward" were both in use. Both offices may have existed simultaneously, with the beadle primarily responsible for collecting rents and the fines levied in court. The beadle's compensation consisted of partial board at the manor house plus exemption from his labor obligation (half the reeve's, or 58½ days a year, since he owed for a half rather than a full virgate). At Elton a reap-reeve was sometimes appointed in late summer to help police the harvest work, a function otherwise assigned to two "wardens of the autumn."[44]

The primary aim of estate management was to provide for the lord's needs, which were always twofold: food for himself and his household, and cash to supply needs that could not be met from the manors. Many lay barons collected their manorial product in person by touring their estates annually manor by manor. Bishop Grosseteste advised careful planning of the tour. It should begin after the post-Michaelmas "view of account," when it would be possible to calculate how lengthy a visit each manor could support. "Do not in any wise burden by debt or long residence the places where you sojourn," he cautioned, lest the manorial economy be so weakened that it could not supply from the sale of its products cash for "your wines, robes, wax, and all your wardrobe."[45]

For Ramsey Abbey and other monasteries, such peripatetic victualing was not practical. Instead, several manors, of which Elton was one, were earmarked for the abbey food supply and assigned a quota, or "farm," meaning sufficient food and drink to answer the needs of the monks and their guests for a certain period.[46]

Whatever the arrangement for exploitation of the manors, the thirteenth-century lord nearly always received his income in both produce and cash. The demesne furnished the great bulk of the produce, plus a growing sum in cash from sales at fair or market. The tenants furnished the bulk of the cash by their rents, plus some payments in kind (not only bread, ale, eggs, and cheese, but in many cases linen, wool cloth, and handicraft products). Cash also flowed in from the manorial court fines. Only a few lords, such as the bishop of Worcester, enjoyed the convenience of a revenue paid exclusively in cash.[47]

Cultivation of the demesne was accomplished by a combination of the villein tenants' contribution of week-work and the daily labor of the demesne staff, the *famuli*. In England the tenants generally contributed about a fourth of the demesne plowing, leaving three fourths to the *famuli*. [48] At Elton these consisted of eight plowmen and drivers, a carter, a cowherd, a swineherd, and a shepherd, all paid two to four shillings a year in cash plus "livery," an allowance of grain, flour, and salt, plus a pair of gloves and money for their Christmas oblation.[49] Smaller emoluments were paid to a cook, a dairyman or dairymaid, extra shepherds, seasonal helpers for the cowherd and swineherd, a keeper of bullocks, a woman who milked ewes, and a few other seasonal or temporary hands.[50] On some manors the *famuli* were settled on holdings, one version of which was the "sown acre," a piece of demesne land sown with grain. Ramsey Abbey used the sown acre to compensate its own huge *familia* of eighty persons.[51] Another arrangement was the "Saturday plow," by which the lord's plow cohort was lent one day a week to plow the holdings of *famuli*. [52]

The manorial plowman was responsible for the well-being of his plow animals and the maintenance of his plows and harness. *Seneschaucie* stressed the need for intelligence in a plowman, who was also expected to be versed in digging drainage ditches. As for plow animals, Walter of Henley judiciously recommended both horses and oxen, horses for their superior work virtues, oxen for their economy. An old ox was edible and, fattened up, could be sold for as much as he had cost, according to Walter (actually, for 90 percent of his cost, according to a modern scholar; in the 1290s, about 12 shillings). Pope Gregory III had proscribed horsemeat in 732, and though most of Europe ignored the ban, in the Middle Ages and long after, in England horsemeat was never eaten. Consequently an old plow horse fetched less than half his original cost of ten to eleven shillings.[53]

Elton's bailiff or the Ramsey steward may have studied Walter of Henley, because the eight Elton demesne plowmen and drivers used ten stots (work horses) and eighteen oxen in their four plow teams. Horses and oxen were commonly harnessed together, a practice also recommended by Walter. In the Elton region (East Midlands) a popular combination was two horses and six oxen.[54]

Sheepfold. Man at center is doctoring a sheep, while woman on the left milks and women on the right carry jars of milk. British Library, Luttrell Psalter, Ms. Add. 42130, f. 163v.

Cattle being driven by herdsmen. British Library, Queen Mary's Psalter, Ms. Royal 2B Vii, f. 75.

On every manor the tenants' labor was urgently required in one critical stretch of the annual cycle, the boon-works of autumn and post-autumn. To get the demesne harvest cut, stacked, carted, threshed, and stored and the winter wheat planted before frost called for mass conscription of villeins, free tenants, their families, and often for recruitment of extra labor from the floating population of landless peasants. At Elton, two *meiatores*, professional grain handlers, and a professional winnower were taken on at harvest time.[55]

Threshing, done in the barn, was a time-consuming job, winnowing an easy one. Hired labor was paid a penny per ring of threshed wheat, a penny per eight rings winnowed.[56]

The staple crops at Elton were those of most English manors: barley, wheat, oats, peas, and beans, and, beginning in the late thirteenth century, rye. The proportions in the demesne harvest of 1286 were about two thousand bushels of barley, half as much wheat, and lesser proportions of oats, drage (mixed grain), and peas and beans.[57] Yields were four to one for barley, four to one for wheat, a bit over two to one for oats, and four to one for beans and peas. The overall yield was about three and two-thirds to one, better than the three and one-third stipulated in the

Harrowing. Man following the harrow is planting peas or beans, using a stick as a seed drill. British Library, Luttrell Psalter, Ms. Add. 42130, f. 171.

Rules of St. Robert.[58] In 1297 the Elton wheat yield reached fivefold, but overall the ratio remained about the same, a third to half modern figures.[59] Prices fluctuated considerably over the half-century from 1270 to 1320, varying from five to eight shillings a quarter (eight bushels) for wheat.[60] Half a ring (two bushels) planted an acre. Even without drought or flood, labor costs and price uncertainty could make a lord's profit on crops precarious.

The treatises offered extensive advice on animal husbandry—standards for butter and cheese production, advice on milk versus cheese, on suspension of the milking of cows and ewes to encourage early breeding, on feeding work animals (best for the reeve or hayward to look to, since the oxherd might steal the provender), and on branding the lord's sheep so that they could be distinguished from those of the tenants. The cowherd should sleep with his animals in the barn, and the shepherd should do the same, with his dog next to him.[61]

In the realm of veterinary medicine, the best that can be said is that it was no worse than medieval human medicine. Without giving specific instructions, Walter of Henley advocated making an effort to save animals: "If there be any beast which begins to fall ill, lay out money to better it, for it is said in the proverb, 'Blessed is the penny that saves two.' "[62] Probably more practical was Walter's advice to sell off animals quickly when disease threatened the herd. Verdigris (copper sulfate), mercury, and tar, all items that appear frequently in the Elton manorial accounts, were applied for a variety of animal afflictions, with little effect on the prevailing rate of mortality, averaging 18 percent among sheep.[63] Sheep pox, "Red Death," and murrain were usually blamed, the word "murrain" covering so many diseases that it occurs more often in medieval stock accounts than any other.[64]

The Elton dairy produced some two hundred cheeses a year, most if not all from ewes' milk, with the bulk of the product going to the cellarer of the abbey, some to the *famuli* and boon-workers.[65] Most of the butter was sold, some of the milk used to nurse lambs. The medieval practice of treating ewes as dairy animals may have hindered development of size and stamina. But though notoriously susceptible to disease, sheep were never a total loss since their woolly skins (fells) brought a good price. The relative importance of their fleece caused medieval flocks to have a composition which would seem odd to modern sheep farmers. Where modern sheep are raised mainly for meat and the wethers (males) are slaughtered early, in the Middle Ages the wethers' superior fleece kept them alive for four to five years.[66]

Poultry at Elton, as on most manors, was the province of a dairymaid, who, according to *Seneschaucie,* ought to be "faithful and of good repute, and keep herself clean, and . . . know her business." She should be adept at making and salting cheese, should help with the winnowing, take good care of the geese and hens, and keep and cover the fire in the manor house.[67]

The only other agricultural products at Elton were flax, apples, and wax, all cultivated on a modest or insignificant scale.[68] The wax was a scanty return on a beekeeping enterprise that failed through a bee disease. On other English manors a variety of garden vegetables, cider, timber, and brushwood were market products. Wine, a major product on the Continent, was a minor one in England.

In the old days of subsistence agriculture, when the manor's produce went to feed the manor and the clink of a coin was

Beehive. British Library, Luttrell Psalter, Ms. Add. 42130, f. 204.

seldom heard in the countryside, the surplus of an exceptional season, beyond what everyone could eat, went to waste. But for some time now a momentous change had been under way. The growth of town markets "put most men within the reach of opportunities of buying and selling."[69] The man most affected was the lord, if he awoke to his opportunity. Robert Grosseteste, the practical-minded bishop of Lincoln, urged his readers to ask "how profitable your plow and stock are."[70] Generally the answer was satisfactory. Not only that, but revenue from cash rents was increasing rapidly as the tenants took advantage of the market. One study of central England in 1279 indicates that even the villeins were now paying more than half their dues in money.[71] Besides rents, these included a long list of servile fees and the fines of the manorial court. The very number and variety of the lord's revenues probably helped blind everyone to the inefficiency of the system that supplied them. Like slavery, serfdom required continuous year-round maintenance of a labor force whose labor was needed only in varying degrees in different seasons.

Hired labor and cash rents were the wave of the future. So was the application of technical improvements. Some lords made an effort. Henry de Bray's account book records a number of improvements added to his single manor, including building cottages for tenants, widening a stream to provide fish ponds, and constructing a mill and a bridge.[72] At Wharram Percy a wholesale reconstruction of the village was executed, evidently a rare seizure of the opportunity afforded a lord by his legal ownership of the village houses and land.[73] In the towns such a large-scale project was impossible; over centuries changes were restricted to individual building sites.

Naive but intelligent Walter of Henley has been credited with pioneering scientific agriculture for his recommendations, admittedly general, for improving seed ("Seed grown on other ground will bring more profit than that which is grown on your own")[74] and breed ("Do not have boars and sows unless of a good breed").[75] The Elton records show evidence of attempts to improve the demesne seed by trading among manors. In 1286–1287, thirty rings of wheat were sent to the reeve of Abbot's Ripton and twenty received from the reeve of Weston.[76] *Seneschaucie* was more specific than Walter in respect to improving breeds, assigning the cowherd responsibility for choosing large bulls of good pedigree to pasture and mate with the cows.[77] Robert Trow-Smith believes the experts were heeded to some extent. Progressive lords such as the Hungerfords of Wiltshire imported rams from Lincolnshire and other regions of England, and Trow-Smith ventures a surmise that "the owners of the great ecclesiastical estates in particular" imported breeding stock from the Continent.[78]

Yet the only really widely used device for increasing agricultural production remained the old one of assarting, of enlarging the area of land by cutting down forest or draining marsh. In earlier centuries, when forest and marsh covered the countryside of northwest Europe, a pioneering effort with axe and spade was natural and obvious. Now, in the late thirteenth century, as villages filled the landscape, scope for assarting was disappearing.

At the same time an opportunity was opening in the booming wool market. Exceeding in volume the demand for grain, meat, leather, and everything else were the purchases by the great merchant-manufacturers of the cloth cities of Flanders, France, and Italy. English wool was especially prized for its fineness, the most sought-after single characteristic of a fiber. Agents of the great wool firms often contracted with a monastic house like Ramsey Abbey for an entire year's clip, or even several years' clip, in advance. Prices remained very steady at four to five shillings a stone (1270–1320). The Elton demesne, which delivered 118 fleeces to Ramsey in 1287, in 1314 carted 521 to the abbey.[79] Clumsy, fragile, and vulnerable, but easy to feed, easy to handle, and producing its fleece reliably every year, the sheep was on its way to becoming England's national treasure.

Appreciative though they were of the wonderful wool market, most lords remained conservative in respect to change, "reluctant to spend heavily from current revenue upon improvements."[80] The most profitable part of the lord's land was meadow, and the most valuable crop he could raise was hay for winter feed, but on most manors grain remained the top priority. Cereal agriculture retained a mystic prestige among the landholding class as it did, for sounder material reasons, among the peasants.[81]

When foreign wool buyers, their eye on long-term investments, insisted that the sheds where fleeces were shorn and stored be given boarded floors, as did a consortium of merchants

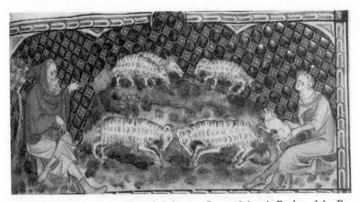

Shepherds watching sheep. British Library, Queen Mary's Psalter, Ms. Royal 2B VII, f. 74.

Donkey carrying wool-sacks to market. Bodleian Library, Ms. Ashmole 1504, f. 30.

from Cahors in dealing with the Cistercian abbey of Pipewell, the abbey gave in and boarded the floors, but that was as far as the lord cared to go in welcoming improvement.[82] The historic shift in British agriculture marked by the enclosure movement got under way, very slowly, only in the fifteenth century.

Content to see their revenues rise and their luxuries multiply, most lords preferred to assure themselves of all that was coming to them under the system rather than striving to improve the system. Manorial custom still ruled the countryside, its authority fortified by the new commitment to the written record, and neither lord nor peasant was sufficiently dissatisfied to press for change. The lord counted on custom to bring laborers to his fields, coins to his coffers, and poultry, cheese, meat, and ale to his table. The villager relied on custom to limit his services and payments, and to guarantee him his house, his croft, his strips of arable, and his grazing rights.

4

THE VILLAGERS: WHO THEY WERE

THREE CONSIDERATIONS GOVERNED THE CONDItion of the Elton villager: his legal status (free versus unfree), his wealth in land and animals, and (related to the first two criteria but independent of them) his social standing. How the villagers interacted has only recently drawn attention from historians. Earlier, the peasant's relationship with his lord dominated scholarly investigation. This "manorial aspect" of the peasant's life overshadowed the "village aspect," which, however, is older and more fundamental, the village being older than the manor. The fact that information about the village is harder to come by than information about the manor in no way alters this conclusion. The manor has been described historically as "a landowning and land management grid superimposed on the settlement patterns of villages and hamlets."[1]

Both village and manor played their part in the peasant's life. The importance of the manor's role depended on the peasant's status as a free man or villein, a distinction for which the lawyers strove to find a clear-cut criterion. Henry de Bracton, leading jurist of the thirteenth century, laid down the principle, *"Omnes homines aut liberi sunt aut servi"* (All men are either free or servile).[2] Bracton and his colleagues sought to fit the villein into Roman law, and in doing so virtually identified him as a slave. Neat though that correspondence might be in legal theory, it did not work in practice. Despite their de jure unfree status, many villeins succeeded de facto in appropriating the privileges of freedom. They bought, sold, bequeathed, and inherited property, including land. Practical need created custom, and custom overrode Roman legal theory.

Back at the time of the Domesday survey, the English villein was actually catalogued among the free men, "the meanest of the free," according to Frederic Maitland, ranking third among the five tiers of peasantry: *liberi homines* (free men); sokemen; villeins; cotters or bordars, equivalent to the serfs of the Continent; and slaves, employed on the lord's land as laborers and servants.[3] In the century after Domesday, slaves disappeared in England, by a process that remains obscure, apparently evolving into either manorial servants or villein tenants. But meanwhile by an equally obscure process the villein slipped down into the category of the unfree. Historians picture a series of pendulum swings in peasant status reflecting large external economic shifts, especially the growth of the towns as markets for agricultural produce. R. H. Hilton believes that the new heavy obligations were imposed on the English villein mainly in the 1180s and 1190s.[4]

The unfreedom of the villein or serf was never a generalized condition, like slavery, but always consisted of specific disabilities: he owed the lord substantial labor services; he was subject to a number of fines or fees, in cash or in kind; and he was under the jurisdiction of the lord's courts. In Maitland's words, the serf, or villein, remained "a free man in relation to all men other than his lord."[5]

The very concepts of "free" and "unfree" involved a tangle of legal subtleties. On the Continent, nuances of freedom and servility developed early, and with them an array of Latin terms for the unfree: *mancipium, servus, colonus, lidus, collibertus, nati-*

vus. [6] In England, terminology became even more complicated. The variety of nomenclature in Domesday Book, which derived in part from regional patterns of settlement, multiplied in the two subsequent centuries to a point where in Cambridgeshire in 1279 villagers were described by twenty different terms, some meaning essentially the same thing, some indicating slight differences. A few miles north, in southern Lincolnshire, eight more designations appeared. To what Edward Miller and John Hatcher call a "positive jungle of rules governing social relationships" was added the fact that land itself was classified as free or villein, meaning that it owed money rents or labor services. Originally villein tenants had held villein land, but by the thirteenth century many villeins held some free land and many free men some villein land.[7]

But if legal status was clouded by complexity, economic status tended to be quite clear, visible, and tangible: one held a certain number of acres and owned a certain number of cattle and sheep. Georges Duby, speaking of the Continent, observes, "Formerly class distinctions had been drawn according to hereditary and juridical lines separating free men from unfree, but by 1300 it was a man's economic condition which counted most."[8] In England the shift was perhaps a little slower, but unmistakably in the same direction. A rich villein was a bigger man in the village than a poor free man.

In the relations among villagers, what might be called the sociology of the village, much remains obscure, but much can be learned through analysis of the rolls of the manorial courts, which recorded not only enforcement of manorial obligations but interaction among the villagers, their quarrels, litigation, marriages, inheritance, sale and purchase of land, economic activities, and crimes.

Just at this moment a major aid in identification of individuals and families of villagers made its historic appearance: the introduction of surnames. A survey of Elton of about 1160 included in the Ramsey Abbey cartulary and listing current tenants, their

fathers, and their grandfathers, gives only a handful of sur-
names. Where these occur they are taken from place of origin
(Ralph of Asekirche, Ralph of Walsoken, Gilbert of Newton);
from occupation (Thurold Priest [Presbyter], Thomas Clerk
[Clericus], Gilbert Reeve [Praepositus], Ralph Shoemaker
[Sutor]); or from paternity (Richard son of Reginald). But most
of the villagers are listed only by their first names: Walter,
Thomas, Ralph, Roger, Robert, Edward.[9]

A century later, manorial court rolls and a royal survey attach
surnames to nearly all the Elton tenants. Some are in Latin, like
the given names, some simply in English: Robertus ad Crucem
(Robert at the Cross) and Henricus Messor (Henry Hayward),
but Iohannes Page (John Page), Henricus Wollemonger (Henry
Woolmonger), and Robertus Chapman (whose Old English
name, meaning merchant, is cited in Latin elsewhere in the
records as Robertus Mercator). Often it is difficult to tell
whether the Latin represents a true surname or merely a trade
or office: thus "Henricus Faber" may be Henry Smith; or he may
be Henry the smith, and may be mentioned elsewhere in the
records as Henry son of Gilbert, or Henry atte Water, or Henry
of Barnwell. John Dunning's son who left the village and became
a tanner at Hayham is always referred to as "John Tanner."

Nearly all surnames derived from the same three sources:
parental (or grandparental) Christian names; occupations, offices, or occasionally legal status; and places, either of origin or
in the village. In the first category are the Fraunceys family,
possibly deriving from a "Franceis" in the twelfth-century survey who held a virgate and six acres; the Goscelins; the Blundels
(in the twelfth century a Blundel held three virgates); the Benyts
(Benedicts); the Huberts; and numerous names prefaced by "son
of" (Alexander son of Gilbert, Nicholas son of Henry, Robert
son of John). In a few cases villagers are identified by their
mothers' first names: William son of Letitia, Agnes daughter of
Beatrice. J. A. Raftis in his study of the village of Warboys
observed that surnames derived from parental Christian names
gradually dropped the "son of" and became simply Alexander
Gilbert, Nicholas Henry, Robert John. Finally, in the latter half

of the fourteenth century, the "son" sometimes reappeared as a suffix: Johnson, Jameson, Williamson.[10]

In the category of occupations and offices, Elton names included Miller, Smith, Shoemaker, Carter, Carpenter, Chapelyn, Comber, Cooper, Dyer, Webster (weaver), Chapman (merchant), Shepherd, Tanner, Walker, Woolmonger, Baxter (baker), Tailor, Painter, Freeman, Hayward, and Beadle. No fewer than eight men in the court rolls in the last two decades of the thirteenth century bear the name Reeve, three in one court roll, and one man is given the name (in English) of Reeveson.

The category of names indicating origin usually derived from villages in the immediate vicinity of Elton: Warmington, Morburn, Water Newton, Stanground, and Alwalton; Barnwell, Keyston, and Brington to the south; Barton in Bedfordshire; Clipsham in Lincolnshire; and Marholm, northwest of Peterborough. Surnames that derived from the part of the village where the family lived mix Latin and English, and occasionally French: Abovebrook, Ad Portam (at the gate), Ad Pontem (at the bridge), Ad Furnam (at the oven), atte (at the) Brook, atte Water, atte Well, Ordevill (hors de ville or Extra Villam, outside the village), In Venella (in the lane), In Angulo (in the nook or corner), Ad Ripam (at the riverbank). In time these were smoothed and simplified into plain Brooks, Gates, Bridges, Lane, Banks, Atwater, or Atwell.

A few Elton surnames seem to have come from personal characteristics or obscurely derived nicknames: L'Hermite (the hermit), Prudhomme (wise man), le Wyse, Child, Hering, Saladin, Blaccalf, Le Long, Le Rus. One family was named Peppercorn, one Mustard.*

Evidence suggests that village society everywhere was stratified into three classes. The lowest held either no land at all or

---

*Surnames are spelled in a variety of ways in the records—for example, Prudhomme, Prodhomme, Prudomme, Prodom, Produmie, Prodome, Produme, Prodomme; Saladin, Saladyn, Saldy, Saldyn, Saldin, Salyn, Saln; Blaccalf, Blacchalf, Blacchelf, Blacchal, Blakchalf. We have chosen one spelling and used it throughout.

too little to support a family. The middle group worked holdings of a half virgate to a full virgate. A half virgate (12 to 16 acres) sufficed to feed father, mother, and children in a good season; a full virgate supplied a surplus to redeem a villein obligation or even purchase more land. At the top of the hierarchy was a small class of comparatively large peasant landholders, families whose 40, 50, or even 100 acres might in a few generations raise them to the gentry, though at present they might be villeins.

A statistical picture of the pattern was compiled by Soviet economic historian E. A. Kosminsky, who analyzed the land-holding information supplied by the Hundred Rolls survey of 1279 of seven Midland counties, including Huntingdonshire. He found that 32 percent of all the arable land formed the lord's demesne, 40 percent was held by villeins, and 28 percent by freeholders. About a fifth of the peasantry held approximately a virgate and more than a third held half-virgates. A few highly successful families had accumulated 100 acres or more. In general, the size of holdings was diminishing as the population grew. Out of 13,500 holdings in 1279, 46 percent amounted to 10 acres or less, probably near the minimum for subsistence.[11]

The Hundred Rolls data for Elton are in rough accord with the overall figures. The survey lists first the abbot's holdings; then the tenants, their holdings and legal status, and their obligations to abbot and king.[12]

The abbot's demesne contained the curia's acre and a half, his three hides of arable land, his sixteen acres of meadow and three of pasture, his three mills, and the fishing rights he held on the river.

The list of tenants was headed by "John, son of John of Elton," a major free tenant who held a hide (6 virgates, or 144 acres) of the abbot's land, amounting to a small estate within the manor, with its own tenants: one free virgater and nine cotters (men holding a cottage and a small amount of land).

Next were listed the abbot's other tenants, twenty-two free men, forty-eight villeins, and twenty-eight cotters; and finally the rector and four cotters who were his tenants.

These 114 names of heads of families by no means accounted

for all the inhabitants of the village, or even the male inhabitants; at least 150 other identifiable names appear in the court rolls of 1279–1300, representing other family members, day laborers, manorial workers, and craftsmen.

John of Elton—or "John le Lord," as he is referred to in one court record—was the village's aristocrat, though devoid of any title of nobility. His miniature estate had been assembled by twelfth-century ancestors by one means or another.* Of his hide of land, thirty-six acres formed the demesne. He owed suit (attendance) to the abbot's honor court at Broughton, the court for the entire estate, as well as "the third part of a suit" (attendance at every third session) to the royal shire and hundred courts. His one free tenant, John of Langetoft, held a virgate "by charter" (deed), and paid a token yearly rent of one penny. Half a virgate of the hide belonged to the abbot "freely in perpetual alms." The rest was divided among nine cotters (averaging out to eight acres apiece).

The abbot's twenty-two other tenants listed as free in the Hundred Rolls survey held varying amounts of land for which they owed minor labor services and money rent ranging from four shillings one penny a year to six shillings. Among them were three whose claim to freedom was later rejected by the manorial court, an indication of the uncertainty often surrounding the question of freedom.

The size of the holdings of these twenty-two tenants and the duties with which the holdings were burdened suggest a history that illustrates the changeable nature of manorial landholding. A given piece of land did not necessarily pass intact from father to son through several generations. Divided inheritance, gifts to younger sons, dowries to daughters, purchase and sale, all produced a shifting pattern which over time subdivided and multi-

---

*He apparently traced his family back to a "Richard son of Reginald," a free tenant in the survey of 1160, to whom Abbot Walter had granted two virgates of land formerly held by Thuri Priest. Richard may have inherited another virgate from his father, and the family seems to have acquired three virgates belonging to another landholder in the survey, one Reiner son of Ednoth.[13] In a survey of 1218, "John son of John of Elton" is listed as holding a hide of land "of the lord abbot of Ramsey."

plied holdings. In 1160 the twenty-two free tenants had been only nine, and in 1279 nine principal tenants still held the land from the lord abbot. But five of the nine had given (as dowry or inheritance) or sold parcels of their land to thirteen lesser tenants, who paid the principal tenants an annual rent.

One of these lesser tenants was Robert Chapman, listed in the rolls as a cotter on John of Elton's land, but whose name, meaning merchant, suggests his status as a rising parvenu. Evidently a newcomer to Elton, Robert in 1279 held in addition to his cottage three parcels of land totaling eighteen acres which he had undoubtedly purchased. On the other side of the social ledger was Geoffrey Blundel, whose ancestor in 1160 had held three virgates (seventy-two acres), but who in 1279 retained only a virgate and a half, and that divided among five lesser tenants. In the fluctuations of peasant landholding, as in that of their betters, some rose, some sank.

The forty-eight villeins of Elton—"customary tenants," subject to the "custom of the manor," meaning its labor services and dues—included thirty-nine virgaters and nine half-virgaters. Growth of population had turned some family virgates into half-virgates, a process that had advanced much farther elsewhere, often leaving no full virgaters at all. No Elton villein held more than a virgate, though land-rich villeins were a well-known phenomenon elsewhere.[14]

Elton's villeins performed substantial labor services, which were spelled out in detail in the survey, the half-virgaters owing half the work obligations of the virgaters. This work had a monetary value, and exemption could be purchased by the tenant, with the price paid going to pay hired labor.

Every "work," meaning day's work, owed by the villein was defined. One day's harrowing counted as one work; so did winnowing thirty sheaves of barley or twenty-four sheaves of wheat; collecting a bag of nuts "well cleaned"; or working in the vineyard; or making a hedge in the fields of a certain length; or carrying hay in the peasant's cart; or if he did not have a cart, hens, geese, cheese, and eggs "on his back."[15]

The time of year affected the price of the work. Works done between August 1 and Michaelmas (September 29), the season of intensive labor, were more expensive. One Elton account records the price of a single work at a halfpenny for most of the year (September 29 to August 1), 2½ pence from August 1 to September 8, and a penny from then to September 29.[16] Later, works were simply priced at a halfpenny from Michaelmas to August 1 and a penny from August 1 to Michaelmas.[17]

In 1286, sixteen of the forty-eight customary tenants had all their year-round works commuted to money payments, and owed only the special works at harvest time.[18] From the annual fee paid by these tenants, called the *censum* (quit-rent), they were said to be tenants *ad censum,* or *censuarii.* The other customary tenants were *ad opus* (at work [services]) and were *operarii.* Though such substitution of money payments for labor services was convenient for the villein in many ways, in other ways it was a disadvantage. Much, obviously, depended on the size of the payment. J. A. Raftis has calculated that the amount of the *censum* paid by a Ramsey Abbey villein was substantially larger than the total sum of the prices of his individual works.[19] The Elton court rolls imply that it was not desirable to be placed *ad censum,* and in fact that tenants were so classed arbitrarily. In 1279 two villagers accused the reeve of "taking the rich off the *censum* and putting the poor on it," apparently in exchange for bribes.[20]

In addition to work services or the *censum,* the customary tenants were subject to a long list of special exactions not imposed on the free tenants. These fell into four categories: charges paid only by the villeins *ad opus;* those paid only by the *censuarii;* those paid by both groups; and the monopolies held by the lord.

The first category included several fines or fees that seem to be relics of services or of contributions in kind: "woolsilver," probably a substitute for a shearing service; "wardpenny" for serving as public watchman; "maltsilver" for making malt for the abbot's ale; "fishsilver" for supplying fish for his Lenten meals; and "vineyard silver" for work in the vineyard. "Fodder-corn" was a payment in kind of a ring of oats from each virgate.

"Filstingpound" seems to have been an insurance premium paid by the villeins to protect themselves against corporal punishment or against excessive fines in the manorial court. If a villein's daughter had sex out of wedlock, she or her father paid *leirwite* or *legerwite.*

The second category consisted of a special charge owed only by the *censuarii:* 120 eggs from each virgater, 60 at Christmas and 60 at Easter.[21]

In the third category were "heushire," or "house hire," rent for the house on the holding, and several charges whose French names indicate importation to England by the Conquest. Tallage was a yearly tax at Elton, set at eight pence,[22] but on some manors it was levied "at the lord's will"—whenever and however much he chose. When the villein succeeded to a holding, he paid an entry fine or *gersum,* in effect a tax on land. On most manors, when the villein died his family paid heriot, usually his "best beast," the "second best beast" commonly going to the rector of the church; this was a tax on chattels. If the villein's daughter married, she or her father paid merchet.

If the villein wished to leave the manor, he could do so with the payment of a yearly fee, at Elton usually two chickens or capons. This payment, known as *chevage,* was not always easy to collect. Some villagers paid regularly—Henry atte Water, Richard in the Lane, Richard Benyt who had left "to dwell on a free tenement," Simon son of Henry Marshal. Others balked, such as Henry Marshal's son Adam, dwelling at Alwalton with his three sisters in 1300. They were "to be distrained if they come upon the fee," but in 1308 they were still living outside the manor.[23] Another Marshal brother, Walter, refused to pay and in 1308 Robert Gamel and John Dunning, who had stood surety for him, were fined twelve pence and twelve capons "because the same Walter has not yet paid to the lord two capons which he is bound to pay him each year at Easter while he dwells with his chattels outside the fee of the said lord, and because they are in arrears during the four years past."[24]

Even more intractable was John Nolly, who was recorded as living "outside the lord's fee" in 1307. John was arrested in 1312 "in the custody of the reeve and beadle, until he finds security to make corporeal residence upon the lord's fee with his chattels, and to make satisfaction to the lord for five capons which are in arrears." The record added: "And because the bailiff witnesses that he is excessively disobedient and refuses to pay the said capons, and that he owes five capons in arrears for the space of five years, it is commanded that he be arrested until he pays the aforesaid capons, and henceforth he is to make corporeal residence upon the lord's fee." In 1322, however, the court was still calling for the arrest of John, "a bondman of the lord, who withdraws himself with his chattels from the lord's fee without license." The chattels—in legal theory the lord's property—were usually mentioned along with the villein himself; he "withdrew himself with his chattels" and was ordered to return and bring them back, or to pay the annual fee.[25]

The fourth class of villein obligation, deriving from the lord's monopolies, included the common mill, the common oven, his sheepfold, and his manorial court.

Next in the Hundred Rolls' list of tenants were the abbot's twenty-eight cotters, who in Elton were also villeins in legal status (though on other manors cotters might be free), but who held little or no land and consequently owed little labor. Each held a cottage and yard theoretically "containing one rod," in return for which they helped with the haying, harvesting, sheepshearing, and threshing but not the plowing (they lacked plows and plow beasts), and paid tallage, merchet, and a small rent. Four had besides their cottage and farmyard a croft of half an acre, but eight had only half a rod of yard, two had a sixth of a rod, and one, paying a minimum rent of sixpence a year, only a "messuage," a house and yard with no specification of its size. Like most cotters, they scraped a precarious livelihood by turning their hand to any kind of labor they could find. Most worked as day laborers, but some had craft skills. Among their suggestive names are Comber, Shepherd, Smith, Miller, Carter, and Dyer.

Last on the Hundred Rolls' list came the rector, who held as a free tenant a virgate of land pertaining to the church and another ten acres for which he paid the abbot a yearly rent of half a mark. Four cotters were settled on his land. One was Roger Clerk (Clericus), probably the curate. The other three were all from the same family, and may have been the rector's servants.

Not mentioned in the Hundred Rolls survey, though present in the twelfth-century Ramsey Abbey extent, was a special category of tenant in Elton and some of the other abbey villages, the *akermen* or *bovarii*, descendants of manorial plowmen of a century earlier who were endowed with land of their own, for which they paid a yearly rent. Very little can be gathered about them from the records, except that their combined rent for five virgates of land, 7 pounds 10 shillings, was high (30 shillings per virgate).[26]

Servants of the villagers are omitted from the Hundred Rolls, but are mentioned occasionally in the rolls of the manorial court: Edith Comber, maidservant *(ancilla)* to William son of Letitia, "carried away some of the lord's peas";[27] Alice, servant of Nicholas Miller, was fined for stealing hay and stubble;[28] John Wagge's male servant was fined for careless planting of beans in the lord's field;[29] Matilda Prudhomme's servant Hugh was attacked and wounded by John Blaccalf.[30]

Among the tenants listed in the Hundred Rolls were many of the village's principal craftsmen. In Elton, the two gristmills were kept under the management of the manorial officials and the profits paid to the abbot. The miller was probably recompensed by a share of the "multure," the portion of flour kept as payment. In most villages the miller "farmed" the mill, paying a fixed sum to the lord and profiting from the difference between that and the multure. The popular reputation of the miller was notorious. Chaucer's miller

. . . was a master-hand at stealing grain.
He felt it with his thumb and thus he knew
Its quality and took three times his due—
A thumb of gold, by God, to gauge an oat![31]

At Elton, the miller collected the toll from persons using the mill as a bridge to cross the Nene. One was relieved of his office in 1300 for "letting strangers cross without paying toll," in exchange for "a gift."

Two others, Matefrid and Stephen Miller, successfully sued William of Barnwell in 1294 for slander in saying that they had taken two bushels of his malt "in a wrongful manner."[32] At the same court, however, the jurors found that another miller and his wife, Robert and Athelina Stekedec, had "unjustly detained" one whole ring of barley (four bushels). They were fined sixpence and ordered to make restitution.[33]

Two bakers farmed Elton's communal ovens in 1286, Adam Brid paying an annual rent of 13 shillings 4 pence for one and Henry Smith 33 shillings 4 pence for the other.[34] The smithy was not nearly as valuable. Robert son of Henry Smith was recorded as paying an annual rent of two shillings in 1308.[35]

Other tradesmen appear in the court rolls: Thomas Dyer was accused by Agnes daughter of Beatrice of "unjust detention of one cloth of linen weave," for the dyeing of which she had promised him a bushel of barley. The jurors decided that Thomas had "only acted justly," since Agnes had not paid him the grain, and that he was entitled to hold on to the cloth until she did so.[36]

Several villagers were part-time butchers and paid, "for exercising the office," an annual fee of two capons: Ralph Hubert, Geoffrey Abbot, William of Bumstead, Robert Godswein, William of Barnwell, Thomas Godswein, Robert Stekedec (who was also a miller), and Richard Tidewell.

Robert Chapman cultivated land while at the same time practicing the trade of merchant. Robert is recorded as selling a bushel of wheat to Emma Prudhomme in 1294,[37] and later of suing her for a hood which she agreed to deliver to John son of John of Elton, but Emma "did not undertake to pay" for it.[38]

Other villagers whose names suggest that they practiced trades were Ralph and Geoffrey Shoemaker, Elias and Stephen Carpenter, Roger and Robert Taylor (who may have made shoes, built houses, or made clothing), and William and Henry Woolmonger.

Dwelling uneasily on the fringes of the village, outside its organization, were a shifting set of "strangers." Several times villagers were fined for "harboring" them. They are characterized as "outside the assize": day laborers, itinerant craftsmen, and vagabonds, the latter a class who turn up frequently in the royal coroners' rolls. In 1312 six villagers were fined and commanded to desist from harboring strangers. Richard le Wyse harbored Henry the Cooper and his wife "to the harm of the village"; Robert Gamel harbored Gilbert from Lancashire; Margery daughter of Beatrice harbored Youn the Beggar; John Ballard, Geoffrey atte Cross, and Richard le Wyse commonly entertained strangers "to the terror of the villagers."[39]

In addition to these suspect outsiders, the village had its eccentrics and mentally ill. In 1306 John Chapman was admonished by the court to see that his son Thomas "who is partly a lunatic" (in parte lunaticus) should "henceforth behave himself among his neighbors."[40] The coroners' rolls record other cases involving mental aberration. In 1316 a peasant woman at Yelden, Bedfordshire, afflicted with "an illness called frenzy," got out of bed, seized an axe, slew her son and three daughters, and "hanged herself in her house on a beam with two cords of hemp."[41]

The peasants of a medieval village were once pictured as coexisting in a state of what might be called mediocre equality. Actually wide differences in wealth existed. Land was the most important kind of wealth, and the distribution of land was far from equal. Furthermore, some tenants, both villein and free, were increasing their holdings by buying or leasing from the others.

In theory, all land needed to be preserved and transmitted intact to heirs, both to protect the integrity of the holding for the family and to assure the lord of his rents and services.

Alienation—sale—was therefore theoretically forbidden. In reality, sale and lease of land were prominent features of the court rolls of the late thirteenth century, and not new phenomena. The lord's acquiescence reflected the profits to be made from the transaction—the opportunity of raising rents and collecting license fees.

In Elton, where a substantial number of the tenants were free, many of the sales recorded were by free men, some of whom sold consistently, some of whom bought, some of whom both bought and sold. Transactions were nearly all small. John Hering appears in the court rolls in 1292 selling two and a half rods to Alice daughter of Bateman of Clipsham,[42] and again in 1300 selling an acre to Joan wife of Gilbert Engayne of Wansford and also half an acre to Richard of Thorpe Waterville.[43] In 1312 Thomas Chausey sold half an acre to Reginald of Yarwell and two rods to Richard Carpenter.[44] In 1322 Richard Fraunceys sold half an acre to John Smith and half an acre to Richard Eliot;[45] Richard Eliot, meanwhile, acquired another two acres from John Ketel, who also sold a rod of land to Richard Chapleyn of Wansford;[46] John Ketel at the same time bought half an acre of meadow from Clement Crane.[47] Among the villeins, Muriel atte Gate and William Harpe each sold an acre to Nicholas Miller "without the license of the lord" and were fined sixpence each.[48] The only sizable transaction before 1350 was that of Reginald Child and John son of Henry Reeve, who in 1325 divided between them a virgate of land that had belonged to John Wagge. Apparently because they had done so without license, they were fined two shillings "for having the judgment of the court," though the transaction seems to have stood.[49]

Anne De Windt, analyzing land transfers in the Ramsey Abbey village of King's Ripton, where only one of the tenants was free, found 292 transfers among the unfree tenants between 1280 and 1397, the majority dealing with plots of between one-half and two and a half acres in the open fields, the others houses, auxiliary buildings, houseplots, and closes. Approximately one-third of the population participated at one time or another in the real-estate market. Thirty-six percent of the deals involved less than an acre of land, 57 percent from one to ten acres, 7 percent from ten to twenty acres. Some of the buyers were evidently newcomers to the village, purchasing holdings. Others apparently bought to satisfy the needs of daughters and younger sons. Still others leased the land they had acquired to subtenants, becoming peasant landlords. By the last half of the fourteenth century, a few families in nearly every English village had accumulated enough land to constitute an elite peasant class.[50]

Land was not the only form of wealth. Few areas in the thirteenth century as yet put sheep- or cattle-raising ahead of crop farming, but many villagers owned animals. Information about village stock is scanty, but some has been gleaned from the records of royal taxes levied at intervals to finance war. Villagers were assessed on the basis of their livestock, grain, and other products. M. M. Postan has extracted valuable information from the assessment record of 1291, including data on five Ramsey Abbey villages. Elton was not among the five, but the figures may be taken as broadly typical of the region. They show the average taxpaying villager owning 6.2 sheep, 4.5 cows and calves, 3.1 pigs, and 2.35 horses and oxen. These figures do not mean that each villager owned approximately 16 animals. Exempt were the poor cotters who owned property worth less than 6 shillings 8 pence, about the value of one ox or cow. Furthermore, as Postan demonstrates, many taxpaying villagers owned no sheep, while a few rich peasants held a large fraction of the total village flock. Plow animals, cows, and pigs appear to have been distributed more evenly,[51] though another scholar, speaking of England in general, asserts that "the bulk of the people owned no more working animals, cows, and sheep, than were necessary for their own subsistence."[52]

The Elton manorial court rolls of the early 1300s list numbers of villagers, mostly customary tenants with virgates, but also a few cotters, whose "beasts" or "draught beasts" had committed trespasses "in the lord's meadow" or "in the lord's grain." In 1312 the beasts of twelve villagers grazed in the fields at a time prohibited by the village bylaws, or "trod the grain" of fellow villagers.[53] A number of villagers are mentioned as having horses, many as having sheep or pigs.

The village poor are specifically identified many times in the court rolls when they are forgiven their fines for offenses. Most are cotters. The coroners' rolls record the small tragedies of destitute villagers who "went from door to door to seek bread." Beatrice Bone, "a poor woman," was begging in Turvey, Bedfordshire, in 1273 when she "fell down because she was weak and infirm and died there . . . between prime and tierce," to be found two days later by a kinswoman.[54] Joan, "a poor child aged five," walked through Risely begging for bread, fell from a bridge, and drowned.[55]

Perhaps as important as either legal status or wealth to most villagers was their standing among their neighbors, their place in the community. As in two other Ramsey Abbey villages studied by Edward Britton (Broughton)[56] and Edwin De Windt (Holywell-cum-Needingworth),[57] Elton shows evidence of a village hierarchy, signaled by the repeated service of certain families in village office, as reeve, beadle, jurors, ale tasters, and heads of tithings. All these officials were chosen by the villagers themselves. All the offices were positions of responsibility, served under oath, and subject to fines for dereliction. A total of over two hundred Elton families can be identified by name in the records between 1279 and 1346.* Of these two hundred families, only forty-nine are recorded as providing village officials. The service of these elite families, moreover, was unevenly distributed:

> 8 families had four or more members who served in a total of 101 offices
>
> 14 families had two members who served in a total of 39 offices
>
> 27 families had one member who served in a total of 41 offices

*The Hundred Rolls of 1279, seventeen manorial court rolls (1279–1342), and ten manorial accounts (1286–1346).

Thus eight families, 3.5 percent of the total village households, filled well over half the terms of office. The number of terms per individual officeholder varied from one to six.

Most of Elton's families who were active in public service, including all eight very active families, were villein virgaters. Four members of the In Angulo family (literal translation: in the nook or corner, English equivalent unknown), accounted for a total of fourteen offices: Geoffrey, listed in the Hundred Rolls of 1279 as a villein and a virgater, served as juror in 1279; Michael as juror in 1294, 1300, 1306, 1307, and 1312; Hugh as juror in 1300, 1307, 1312, and 1331, as reeve in 1323–1324 and again in 1324–1325; and William as juror in 1318 and 1322. Five members of the Gamel family served: Roger as juror in 1279 and 1294, ale taster in 1279; Robert as juror in 1292 and 1308; Philip as juror in 1300, ale taster in 1312; John as juror in 1308 and 1312 and ale taster in 1331; and Edmund as juror in 1342 and ale taster the same year. Four members of the Brington family served as juror, Reginald three times. Four of the Child family served in eight offices, three as jurors, William Child three times as reeve. Four Abovebrooks were jurors, and one was also an ale taster. Four atte Crosses served, Alexander four times as juror and once as reeve. The Goscelins contributed jurors, two reeves, and a beadle. The Reeves were jurors, ale tasters, and, naturally, reeves.

That these same families also figure prominently in the court rolls for quarrels, suits, infractions, and acts of violence is a striking fact, corroborating Edward Britton's observations to the same effect about Broughton. Members of three of the most active families were fined and assessed damages in 1279 when Alexander atte Cross, Gilbert son of Richard Reeve, and Henry son of Henry Abovebrook "badly beat" the son of another virgater, Reginald le Wyse.[58] In 1294 Roger Goscelin "drew blood from Richer Chapeleyn," while the wives of two of the In Angulo men quarreled and Michael's wife, Alice, "did hamsoken" on Geoffrey's wife, also named Alice—that is, assaulted her in her own house; Michael's wife paid a fine and also gave sixpence for "license to agree" with her sister-in-law. Richard

Benyt, twice a juror, "badly beat Thomas Clerk and did ham-soken upon him in his own house." John son of John Above-brook, both father and son officeholders, "took the beasts of Maud wife of John Abovebrook," apparently his stepmother, "and drove them out of her close."[59]

In 1306 what sounds like a free-for-all involving the members of several of the elite families occurred. John Ketel, twice juror and twice ale taster, "broke the head" of Nicholas son of Rich-ard Smith and badly beat Richard Benyt, "and moreover did hamsoken upon him"; John son of Henry Smith, four times juror, "struck Robert Stekedec and drew blood from him," while his brother Henry Smith "pursued John [Smith] . . . with a knife in order that he might strike and wound him."[60]

Members of the elite families sued each other for debt, ac-cused each other of libel, and committed infractions such as coming late to the reaping in the fall or not sending all of their household or "not binding the lord's wheat in the autumn as [their] neighbors did." Their daughters were convicted of "for-nication": in 1303, Matilda daughter of John Abovebrook;[61] in 1307, Athelina Blakeman;[62] in 1312, Alice daughter of Robert atte Cross;[63] in 1316, two women of the In Angulo family, Muriel and Alice.[64]

In short, a handful of village families were active leaders in village affairs, on both sides of the law. Their official posts may have helped them maintain and improve their status, which in turn perhaps lent them a truculence reminiscent of the Tybalts and Mercutios of the Italian cities, with somewhat similar re-sults.

From the terse wording of the court records, a few village per-sonalities emerge. One is that of Henry Godswein, virgater, ale taster, and juror, who in 1279 was fined "because he refused to work at the second boon-work of the autumn and because he impeded said boon-work by ordering that everyone should go home early and without the permission of the bailiffs, to the lord's damage of half a mark."[65] Another is that of John of Elton the younger, whose troubles with his neighbors recur with regularity: a quarrel with his free tenant, John of Langetoft in 1292;[66] one with Emma Prudhomme in 1294;[67] a conviction of adultery in 1292 with Alice wife of Reginald le Wyse;[68] then an accusation of trespass by John Hering in 1306;[69] and finally an episode in 1306 in which John attacked one of his own tenants, John Chapman, "drove him out of his own house," and carried off the hay of Joan wife of Robert Chapman.[70]

Not all the troublemakers were from the elite families. One family that never appeared in the lists of officials but often in the court rolls was the Prudhommes, of whom William was one of John of Elton's cotters and Walter a free virgater. Walter's wife Emma and Matilda, possibly William's wife, appear a number of times, quarreling with their neighbors, suing or being sued, or as brewers. The family produced the only murderer among the Elton villagers to be named in the court rolls (homicides were judged in royal courts): Richard Prudhomme, who in 1300 was convicted of killing Goscelyna Crane.[71] The Sabbes, also, were prominent mainly for their participation in quarrels and violence, and one of their members, Emma, was fined for being a *"fornicatrix"* and "as it were a common woman," a whore.[72]

Through the formulas and the abbreviated Latin of the court rolls, the villagers' speech echoes only remotely. Prudence Andrew, in *The Constant Star,* a novel about the Peasants' Rebellion of 1381, follows a popular tradition by recording her hero's speech as on an intellectual level just above that of the donkey with whom he sometimes sleeps. No reliable real-life source exists for the everyday speech of the English peasantry (though Chaucer yields hints), but the Inquisition records for the village of Montaillou, in the Pyrenees, roughly contemporary with the court records of Elton, cast valuable light.[73] The Montaillou peasants talk freely, even glibly, about politics, religion, and morality, philosophizing and displaying lively intelligence, imagination, humor, and wisdom. The Elton court records give us a single glimpse of peasants in an informal dialogue. The villagers were gathered in the churchyard on the Sunday before All Saints, when three people belonging to the elite families, Richer son of Goscelin and Richard Reeve and his wife, confronted Michael Reeve "with most base words in front of the whole parish." They accused Michael of a number of corrupt practices often imputed to reeves: "that he reaped his grain in the autumn by boon-works performed by the abbot's customary tenants, and plowed his land in Eversholmfield with the boon plows of the village; that he excused customary tenants from works and carrying services on condition that they leased their lands to him at a low price"; and finally "that he had taken bribes from the rich so that they should not be *censuarii,* and [instead] put the poor *ad censum.*"

Michael sued for libel, and the jurors pronounced him "in no article guilty," fined Richard Reeve and Richer Goscelin two shillings and 12 pence respectively, and ordered Richard Reeve to pay Michael the substantial sum of ten shillings in damages. Michael later forgave all but two shillings of the award.[74]

5

THE VILLAGERS: HOW THEY LIVED

ALL THE VILLAGERS OF ELTON, FREE, VILLEIN, AND of indeterminate status, virgaters, half-virgaters, cotters, servants, and craftsmen, lived in houses that shared the common characteristic of impermanence. Poorly built, of fragile materials, they had to be completely renewed nearly every generation. At Wharram Percy, nine successive transformations of one house can be traced over a span of little more than three centuries. The heir's succession to a holding probably often supplied an occasion for rebuilding. For reasons not very clear, the new house was often erected adjacent to the old site, with the alignment changed and new foundations planted either in postholes or in continuous foundation trenches.[1]

Renewal was not always left to the tenant's discretion. The peasant taking over a holding might be bound by a contract to build a new house, of a certain size, to be completed within a certain time span. Sometimes the lord agreed to supply timber or other assistance.[2] The lord's interest in the proper maintenance of the houses and outbuildings of his village was sustained

Fourteenth-century peasant house, St. Mary's Grove cottage, Tilmanstone, Kent. Originally of one story, the house has retained the studs of the medieval partition that divided it into two rooms, and the framing of the window wall. Upper story and chimney were added in the seventeenth century, and the walls have been largely rebuilt. Royal Commission on the Historic Monuments of England.

by the manorial court. In Elton in 1306, Aldusa Chapleyn had to find pledges to guarantee that she would "before the next court repair her dwelling house in as good a condition as she received it."[3] Two years later, William Rouvehed was similarly enjoined to "repair and rebuild his dwelling house in as good a condition as that in which he received it for a gersum [entry fee],"[4] and in 1331 three villagers were fined 12 pence each because they did not "maintain [their] buildings."[5]

All the village houses belonged to the basic type of medieval building, the "hall," as did the manor house, the barns, and even the church: a single high-ceilinged room, varying in size depending on the number of bays or framed sections. In peasants' houses, bays were usually about fifteen feet square.[6]

The house of a rich villager such as John of Elton might

Outline of foundation of house at Wharram Percy, with entry in middle of long side.

consist of four or even five bays, with entry in the middle of a long side. Small service rooms were probably partitioned off at one end: a buttery, where drink was kept, and a pantry, for bread, dishes, and utensils, with a passage between leading to a kitchen outside. A "solar," a second story either above the service rooms or at the other end, may have housed a sleeping chamber. A large hall might retain the ancient central hearth, or be heated by a fireplace with a chimney fitted into the wall. Early halls were aisled like churches, with the floor space obstructed by two rows of posts supporting the roof. Cruck construction had partially solved the problem, and by the end of the thirteenth century, carpenters had rediscovered the roof truss, known to the Greeks and Romans. Based on the inherent strength of the triangle, which resists distortion, the truss can support substantial weight.[7]

A middle-level peasant, a virgater such as Alexander atte Cross, probably lived in a three-bay house, the commonest type. A cotter like Richard Trune might have a small one- or two-bay house. Dwellings commonly still lodged animals as well as human beings, but the byre was more often partitioned off and sometimes positioned at right angles to the living quarters, a configuration that pointed to the European farm complex of the future, with house and outbuildings ringing a central court.[8]

Interiors were lighted by a few windows, shuttered but unglazed, and by doors, often open during the daytime, through which children and animals wandered freely. Floors were of beaten earth covered with straw or rushes. In the center, a fire of wood, or of peat, commonly used in Elton,[9] burned on a raised stone hearth, vented through a hole in the roof. Some hearths were crowned by hoods or funnels to channel the smoke to the makeshift chimney, which might be capped by a barrel with its ends knocked out. The atmosphere of the house was perpetually smoky from the fire burning all day as water, milk, or porridge simmered in pots on a trivet or in footed brass or iron kettles. At night a fire-cover, a large round ceramic lid with holes, could be put over the blaze.[10]

A thirteenth-century writer, contrasting the joys of a nun's life with the trials of marriage, pictured the domestic crisis of a

Woman stirs footed pot on central hearth while holding baby. Trinity College, Cambridge, Ms. B 11.22, f. 25v.

Central hearth of house in reconstruction of Anglo-Saxon settlement at West Stow.

wife who hears her child scream and hastens into the house to find "the cat at the bacon and the dog at the hide. Her cake is burning on the [hearth] stone, and her calf is licking up the milk. The pot is boiling over into the fire, and the churl her husband is scolding."[11]

Medieval sermons, too, yield a glimpse of peasant interiors: the hall "black with smoke," the cat sitting by the fire and often singeing her fur, the floor strewn with green rushes and sweet flowers at Easter, or straw in winter. They picture the housewife at her cleaning: "She takes a broom and drives all the dirt of the house together; and, lest the dust rise . . . she casts it with great violence out of the door." But the work is never done: "For, on Saturday afternoon, the servants shall sweep the house and cast all the dung and the filth behind the door in a heap.

But what then? Come the capons and the hens and scrape it around and make it as ill as it was before." We see the woman doing laundry, soaking the clothes in lye (homemade with ashes and water), beating and scrubbing them, and hanging them up to dry. The dog, driven out of the kitchen with a basinful of hot water, fights over a bone, lies stretched in the sun with flies settling on him, or eagerly watches people eating until they throw him a morsel, "whereupon he turns his back."[12]

The family ate seated on benches or stools at a trestle table, disassembled at night. Chairs were rarities. A cupboard or hutch held wooden and earthenware bowls, jugs, and wooden spoons. Hams, bags, and baskets hung from the rafters, away from rats and mice. Clothing, bedding, towels, and table linen were stored in chests. A well-to-do peasant might own silver spoons, brass pots, and pewter dishes.[13]

When they bathed, which was not often, medieval villagers used a barrel with the top removed. To lighten the task of carrying and heating water, a family probably bathed serially in the same water.[14]

At night, the family slept on straw pallets, either on the floor of the hall or in a loft at one end, gained by a ladder. Husband and wife shared a bed, sometimes with the baby, who alternatively might sleep in a cradle by the fire.

Manorial accounts yield ample information about what the abbot of Ramsey ate, especially his feast-day diet, which included larks, ducks, salmon, kid, chickens at Easter, a boar at Christmas, and capons and geese on other occasions.[15] The monks ate less luxuriously. For their table, Elton (and other manors) supplied the cellarer at Ramsey with bacon, beef, lambs, herring, butter, cheese, beans, geese, hens, and eggs, as well as flour and meal. The inhabitants of the curia, including the reeve, the beadle, some of the servants, and "divers workmen and visitors from time to time," also ate comparatively well, consuming large quantities of grain in various forms as well as peas, beans, bacon, chickens, ducks, cheese, and butter. Food was no small part of

the remuneration of servants and staff of a manor. Georges
Duby cites the carters of Battle Abbey, who demanded rye
bread, ale, and cheese in the morning, and meat or fish at
midday.[16]

Less evidence exists for the diet of the average peasant. The
thirteenth-century villager was a cultivator rather than a herdsman because his basic need was subsistence, which meant food
and drink produced from grain. His aim was not exactly self-
sufficiency, but self-supply of the main necessities of life.[17] These
were bread, pottage or porridge, and ale. Because his wheat went
almost exclusively to the market, his food and drink crops were
barley and oats. Most peasant bread was made from "maslin,"

Netting small birds. British Library, Luttrell Psalter, Ms. Add. 42130, f. 63.

The abbot's kitchen at Glastonbury Abbey contained four fireplaces for cooking.

a mixture of wheat and rye or barley and rye, baked into a coarse dark loaf weighing four pounds or more, and consumed in great quantities by men, women, and children.[18]

For the poorer peasant families, such as the Trunes or the Saladins of Elton, pottage was favored over bread as more economical, since it required no milling and therefore escaped both the miller's exaction and the natural loss of quantity in the process. Barley grains destined for pottage were allowed to sprout in a damp, warm place, then were boiled in the pot. Water could be drawn off, sweetened with honey, and drunk as barley water, or allowed to ferment into beer. Peas and beans supplied scarce protein and amino acids to both pottage and bread. A little fat bacon or salt pork might be added to the pottage along with onion and garlic from the garden. In spring and summer a variety of vegetables was available: cabbage, lettuce, leeks, spinach, and parsley. Some crofts grew fruit trees, supplying apples, pears, or cherries. Nuts, berries, and roots were gathered in the woods. Fruit was usually cooked; raw fruit was thought unhealthy. Except for poisonous or very bitter plants, "anything that grew went into the pot, even primrose and strawberry leaves."[19] The pinch came in the winter and early spring, when the grain supply ran low and wild supplements were not available.

Stronger or weaker, more flavorful or blander, the pottage kettle supplied many village families with their chief sustenance. If possible, every meal including breakfast was washed down with weak ale, home-brewed or purchased from a neighbor, but water often had to serve. The most serious shortage was protein. Some supplement for the incomplete protein of beans and peas was available from eggs, little from meat or cheese, though the wealthier villagers fared better than the poor or middling. E. A.

Gathering fruit. British Library, Luttrell Psalter, Ms. Add. 42130, f. 196v.

Kosminsky believed that the virgater and half-virgater could have "made ends meet without great difficulty, had it not been for the weight of feudal exploitation"—that is, the labor services and other villein obligations—but that a quarter virgate (five to eight acres) did not suffice even in the absence of servile dues.[20] H. S. Bennett calculated the subsistence level as lying between five and ten acres, "probably nearer ten than five." The most recent scholarly estimate, by H. E. Hallam (1988), is that twelve acres was needed for a statistical family of 4.75. J. Z. Titow pointed out that more acreage was needed per family in a two-field system than a three-field system, since more of each holding was lying fallow. Cicely Howell, studying data from the Midland village of Kibworth Harcourt, concluded that not until the mid–sixteenth century could the half-virgater provide his family with more than eight bushels of grain a year per person from his own land. Poor families survived only by their varied activities as day laborers.[21]

Besides the shortage of protein, medieval diets were often lacking in lipids, calcium, and vitamins A, C, and D.[22] They were also often low in calories, making the inclusion of ale a benefit on grounds of health as well as recreation. Two positive aspects of the villagers' austere regimen—its low protein and low fat content—gave it some of the virtues of the modern "heart-smart" diet, and its high fiber was a cancer preventative.

A middling family like that of Alexander atte Cross or Henry Abovebrook probably owned a cow or two or a few ewes, to provide an intermittent supply of milk, cheese, and butter. Most households kept chickens and pigs to furnish eggs and occasional meat, but animals, like wheat, were often needed for cash sales to pay the rent or other charges. Salted and dried fish were available for a price, as were eels, which also might be fished from the Nene or poached from the millpond.

Medieval literature voiced the popular hunger for protein and fat. A twelfth-century Irish poet describes a dream in which a coracle "built of lard/ Swam a sweet milk sea," and out of a lake rose a castle reached by a bridge of butter and surrounded by a palisade of bacon, with doorposts of whey curds, columns of

Men fishing with nets. British Library, Queen Mary's Psalter, Ms. Royal 2B VII, f. 73.

aged cheese, and pillars of pork. Across a moat of spicy broth covered with fat, guards welcomed the dreamer to the castle with coils of fat sausages.[23]

It was a hungry world, made hungrier by intermittent crop failures, one series of which in the early fourteenth century brought widespread famine in England and northwest Europe. The later, even more devastating cataclysm of the Black Death so reduced the European population that food became compara- tively plentiful and the peasants took to eating wheat. The poet John Gower (d. 1408) looked back on the earlier, hungrier period not in sorrow but rather with an indignant nostalgia that reflected the attitude of the elite toward the lower classes:

> Laborers of olden times were not wont to eat wheaten bread; their bread was of common grain or of beans, and their drink was of the spring. Then cheese and milk were a feast to them; rarely had they any other feast than this. Their garment was of sober gray; then was the world of such folk well ordered in its estate.[24]

The peasant's "garment" has often been pictured in the il- luminations of manuscripts, but only occasionally in "sober gray"; the colors shown are more often bright blues, reds, and greens. Whether Gower's memory was accurate is uncertain. Peasants did have access to dyestuffs, and Elton had a dyer.

Over the period of the high Middle Ages, styles of clothing of nobles and townspeople changed from long, loose garments for both men and women to short, tight, full-skirted jackets and close-fitting hose for men and trailing gowns with voluminous sleeves, elaborate headdresses, and pointed shoes for women. Peasant dress, however, progressed little. For the men, it consisted of a short tunic, belted at the waist, and either short stockings that ended just below the knee or long hose fastened at the waist to a cloth belt. A hood or cloth cap, thick gloves or mittens, and leather shoes with heavy wooden soles completed the costume. The women wore long loose gowns belted at the waist, sometimes sleeveless tunics with a sleeved undergarment, their heads and necks covered by wimples. Underclothing, when it was worn, was usually of linen, outer garments were woolen.

The tunic of a prosperous peasant might be trimmed with fur, like the green one edged with squirrel found by three Elton boys in 1279 and turned over to the reeve.[25] A poor peasant's garb, on the other hand, might resemble that of the poor man in Langland's fourteenth-century allegory, *Piers Plowman*, whose "coat was of a [coarse] cloth called cary," whose hair stuck through the holes in his hood and whose toes stuck through those in his heavy shoes, whose hose hung loose, whose rough mittens had worn-out fingers covered with mud, and who was himself "all smeared with mud as he followed the plow," while beside him walked his wife carrying the goad, in a tunic tucked up to her knees, wrapped in a winnowing sheet to keep out the cold, her bare feet bleeding from the icy furrows.[26]

The village world was a world of work, but villagers nevertheless found time for play. Every season was brightened by holiday intervals that punctuated the Christian calendar. Many of these were ancient pagan celebrations, appropriated by the Church, often with little alteration of their character. Each of the seasons of the long working year, from harvest to harvest, offered at least one holiday when work was suspended, games were played, and meat, cakes, and ale were served.

On November 1, bonfires marked All Hallows, an old pagan rite at which the spirits of the dead were propitiated, now re-named All Saints. Martinmas (St. Martin's Day, November 11) was the feast of the plowman, in some places celebrated with seed cake, pasties, and a frumenty of boiled wheat grains with milk, currants, raisins, and spices.

The fortnight from Christmas Eve to Twelfth Day (Epiphany, January 6) was the longest holiday of the year, when, as in a description of twelfth-century London, "every man's house, as also their parish churches, was decked with holly, ivy, bay, and whatsoever the season of the year afforded to be green."[27] Vil-lagers owed extra rents, in the form of bread, eggs, and hens for the lord's table, but were excused from work obligations for the fortnight and on some manors were treated to a Christmas dinner in the hall.

This Christmas bonus often reflected status. A manor of Wells Cathedral had the tradition of extending invitations to two peasants, one a large landholder, the other a small one. The first was treated to dinner for himself and two friends and served "as much beer as they will drink in the day," beef and bacon with mustard, a chicken stew, and a cheese, and provided with two candles to burn one after the other "while they sit and drink." The poorer peasant had to bring his own cloth, cup, and trencher, but could take away "all that is left on his cloth, and he shall have for himself and his neighbors one wastel [loaf] cut in three for the ancient Christmas game to be played with the said wastel."[28] The game was evidently a version of "king of the bean," in which a bean was hidden in a cake or loaf, and the person who found it became king of the feast. On some Glaston-bury Abbey manors, tenants brought firewood and their own dishes, mugs, and napkins; received bread, soup, beer, and two kinds of meat; and could sit drinking in the manor house after dinner.[29] In Elton the manorial servants had special rations, which in 1311 amounted to four geese and three hens.[30]

In some villages, the first Monday after Epiphany was cele-brated by the women as Rock (distaff) Monday and by the men as Plow Monday, sometimes featuring a plow race. In 1291 in the Nottinghamshire village of Carlton, a jury testified that it was an ancient custom for the lord and the rector and every free man of the village to report with his plow to a certain field that was common to "the whole community of the said village" after sunrise on "the morrow of Epiphany" and "as many ridges as he can cut with one furrow in each ridge, so many may he sow in the year, if he pleases, without asking for license."[31]

Candlemas (February 2), commemorating Mary's "churching," the ceremony of purification after childbirth, was celebrated with a procession carrying candles. It was followed by Shrove Tuesday, the last day before Lent, an occasion for games and sports.

At Easter, the villagers gave the lord eggs, and he gave the manorial servants and sometimes some of the tenants dinner. Like Christmas, Easter provided villeins a respite—one week— from work on the demesne. Celebrated with games, Easter week ended with Hocktide, marked in a later day, and perhaps in the thirteenth century, by the young women of the village holding the young men prisoner until they paid a fine, and the men retaliating on the second day.[32]

On May Day the young people "brought in the May," scouring the woods for boughs from flowering trees to decorate their houses. Sometimes they spent the night in the woods.

Summertime Rogation Days, when the peasants walked the boundaries of the village, were followed by Whitsunday (Pentecost), bringing another week's vacation for most villeins. St. John's Day (June 24) saw bonfires lit on the hilltops and boys flourishing brands to drive away dragons. A fiery wheel was rolled downhill, symbolizing the sun's attaining the solstice.[33]

Lammas (August 1) marked the end of the hay harvest and the beginning of grain harvest, with its "boons" or precarias, when all the villagers came to reap the lord's grain and were treated to a feast that in Elton in 1286 included an ox and a bullock, a calf, eighteen doves, seven cheeses, and a quantity of grain made into bread and pottage.[34] On one Oxfordshire manor it was customary for the villagers to gather at the hall for a songfest—"to sing harvest home."[35] Elton records mention an occasional "repegos," a celebration at which the harvesters feasted on roast goose.[36]

One holiday, Wake Day, the feast of the local parish saint, varied from place to place. Probably in the thirteenth century, as later, the villagers kept vigil all night, in the morning heard Mass in honor of their patron saint, then spent the day in sports. Often the churchyard was turned into a sports arena, a usage deplored by the clergy. Robert Manning wrote in his *Handlyng Synne* (1303), a verse translation of a thirteenth-century French *Manuel des Pechiez* (Manual of Sins):

Carols, wrestling, or summer games
Whosoever haunteth any such shames
In church, or in churchyard
Of sacrilege he may be afraid;
Or interludes, or singing,
Or tambour beat, or other piping,
All such thing forbidden is
While the priest standeth at Mass.*[37]

A preacher condemned the common people's enjoyment of "idle plays and japes, carolings, making of fool countenances . . . [giving] gifts to jongleurs to hear idle tales . . . smiting . . . wrestling, in other doing deeds of strength."[38]

Many of the games enjoyed by the villagers were played alike by children, adolescents, and adults, and endured into modern times: blind man's buff, prisoner's base, bowling. Young and old played checkers, chess, backgammon, and most popular of all, dice. Sports included football, wrestling, swimming, fishing, archery, and a form of tennis played with hand coverings instead of rackets. The Luttrell Psalter (c. 1340) portrays a number of mysterious games involving sticks and balls and apparatus of various kinds, remote ancestors of modern team sports. Bull-baiting and cockfighting were popular spectator sports.

---

*Like all other excerpts in Middle English in this book, this is translated into modern English.

Yet the favorite adult recreation of the villagers was undoubtedly drinking. Both men and women gathered in the "tavern,"
usually meaning the house of a neighbor who had recently
brewed a batch of ale, cheap at the established price of three
gallons for a penny. There they passed the evening like modern
villagers visiting the local pub. Accidents, quarrels, and acts of
violence sometimes followed a session of drinking, in the thirteenth century as in subsequent ones. Some misadventures may
be deduced from the terse manorial court records. The rolls of
the royal coroners, reporting fatal accidents, spell many out in
graphic detail: In 1276 in Elstow, Osbert le Wuayl, son of William Cristmasse, coming home at about midnight "drunk and
disgustingly over-fed," after an evening in Bedford, fell and
struck his head fatally on a stone "breaking the whole of his
head."[39] One man tumbled off his horse riding home from the
tavern; another fell into a well in the marketplace and drowned;
a third, relieving himself in a pond, fell in; still another, carrying
a pot of ale down the village street, was bitten by a dog, tripped
while picking up a stone to throw, and struck his head against
a wall; a child slipped from her drunken mother's lap into a pan
of hot milk on the hearth.[40]

Many violent quarrels followed drinking bouts, as the Bedfordshire coroners' rolls attest. In 1266, "about bedtime," three
men who had been drinking in a Bedford tavern fell to quarreling on the king's highway, two attacking the third and stabbing
him in the heart with a sickle.[41] In 1272 in Bromham, four men
who had been drinking in a tavern accosted a passerby, Ralph,
son of the vicar of Bromham, and demanded to know who he
was. Ralph replied defiantly, "A man, who are you?" Whereupon one of the men, Robert Barnard of Wooton, "because he
was drunk," struck Ralph over the head with an axe. Ralph's
widow testified that all four men had assaulted her husband with
axes and staves, and accused the tavern keeper and his wife of
having instigated the attack.[42] In another case, an innocent
bystander was killed. Four villagers of Wooton who had been
drinking in Bedford were returning home when one of them

suddenly "and with no ulterior motive" turned, drew his bow, and took aim at a man who was following them. The only woman in the party, Margery le Wyte, threw herself between the two men and received the arrow in her throat "so that she immediately died."[43]

Not all village violence was drink-related. The subject of the numerous altercations recorded in the Elton court records is not usually given, but the coroners' rolls report quarrels about debt, in one case a halfpenny one brother lent another, thefts (a bushel of flour, a basket, a hen), trespass, and once simply "an old hatred." Occasionally the subject was a woman: two brothers in Radwell, Bedfordshire, found their sister Juliana "lying under a haystack" with a young man who "immediately arose and struck [one of the brothers] on the top of the head, to the brain, apparently with an axe, so that he immediately died." The lovers fled.[44] Domestic quarrels got out of hand, as when Robert Haring of Aston, Bedfordshire, and his wife Sybil fell to quarreling, and a friend eating lunch with them tried to intervene as peacemaker and was slain by an axe blow.[45]

Occasionally violence came on a larger scale. The Bedfordshire coroner reported homicides resulting from a melee between the men of a knight's household and those of the prior of Lanthony; from the siege of a church in a dispute over the right to a piece of land, involving large numbers of attackers and besiegers; and from a pitched battle between the villages of St. Neots and Little Barford.[46]

Besides such amateur lawbreakers, bands of professional criminals roamed the countryside. Bedfordshire coroners recorded the depredations of one gang of thieves who in 1267 came to the village of Honeydon at about vespers, armed with swords and axes, seized a boy named Philip "who was coming from his father's fold," "beat, ill-treated, and wounded him," and forced him to accompany them to the house of Ralph son of Geoffrey. Recognizing the boy's voice, Ralph opened the door, the thieves fell upon him, wounded him, and tied him up, killed his mother and a servant, and ransacked the house. They then broke into and burglarized seven more houses, killing and wounding several more people. The boy Philip at last managed to escape and give the alarm, but the gang fled and apparently was never apprehended.[47]

Another band of "felons and thieves" committed a similar assault on the village of Roxton in 1269, breaking through the wall of a house and carrying away "all the goods," breaking into the house next door and murdering a woman in her bed, finally invading the house of John the Cobbler by breaking a door and windows, dragging John out and killing him, and wounding his wife, daughter, and a servant. A second daughter hid "between a basket and a chest" and escaped to give the alarm. In this case the thieves were identified by the dying wife of John the Cobbler, one as a former servant of the prior of Newnham, the others as men who had collected the tithes for the prior of Cauldwell and as "glovers of Bedford." They were arrested and brought to justice.[48]

One thief became a victim of his own crime when he entered a house by a ladder to purloin a ham hanging from a roof beam. When the householder, Matilda Bolle, saw him leaving and gave the alarm, he panicked, tumbled from the ladder, and died of a broken neck.[49]

6

MARRIAGE AND
THE FAMILY

W ITHIN THE VILLAGE COMMUNITY, THE BASIC
social and economic unit was the family household. The
number of its members fluctuated through the generational
cycle: young couple, couple with children, with grandparents,
with brother or sister (or aunt or uncle), solitary widow or
widower. Information about the composition of the average
household is scarce and unreliable, but the consensus among
scholars is that it was small, with no more than five members,
and most commonly nuclear—that is, husband and wife with or
without children. Size of household tended to reflect economic
status, rich households supporting more children, other relatives, and a servant or two.[1]

One important characteristic of the thirteenth-century
peasant household was its autonomy. The larger kinship
groupings (clan, sippe, kindred) that had played an important
role in Anglo-Saxon England and early medieval France and
Germany had lost their powers of protection and supervision,
along with the need for such powers. Their functions had

been taken over by new police and judicial agencies of the community and state.

The two great fundamentals of family history are marriage and inheritance, always closely linked. In open field country, impartible (undivided) inheritance was the general rule, holdings passing to a single heir, usually the eldest son. A study of seventy-five cases of succession in the Midland village of Wakefield showed that a single son inherited from a father in forty-seven cases; in nine, in the absence of a son, a daughter or daughters did so. In the remaining nineteen cases, a son or daughter succeeded a mother, a brother or sisters succeeded a brother, an uncle succeeded a nephew or niece, a cousin succeeded a cousin, and in one case a (presumably second) husband succeeded a wife. If there was no son but two or more daughters, land was divided among the daughters.[2]

Widows had inferior but definite rights that varied from place to place. Under common (feudal) law, a widow's portion of an estate was from one third to one half, but a widow often automatically succeeded a husband in a peasant holding, not as the heiress, but as the surviving co-tenant. This arrangement allowed her to support the family and hold it together. A widow might be pressured by the lord to remarry, to insure that the holding had a man to perform its labor services, but she might preserve her freedom by hiring workers. Most widows eventually married, or turned over the holding to an adult son, but some, like Cecilia Benyt of Cuxham (Oxfordshire), remained in possession of the family holding, never remarrying, although her son was an adult and in fact reeve.[3] Widows' rights, says Rosamond Faith, "seem to have been by far the most durable and firmly established of all inheritance customs."[4] Widows' rights, and inheritance customs in general, were influenced by the long-term fluctuations in availability of land. The scarcer land became, the more attractive a widow became.

A grand principle of inheritance had come to be very widely accepted: "An established holding ought to descend in the blood of the men who . . . held it of old," sometimes expressed as "keeping the name on the land."[5] No one yet disputed the lord's title to his entry fee and even his heriot [death duty], but by now, legal doctrine notwithstanding, the land was felt to belong to the tenant, villein or free, who plowed, harrowed, and planted it. Tradition was even strong enough to inhibit the lord from raising the rent on a holding when a normal succession took place (alert lords and stewards made sure to raise it when a tenant died without heir and a new tenant was found).

The entry fee was substantial, arbitrary, and proportional to the size of the holding: in Elton in 1313, "four shillings from Henry Reed to have one cottage formerly his father's"; "13 shillings 4 pence from Ralph son of Gilbert Shepherd to have one cottage and eight acres of land formerly his father's"; and "60 shillings from John son of Henry Reeve to have one virgate of land formerly his father's." Sometimes the connection between heir and dead tenant is not clear; while Gilbert Shepherd's son Ralph inherited his father's holding, another son, John, paid an entry fee of 2 shillings "to have one cottage formerly belonging to Margery Carter."[6]

Manorial courts sometimes had to rule on complicated inheritance questions. In the Bedfordshire village of Chalgrave in 1279, Richard son of Thomas Ballard presented himself and "demanded the land which was his father's." Investigation showed that Richard had had an elder brother named Walter, who had died, leaving sons. These sons "would have been the next heirs if Walter had held the land while he lived, but he did not have possession of the land, therefore [the jurors] say that Richard himself is the next heir." The custom of the manor, however, was that "no customary tenant can enter such land after the death of his father while his mother is alive, unless the mother shall agree, and . . . his mother will hold the land all her life if she shall wish." Richard therefore agreed to pay his mother, Avice, a yearly ration of winter wheat (*frumentum*), beans, and spring wheat (*tramesium*). Richard paid 12 pence entry fee and promised to do the services "due and accustomed" for the holding, as well as to "maintain the houses of the same tenement."[7]

If the inheriting son was a minor and an orphan and no other relative could be found, the lord might exercise his right of "wardship." Thus at Elton in 1297 John Ketel was "in the custody of the lord," slept and ate in the manor house, and was apparently clothed; at least he was bought a pair of shoes which had to be repaired at the manor's expense.[8] John Daye, who "tore up and carried away" the house on his father's holding "which had come into the hand of the lord through the minority of John son and heir of . . . Richard Daye," was undoubtedly also in wardship.[9]

Where no heir could be found, the lord provided a tenant. "One cottage which John Stabler formerly held in bondage for 12 pence a year is in the hand of the lord," reported the Elton court record in 1342. "Therefore it is commanded to make provision of one tenant. Afterward, they say, Alexander Cook came and paid entry fee."[10]

The Elton accounts also record several cases in which the land of a deceased tenant was rented out by the lord, sometimes to several villagers, in small parcels: "three rods," "an acre," "four acres of land and an acre of meadow." Usually the rent was substantially raised, and the lease made "for the term of life."[11]

Heriot passes unmentioned in Elton documents except for the comment that a widow succeeding to a holding did not pay it (implying that a son succeeding did).[12] Most manors exacted heriot from the widow. A custumal of Brancaster, a Norfolk manor belonging to Ramsey Abbey, states: "If [the villein] virgater dies, the lord has his best beast of the house, if he has a beast. If there is no beast, she gives 32 pence and she holds her husband's land for the service which pertains to it."[13] Usually a person inheriting a virgate gave a cow or horse, one inheriting a half-virgate a sheep. On some Ramsey Abbey manors, the village rector rather than the lord received the best beast, under the name of "mortuary."[14] Sometimes the fine was simply levied in money: at Abbot's Ripton, Hemmingford, and Wistow the widow of a virgater gave five shillings as heriot, half the price of a horse, ox, or cow.[15]

At Chalgrave in 1279, a jury weighed the question of the rival claims of lord and church on the estate of a man who had no animal. The jury decided that the lord "should have the best cloth or grain whichever shall please him the more, before holy church may have anything of the dead person." They cited the precedent of "a certain Ascelina who was the wife of Roger the reeve," and who had held eight acres of land in the time of the grandfather of the present lord, "and had no animal." The lord took in heriot "the best cloth which she had, to wit, one tunic of blanket [cloth], before holy church took away anything. Afterwards a certain Nigel the Knight, holding the same land, died as tenant, and had no animal. Therefore the lord by custom took one tabard [tunic] of gray in the name of heriot, and he can rightly do so from all his customary tenants in the manor of Chalgrave."[16] One study shows that of eighty-six heriots exacted at Langley, St. Albans, Hertfordshire, in 1348, twenty-two were horses, seventeen cows, eight bulls, five sheep, and the remaining thirty-two insignificant chattels such as a mattock or a pitcher, or "nothing because they are poor."[17]

Among the villagers as among the nobility, primogeniture created some problems while solving others. It kept holdings intact, but as land grew scarce, older sons of both nobility and peasantry had to wait until their fathers died or retired before marrying. Younger sons of the nobility traditionally had to leave the family estate to seek their fortunes in war, or embark on careers in the Church. Younger sons of the peasantry might enlist as common soldiers, or (on payment of a fee to the lord) undertake training for the lower ranks of the clergy. Among the better-off peasants, many fathers gave younger sons small grants of land, often purchased in the growing peasant land market. Edward Britton found that in Broughton 44 percent of the elite families had two or more sons established simultaneously in the village. Younger sons of the poor peasants were not so lucky, generally having to choose between staying home, celibate, and taking their chances as day laborers, perhaps slipping into vagabondage and crime.[18]

A few peasants made wills, an increasingly popular measure in the fourteenth century, often recorded in the manorial court rolls. In King's Ripton in 1309, Nicholas Newman bequeathed a rod of land to his daughter Agnes, and Roger Dike an acre to his sister Margaret; in 1322 Nicholas son of Hugh left his sister a house and yard "lying next to the manor of the lord abbot," to be held by her for life and then to pass to Joan daughter of Thomas Cooper, and half an acre of land on the Ramsey road to Ivo son of Henry. Alternatively, land might be transferred to a daughter or sister or younger son on the deathbed, evading the inheritance custom. In the period before the Black Death, such transfers were usually not of land handed down in the family, but of acquisitions that the peasant had made during his own lifetime. In the fifteenth century, peasant wills became common.[19]

The land market also facilitated acquisition of dowries for daughters of the richer villagers, who might seek alliance with another village family of their own class or even with the lesser gentry without sacrificing any of the family holding. The dowry of a middling peasant's daughter might also include an acre or two of land, but more often would consist of money, chattels, or both. A poor peasant's daughter might marry with nothing at all. Substantial dowries came into play mainly in the increasing negotiations for upwardly mobile marriages.[20]

Dowries aside, peasant women inherited, held, bought, sold, and leased land. The Elton records disclose many land transactions carried out by women: "And they say that the wife of Geoffrey in Angulo let one acre of land to Richard of Thorpe Waterville, chaplain."[21] "And they say that Muriel atte Gate demised [sold] one acre of her land to Nicholas Miller."[22]

In all transfers of property held by villeins, the lord had an interest. The tangible sign of his interest in peasant marriage was merchet, the fee or fine usually paid by the bride or her father. The origin of merchet (along with its etymology) is lost in the earlier Middle Ages, but by the late thirteenth century it was so long established that it had become a legal test for villein status. In the Elton manorial court of 1279, Reginald son of Benedict tried to escape jury service by claiming that he was free, but lost his case because his sisters had paid merchet. Elias Freeman also was adjudged unfree (in spite of his name) because his ancestor John Freeman had paid merchet for his daughters.[23]

Merchets were once regarded as taxes on persons, but Eleanor Searle has argued persuasively that the dowry granted to a daughter was a form of inheritance, and that merchet may better be seen as an inheritance tax on property: "Girls were given land, chattels, or coin . . . as their part of the inheritance." Searle observes that merchet was paid only where a substantial dowry was being given the bride. "A foolish girl or a poor one might marry as she liked." Only if she received part of the family inheritance was she obligated.

Significantly, the size of the merchet evidently related to the value of the dowry. A St. Albans formulary for holding a manorial court included the instruction to inquire "whether any bondman's daughter has married without leave, and what her father has given her by way of goods." When the dowry was in the form of land, it was often transferred at the same time that the merchet was paid. Searle sees an analogue to merchet in the fine paid by a villein for having his sons licensed to be educated for the clergy.[24]

Whatever the relationship of merchet to dowry, the Elton records supply evidence of its close relationship to landholding. When Margery daughter of John atte Gate paid two shillings for "giving herself in marriage," the transaction was recorded by the clerk in the accounts of 1286–1287 as an entry fee (gersum),[25] and in the 1307 accounts, entry fees and merchets are mixed together as if they were interchangeable terms.[26] The Ramsey Abbey register known as the *Liber Gersumarum* includes not only gersums but 426 merchets.[27]

Merchet has traditionally been thought of as paid by the bride's father, yet in many cases the daughter paid the fee, and sometimes the prospective bridegroom, or occasionally the mother, or a collateral relative. In the surviving Elton records between 1279 and 1342, eight fathers, eight daughters, and one mother are recorded as paying. A recent study of the *Liber Gersumarum* showed that payments were made as frequently by daughters as by fathers—each in 33 percent of the cases. The bridegroom paid in 26 percent, and some other relative in the remaining 8 percent.[28] Who paid seems to have depended on circumstance. A bride who paid her own merchet was probably marrying late, and may well have earned the money herself, working as a servant or dairymaid, or even at such masculine-sounding tasks as road repair, manuring, thatching, weeding, mowing, sheep-shearing, carrying, and plowing.[29]

When a widow remarried, on the other hand, the merchet was usually paid by the prospective husband, who would benefit from taking possession of her first husband's lands. An unfree woman marrying a free man, however, was the one who bene-fited, and she or her father paid the fee, never the bridegroom.[30]

In short, the decision as to who paid merchet was part of the marriage negotiations, usually depending on who gained the most from the marriage. The amount was subject to haggling with the lord's steward—the villein must "make the best bargain he can," in the words of a Ramsey Abbey custumal.[31] Several circumstances influenced the price: whether the woman was marrying a villein in the same village, or a freeman, or a man from outside the village, or "whomever she wished." It was more expensive to marry a freeman or an outsider, or to marry at will, since the lord risked losing the woman's services, chattels, and future children.[32]

Another important factor was the family's ability to pay. Merchet was highest when the bride was an heiress or a widow, generally ranging from five shillings to four pounds. Where no land was involved but only chattels, the range was far lower, sometimes as little as six pence. Muriel daughter of Richard Smith, an Elton cotter, paid three shillings, while Alexander atte Cross and Hugh in Angulo, both virgaters from the elite fami-lies, gave five for their daughters, and Emma wife of Richard Reeve six shillings eight pence for hers.[33] Many daughters of Elton villeins too poor to be taxed evidently married without paying merchet.

The actual ceremony of rural marriage, or more precisely the lack of ceremony, was a long-standing problem for the Church. Many village couples saw no need for more than a kiss and a promise, which left room for debate over the nature of the alleged promise. The great twelfth-century legal authorities, Gratian and Peter Lombard, had wrestled with the question of what constituted a legal marriage, and Pope Alexander III (1159–1181) had laid down rules: a valid marriage could be accomplished either by "words of the present" (I take thee, John . . .) or by "words of the future," a more indefinite promise, if it was followed by consummation. Consent of the two parties alone was indispensable. The Fourth Lateran Council (1215) stipulated that the wedding must be public and the bride must receive a dowry, but made no provision for witnesses, and did not even insist on Church participation.[34]

Most marriages were arranged between families, and sometimes property considerations resulted in mismatches, such as those described by William Langland:

It is an uncomely couple . by Christ, so me thinketh
To give a young wench . to an old feeble,
Or wed any widow . for wealth of her goods,
That never shall bairn bear . but if it be in [her] arms.[35]

Robert Manning's *Handlyng Synne* had much to say about the evils of such marriages. When couples were married for property and not love, it was "no right wedding." A man who married a woman "for love of her cattle" would have regrets:

When it is gone and is all bare
Then is the wedding sorrow and care.
Love and cattle then are away,
And "wellaway," they cry and say.[36]

Even worse was for a man to "wed any woman against her will,"[37] strictly forbidden by the Church, and improbable in the village, where, unlike the castle, most marriages involved some courtship and even sexual contact.

Peasant couples usually spoke their vows at the church door, the most public place in the village. Here the priest inquired whether there were any impediments, meaning kinship in a degree forbidden by the Church. The bridegroom named the dower which he would provide for his wife, giving her as a token a ring and a small sum of money to be distributed to the poor. The ring, according to a fourteenth-century preacher, must be "put and set by the husband upon the fourth finger of the woman, to show that a true love and cordial affection be between them, because, as doctors say, there is a vein coming from the heart of a woman to the fourth finger, and therefore the ring is put on the same finger, so that she should keep unity and love with him, and he with her."[38]

Vows were then exchanged, and the bridal party might proceed into the church, where a nuptial Mass was celebrated. At one such Mass a fourteenth-century priest addressed the wedding party: "Most worshipful friends, we are come here at this time in the name of the Father, Son, and Holy Ghost, . . . to join, unite, and combine these two persons by the holy sacrament of matrimony, granted to the holy dignity and order of priesthood. Which sacrament of matrimony is of this virtue and strength that these two persons who now are two bodies and two souls, during their lives together shall be . . . one flesh and two souls."[39]

The ceremony was usually followed by a feast, a "bride ale," in a private house or a tavern. In Warboys and some other villages, the groom was obligated to treat the manorial servants to a dinner with "bread, beer, meat or fish" on "the day on which he takes a wife."[40]

Enough couples in the village, however, continued to speak their vows elsewhere—in the woods, in a tavern, in bed—to make "clandestine marriage" a universal vexation for the Church courts. Typically, a girl sued a man who disclaimed his promise, though sometimes the shoe was on the other foot. Not until the Protestant Reformation and the Catholic Church's Council of Trent in the sixteenth century was clandestine marriage effectively abolished by requiring witnesses.[41]

"Clandestine marriage" obviously shaded off into seduction. Robert Manning condemned men who

> . . . beguile a woman with words;
> To give her troth but lightly
> For nothing but to lie by her;
> With that guile thou makest her assent,
> And bringest you both to cumberment.[42]

Court records contain numerous instances of women leaving their villages in company of men without any mention of marriage. They contain even more frequent instances of "leirwite" or "legerwite" (lecher-wite), a fine for premarital sex, literally for lying down. On some manors a separate fine called "childwite" was levied for bearing a child out of wedlock, but in Elton premarital sex and pregnancy were lumped together. Twenty-two cases of leirwite are listed in surviving Elton records between 1279 and 1342, with fines of either sixpence or twelve pence, in a single case three pence. In all but one, only the woman is named, and she paid the fine; in the single exception, in 1286, Maggie Carter and Richard Miller were fined sixpence each.[43]

Daughters of the elite families figure prominently among those convicted. Despite the fine, little social stigma seems to have been attached to premarital sex. One theory is that peasant women may have become pregnant as a prelude to marriage in order to prove their fertility. In Elton in 1307, Athelina Blakeman paid a leirwite of twelve pence; in the same year's accounts her father paid two shillings merchet "for giving his daughter Athelina in marriage."[44] Premarital sex was thus followed by marriage. The village community seems to have taken a liberal attitude toward young people's sexual activities; in 1316 an Elton jury was fined "because they had concealed all these [five] leirwites."[45]

A more serious matter was adultery, a threat to the family. It lay in the province of the Church courts, but the lord exacted a fine too, usually under a curious legal rationale: the parties had "wasted the lord's chattels in chapter." G. G. Coulton once interpreted this recurring phrase as reflecting the lord's control over the marriage of peasant women.[46] The lord, however, had little to do with arranging peasant marriages. The same words are used in regard to men convicted of adultery, and a reasonable explanation is that the lord used the pretext of loss of village resources as an opportunity to collect a fine of his own in a province that was normally the Church's. The Church court identified the guilty parties in a way that neighbors might be reluctant to do in the manorial court.[47] In the Elton records between 1279 and 1342, six cases of adultery are cited, in three of which only the women are mentioned, in two only the men, in one both parties. Edward Britton, studying the Broughton court rolls between 1294 and 1323, found twenty-four adultery cases, ten citing both the guilty parties, eight only the man, six only the woman.[48]

Divorce (*divortium*—synonymous with annulment) was a recurring problem for the Church among the aristocracy, who searched for ways to dissolve a barren or disappointing marriage, but among the peasants it was a rarity. When it did occur among villagers, the commonest ground was bigamy. Couples sometimes separated, however, either informally or under terms arranged by a Church court, though the latter expedient was expensive and therefore not normally undertaken by villagers.

In the village as in castle and city, babies were born at home, their birth attended by midwives. Men were excluded from the lying-in chamber. Literary evidence suggests that the woman in labor assumed a sitting or crouching position.[49] Childbirth was dangerous for both mother and child. The newborn infant was immediately prepared for baptism, lest it die in a state of original sin. If a priest could not be located in time, someone else must perform the ceremony, a contingency for which water must be kept ready. If the baptizer did not know the formula in Latin, he must say it in English or French: "I christen thee in the name of the Father and the Son and the Holy Ghost. Amen."[50]

The words must be said in the right order. If the baptizer said, "In the name of the Son and the Father and the Holy Ghost," the sacrament was invalid. Robert Manning told the story of a midwife who said the wrong words:

> She held it on her lap before,
> And when she saw that it would die,
> She began loud for to cry,
> And said, "God and Saint John,
> Christen the child both flesh and bone."

When the priest heard the formula she had used, he cried, "God and Saint John give thee both sorrow and shame . . . for in default a soul is lost," and he commanded her no longer to deliver babies. Robert Manning concluded,

> Being a midwife is a perilous thing
> Unless she knows the points of christening.[51]

John Myrc in his *Instructions for Parish Priests* (early fifteenth century) advised that if the baby seemed likely to die, "though the child but half be born/ Head and neck and no more," the midwife should "christen it and cast on water." If the mother died before the child could be born, the midwife must free the child with a knife, to save its life, or at least to assure baptism.[52]

Under normal circumstances the child was washed and sometimes (though not universally) swaddled, the godparents were summoned, and godmother or midwife carried the baby to the church, where the font was kept ever ready. The mother was not present, and in fact was not permitted to enter the church until several weeks later, when she had undergone the ritual of "churching," purification after childbirth.

Preliminary baptismal rites were performed, as in marriage, at the church door. The priest blessed the child, put salt in its mouth to symbolize wisdom and exorcise demons, read a Bible text, and ascertained the child's name and the godparents' qualifications. The party then moved into the church to the baptismal font. The child was immersed, the godmother dried it and dressed it in a christening garment, and the priest anointed it with holy oil. The ceremony was completed at the altar with the godparents making the profession of faith for the child. The christening party then repaired to the parents' house for feasting and gift-giving.[53]

Children were usually named for their principal godparents. Variety of Christian names was limited in the thirteenth and fourteenth centuries, usually Norman rather than Anglo-Saxon, the most popular in Elton being John, Robert, Henry, Richard, William, Geoffrey, Thomas, Reginald, Gilbert, Margaret, Matilda, Alice, Agnes, and Emma. Less common were Nicholas, Philip, Roger, Ralph, Stephen, Alexander, Michael, Adam, and Andrew, Sarah, Letitia, Edith, and Beatrice. There were as yet no Josephs or Marys.

Unlike the lady of the castle or many city women, the peasant mother normally nursed her own children. Only if the mother had no milk, or if she died, was a wet nurse employed. The evidence of the coroners' rolls indicates that during the first year of life, infants were frequently left alone in the house while their parents worked in the fields, looked after the animals, or did other chores. Older children were more likely to be left with a sitter, usually a neighbor or a young girl. Although neglect on the part of busy parents might lead to tragedy, little evidence exists of infanticide, a commonplace of the ancient world.[54]

Medieval parents have been accused by certain modern writers of a want of feeling toward their children, but even in the comparative poverty of the kind of literary expressions—correspondence and memoirs—that have recorded such sentiments for more recent times, the charge scarcely stands up. Between the lines in the accounts of the coroners may be read again and again the anguish of parents over a lost child: one father searching for his son, drowned in a ditch, "found him, lifted him from the water, could not save him, and he died";[55] another, whose son was struck by lightning in a field, "came running toward him, found him lying there, took him in his arms to the house . . . thinking to save him";[56] a mother dragged her son out of a ditch "because she believed she could save him";[57] a father whose son fell into the millpond "tried to save [him] and entered the water but could do nothing."[58] Sometimes peasants gave their lives for their children, as in one case when a father was killed defending his young daughter from rape.[59]

A fourteenth-century sermon pictures a mother and her child: "In winter, when the child's hands are cold, the mother takes him a straw or a rush and bids him warm it, not for love of the straw, to warm it, but to warm the child's hands [by pressing them together]." When the child falls ill, "the mother for her sick child takes a candle, and makes a vow in prayers."[60]

The coroners' rolls yield rare glimpses of children at work and play: the baby in the cradle by the fire; little girls following their mothers around, helping stir the pot, draw water, gather fruit; little boys following their fathers to the fields, to the mill, or fishing, or playing with bows and arrows. A sermon pictures a child using his imagination, playing "with flowers . . . with sticks, and with small bits of wood, to build a chamber, buttery, and hall, to make a white horse of a wand, a sailing ship of broken bread, a burly spear from a ragwort stalk, and of a sedge a sword of war, a comely lady of a cloth, and be right busy to deck it elegantly with flowers."[61]

A child, said one preacher, did not bear malice, "nor rancor nor wrath toward those that beat him ever so sorely, as it happened for a child to have due chastising. But after thou hast beaten him, show him a fair flower or else a fair red apple; then hath he forgotten all that was done to him before, and then he will come to thee, running, with his embracing arms, to please thee and to kiss thee."[62]

Small children played; older ones did chores. In their teens, both boys and girls moved into the adult work world, the girls in and around the house, the boys in the fields. Contrary to what was formerly believed, in this period village children were not ordinarily sent away to become servants in other people's households or to be apprenticed at a craft. Most remained at home.[63]

The Middle Ages produced the world's first hospitals and medical schools, but these important advances hardly affected life in the village. Doctors practiced in city and in court. Villagers were left to their own medical devices. Even the barbers who combined shaving with bloodletting (a principal form of therapy) and tooth-pulling (the sole form of dentistry) were rarely seen in villages. Most manorial custumals provided for a period of sick leave, commonly up to a year and a day. "If [the villein] is ill, so that he cannot leave his house," states a Holywell custumal, "he is quit of all work and heusire before the autumn, except plowing [which presumably he would have to pay someone else to do]. In the autumn he is quit of half his work if he is ill, and he will have relaxation for the whole time he is ill, up to a year and a day. And if his illness lasts more than a year and a day, or if he falls ill again, from that time he will do all works which pertain to his land."[64]

Life was short. Even if a peasant survived infancy and childhood to reach the age of twenty, he could not expect to live much beyond forty-five, when old age (senectus) began.[65] The manorial records make no mention of diseases, though to the well-known afflictions of tuberculosis, pneumonia, typhoid, violence, and accident may probably be added circulatory disorders: stroke and heart attack. The coroners' rolls list several cases of fatal accidents from "falling sickness"—epilepsy. Invalids flocked on pilgrimage to Canterbury and other shrines: spastics, cripples, paralytics, the mentally ill, and the scrofulous (skin disease was especially prevalent in a not very well washed society).

The most pathetic of the medieval sick, however, were excluded from the benefits of the shrine. Leprosy, mysteriously widespread, inspired a vague terror that outlasted the Middle Ages. Its victims were isolated, either singly or in colonies, and were permitted to emerge in public only when clothed in a shroud and clacking a pair of castanets in warning. The isolation of lepers represented a remarkable advance in medical theory, the recognition of contagion, but at the same time a sad irony, since leprosy (Hansen's disease) is only slightly contagious. The Elton court rolls record a single possible mention of the disease in the fine in 1342 of "Hugh le Lepere" for carrying away the lord's stubble.[66]

* * *

As in all societies, the old and infirm depended on the younger generation for help when they were no longer able to work their land. The commonest form such help took in the thirteenth century was an arrangement between tenant and heir, in essence an exchange of the older person's land for the younger person's work. The holding was transferred to the heir, who promised in return to maintain the parents, widowed father or mother, or other aged relative, either in a separate dwelling or as free boarders. Typically the son accepted the holding's obligations of work service, rent, and fees, and pledged himself to support his parent or parents, stipulating that he would provide them with a separate house or "a room at the end of the house" that had been theirs, food, fuel, clothing, and again and again "a place by the fire." Most such arrangements must have been informal, leaving no trace in the records, but they were also spelled out in written contracts, entered in the manorial court rolls.[67]

Both sermons and moral treatises warned parents against handing over their land to their sons without such safeguards. Men gave their children land, said Robert Manning, to provide sustenance in their old age; better for them to keep it "than beg

Man warming himself at the fire.
Corpus Christi College, Oxford,
Ms. 385, f. 6v.

it at another's hand." In illustration he told a version of the already old story of the "Divided Horsecloth": a man gave his son "all his land and house and all his cattle in village and field, so that he should keep him well in his old age." The young man married and at first bade his wife "to serve his father well at his will." But soon he had a change of heart, and began to be "tenderer of his wife and child than of his father," and it seemed to him that his father had lived too long. As time passed, the son served him worse and worse, and the father began to rue the day he "gave so much to his son." One day the old man was so cold that he begged his son to give him a blanket. The son called his little boy and told him to take a sack and fold it double and put it over his grandfather. The child took the sack and tore it in two. "Why have you torn the sack?" asked the father. The child replied:

This deed have I done for thee.
Good example givest thou me
How I shall serve thee in thine age.
. . . This half sack shall lie above thy father,
And keep the other part to thy behalf.[68]

Most peasants were more careful. In Upwood in 1311 Nicholas son of Adam turned over his virgate to his son John, stipulating that he should have "a reasonable maintenance in that land until the end of his life," and that John should give him "every year for the rest of his life" specified amounts of grain.[69] At Cranfield in 1294, Elias de Bretendon made a more complicated agreement with his son John; John was to take over his house, yard, and half virgate for the services and money rent owed the lord. "And . . . the above John will provide suitable food and drink for Elias and his wife Christine while they are alive, and they will have residence with John [in his house]." The contract left nothing to chance:

And if it should happen, though may it not, that trouble and discord should in the future arise between the parties so that they are unable to live together, the above John will provide for Elias and Christine, or whichever of them should outlive the other, a house and curtilage [yard] where they can decently reside. And he will give each year to the same Elias and Christine or whichever of them is alive, six quarters of hard grain at Michaelmas, namely three quarters of wheat, one and one-half quarters of barley, one and one-half quarters of peas and beans, and one quarter of oats. [The addition evidently gave trouble, since the total is not six but seven quarters.][70]

If the retiring tenant was childless, the pension was contracted for outside the family, an arrangement that became frequent after the Black Death. In 1332 John in the Hale of Barnet, Hertfordshire, agreed with another peasant, John atte Barre, to turn over his house and land in return for a yearly contribution of "one new garment with a hood, worth 3 shillings 4 pence, two pairs of linen sheets, three pairs of new shoes, one pair of new hose, worth 12 pence, and victuals in food and drink decently as is proper." An unusual feature of the contract was that the retiring tenant agreed to work for his replacement "to the best of his ability," and that the new tenant not only paid an entry fee, as was customary, but "satisfied the lord for the heriot of the said John in the Hale by [the payment of] one mare," although the retiree was not yet dead.[71]

Pension contracts were enforceable in the manor court, a sign of one of their most striking aspects: the community's interest in enforcement. "Dereliction of duty to the old [was] a matter of public concern," observes Elaine Clark.[72] A son undertaking to support his aged parents commonly requested the manorial court to witness his oath, or enlisted as guarantors pledges whose names he reported to the steward. For the court's participation the pensioners paid a fee.[73]

In Ellington in 1278, William Koc acknowledged that he was in arrears for the contributions he owed his father, in wheat, barley, beans, and peas, and promised to make amends.[74] The jurors in Warboys in 1334 reported: "And since Stephen the

Smith did not keep his mother according to their agreement he is [fined] sixpence. And afterwards the above jurors ordered that the said land be given back to his mother and that she should hold it for the rest of her life. And the above Stephen may not have anything of that land while his mother is alive."[75]

Pensions were sometimes negotiated between the parties, sometimes mandated as deathbed settlements—mainly by husbands in favor of their widows—and sometimes ordered by the manorial court. When a tenant's disability rendered him unfit to discharge the obligations of his holding, it was in the interest of the lord to make a change, but the change served the interest of the elderly tenant as well.[76]

A pension contract that dated back to the early Middle Ages was originally developed in the monasteries to provide for the retirement of monks. The corrody consisted of a daily ration of bread and ale, usually two loaves and two gallons, plus one or two "cooked dishes" from the monastic kitchen. In the later Middle Ages, corrodies became available to lay pensioners, who purchased them like life insurance annuities. The purchaser might stipulate for a certain amount of firewood every year, a room in the monastery, sometimes with a servant, clothing, candles, and fodder for horses. A wealthy peasant might buy a corrody that even included a house and garden, pasture, and cash; a poor one might buy only a ration of dark bread, ale, and pottage.[77]

Still other arrangements might be made. A widow and her young son leased their holding at Stoke Pryor to a fellow villager for twelve years in return for an annual supply of mixed grain; presumably in twelve years the son would be old enough to take over the holding.[78]

The pension agreement implied bargaining power on the part of the aging tenant, nearly always meaning landholding. In its absence, an old man or woman might end like those whose deaths are recorded in the coroners' rolls: Sabinia, who in January of 1267 went into Colmworth, Bedfordshire, to beg bread and "fell into a stream and drowned,"[79] or Arnulf Argent of

Ravensden, "poor, weak, and infirm," who was going "from door to door to seek bread," when he fell down in a field and "died of weakness."[80]

When death was imminent, the priest was sent for, and arrived wearing surplice and stole, carrying the blessed sacrament, preceded by a server carrying a lantern and ringing a hand bell. If the case was urgent and no server could be found, the priest might hang the lamp and bell on his arm, or around the neck of his horse. According to Robert Manning, sick men were often reluctant to accept the sacrament because of a belief that if they recovered they must abstain from sex:

> Many a one thus hopes and says,
> "Anoint them not save they should die,
> For if he turns again to life
> He should lie no more by his wife."

Manning counseled against the superstition and recommended more trust in God:

> In every sickness ask for [the sacrament] always;
> God almighty is right courteous.[81]

John Myrc advised that if death was imminent, the priest should not make the sick man confess all his sins, but only counsel him to ask God's mercy with a humble heart. If the dying man could not speak but indicated by signs that he wished the sacraments, the priest should administer them. If, however, the dying man was able to speak, Myrc advised that he should be asked "the seven interrogations": if he believed in the articles of the faith and the Holy Scriptures; if he recognized that he had offended God; if he was sorry for his sins; if he wished to amend and would do so if God gave him more time; if he forgave his enemies; if he would atone for his sins if he lived; and finally, "Do you believe fully that Christ died for you and that you may never be saved but by the merit of Christ's passion, and do you think of God with your heart as much as you may?" The sick man should answer yes and be instructed to say, "with a good steadfast mind, if he can . . . 'Into thy hands I commend my soul.' " If he could not, the priest should say it for him, anoint him, and administer Communion.[82]

Wakes commonly turned into occasions of drinking and merriment, condemned by the Church. Robert Grosseteste warned that a dead man's house should be one of "sorrow and remembrance," and should not be made a house of "laughter and play," and a fourteenth-century preacher complained that people "finally like madmen make . . . merry at our death, and take our burying for a bride ale."[83] In the Ramsey Abbey village of Great Raveley in 1301, ten Wistow men were fined after coming "to watch the body of Simon of Sutbyr through the night," because returning home they "threw stones at the neighbors' doors and behaved themselves badly."[84]

Village funerals were usually starkly simple. The body, sewed in a shroud, was carried into the church on a bier, draped with a black pall. Mass was said, and occasionally a funeral sermon was delivered. One in John Myrc's collection, *Festiall*, ends: "Good men, as ye all see, here is a mirror to us all: a corpse brought to the church. God have mercy on him, and bring him

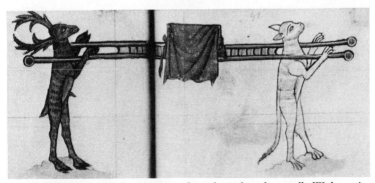

Fanciful funeral: animals carrying a bier draped with a pall. Walters Art Gallery, Baltimore, Psalter and Book of Hours, Ms. 102, f. 76v–77.

into his bliss that shall last for ever. . . . Wherefore each man and woman that is wise, make him ready thereto; for we all shall die, and we know not how soon."[85]

A villager was buried in a plain wooden casket or none at all, in the churchyard, called the "cemetery," from *coemeterium* (dormitory), the sleeping place of the Christian dead. Here men and women could slumber peacefully, their toil finished, until the day of resurrection.

7

THE VILLAGE AT WORK

FOR THE MEDIEVAL VILLAGER, WORK WAS THE ruling fact of life. By sunup animals were harnessed and plows hitched, forming a cavalcade that to the modern eye would appear to be leaving the village to work outside it. Medieval people felt otherwise. They were as much in their village tramping the furrowed strips as they were on the dusty streets and sunken lanes of the village center. If anything, the land which literally provided their daily bread was more truly the village. The geography was a sort of reverse analogue of the modern city with its downtown office towers where people work and its suburban bedroom communities where they eat and sleep.

Whether Elton had two or three fields in the late thirteenth century is unknown. Whatever the number, they were twice subdivided, first into furlongs (more or less rectangular plots "a furrow long"), then into selions, or strips, long and narrow sets of furrows. Depending on the terrain, a village's strips might be several hundred yards long; the fewer turns with a large plow team the better. The strip as a unit of cultivation went far back, probably antedating the open field system itself. Representing the amount of land that could conveniently be plowed in a

Aerial view of the deserted village of Newbold Grounds (Northamptonshire), showing house plots, sunken paths and roads, and the ridge-and-furrow of the surrounding fields. British Crown Copyright/RAF Photograph.

day—roughly half a modern acre—it probably originated in the parcellation of land forced by a growing population. By the late thirteenth century the distribution of a village's strips was haphazard, some villagers holding many, some few, and all scattered and intermingled. The one certainty was that everyone who held land held strips in both or all three fields, in order to guarantee a crop every year regardless of which field lay fallow.

The furlong, or bundle of strips, was the sowing unit, all the strips in a given furlong being planted to the same crop. Many furlongs appear by name in the Elton court records: "Henry in the Lane [is fined] for bad plowing in Hollewell furlong, sixpence," indicating, incidentally, that the lord's demesne land was scattered, like the peasants'.[1] Within each furlong the strips ran parallel, but the furlongs themselves, plotted to follow the ambient pattern of drainage, lay at odd angles to each other, with patches of rough scattered throughout. A double furrow or a balk of unplowed turf might separate strips, while between some furlongs headlands were left for turning the plow. Wedges of land (gores) created by the asymmetry of the furlongs and the character of the terrain were sometimes cultivated by hoe.[2] The total appearance of an open field village, visible in aerial photographs of many surviving sites, is a striking combination of the geometric and the anarchic.

Beyond the crazy-quilt pattern of arable land stretched meadow, waste, and woodland, hundreds of acres that were also part of the village and were exploited for the villagers' two fundamental purposes: to support themselves and to supply their lord. But the most significant component of the open field village was always its two or three great fields of cultivated land. The difference between a two- and a three-field system was slighter than might appear at first glance. Where three fields were used, one lay fallow all year, a second was planted in the fall to winter wheat or other grain, the third was planted in the spring to barley, oats, peas, beans, and other spring crops. The next year the plantings were rotated.

In the two-field system one field was left fallow and the other divided in two, one half devoted to autumn and the other to spring crops. In effect, the two-field system was a three-field system with more fallow, and offered no apparent disadvantage as long as enough total arable was available. If, however, a growing village population pressed on the food supply, or if market demand created an opportunity hard to resist, a two-field system could be converted to three-field. Many two-field systems were so converted in the twelfth and especially the thirteenth century, with a gain of one-third in arable.[3]

Multifield systems, which could accommodate crop rotation, were also common, especially in the north of England. In some places, the ancient infield-outfield system survived, the small infield being worked steadily with the aid of fertilizer, and the large outfield treated as a land reserve, part of which could be cultivated for several successive years (making plowing easier) and then left fallow for several.[4]

But in the English Midlands, and much of northwest Europe, the classic two- or three-field system of open field husbandry prevailed. It involved three essentials: unfenced arable divided into furlongs and strips; concerted agreement about crops and cultivation; and common use of meadow, fallow, waste, and stubble.

Implied was a fourth essential: a set of rules governing details, and a means of enforcing them. Such rules were developed independently in thousands of villages in Britain and on the Continent, at first orally, but by the late thirteenth century in written form as village bylaws. The means of enforcement was provided by the manorial court. Surviving court records include many bylaw enactments and show the existence of many more by citation. For stewards, bailiffs, reeves, free tenants, and villeins, they spelled out a set of restrictions and constraints on plowing, planting, harvesting, gleaning, and carrying. They gave emphatic attention to theft and chicanery, from stealing a neighbor's grain to "stealing his furrow" by edging one's plow into his strip, "a major sin in rural society"[5] (Maurice Beresford). "Reginald Benyt appropriated to himself three furrows under Westereston to his one rod from all the strips abutting upon that rod and elsewhere at Arnewassebroc three furrows to his one headland from all the strips abutting upon that headland," for which Reginald was fined 12 pence by the Elton manorial court of 1279.[6]

Bylaws stipulated the time the harvested crop could be taken from the fields (in daylight hours only), who was allowed to carry it (strangers not welcome), and who was allowed to glean. All able-bodied adults were conscripted for reaping. "And [the jurors] say that Parnel was a gleaner in the autumn contrary to the statutes. Therefore she is in mercy [fined] sixpence."[7] "The wife of Peter Wrau gleaned . . . contrary to the prohibition of autumn."[8] Bylaws ruled the period when the harvest stubble should be opened to grazing, and for which kind of animals, when sheep were barred from the meadows, and when tenants must repair ditches and erect, remove, and mend fences. (Only the lord's land could be permanently fenced, and only if it lay in a compact plot.) Repeatedly, through the year, the village animals were herded into or driven off the open fields as crop, stubble, and fallow succeeded each other.

The regulation of grazing rights was fundamental to the operation of open field farming. The lord's land was especially inviolate to beastly trespass: "Robert atte Cross for his draft-beasts doing damage in the lord's furlong sown with barley, [fined] sixpence."[9] On some manors grazing rights were related to the size of the holding. A Glastonbury survey of 1243 found the holder of a virgate endowed with pasture enough for four oxen, two cows, one horse, three pigs, and twelve sheep, calculated as the amount of stock required to keep a virgate of land fertile.[10]

The open field system was thus not one of free enterprise. Its practitioners were strictly governed in their actions and made to conform to a rigid pattern agreed on by the community, acting collectively.

Neither was it socialism. The strips of plowed land were held individually, and unequally. A few villagers held many strips, most held a few, some held none. Animals, tools, and other movable property were likewise divided unequally. The poor cotters eked out a living by working for the lord and for their better-off neighbors who held more land than their families could cultivate, whereas these latter, by marketing their surplus produce, were able to turn a profit and perhaps use it to buy more land.

How much of his time a villager could devote to cultivating his own tenement depended partly on his status as free or unfree, partly on the size of his holding (the larger the villein holding, the larger the obligation), and partly on his geographical location. In England "the area of heavy villein labor dues—say two or more days each week—was relatively small," consisting mostly of several counties and parts of counties in the east.[11] In the rest of the country, though rules varied from manor to manor, the level of villein obligations tended to be lower. In several counties in the north and northwest they were very light or nonexistent.

Huntingdonshire, containing Ramsey Abbey and Elton, was in the very heart of the heavy-labor region, where the obligation was basically two days' work a week. In Elton, the dozen free tenants owed very modest, virtually token service. The cotters owed little service because they held little or no land. Only the two score villein virgaters owed heavy week-work, amounting to 117 days a year (the nine half-virgaters owed fifty-eight and a half days).[12] In addition, the Elton virgater owed a special service, the cultivation of half an acre of demesne land summer and winter, including sowing it with his own wheat seed, reaping, binding, and carrying to the lord's barn.[13]

Some question exists about the length of the work day required of tenants. A Ramsey custumal for the manor of Abbot's Ripton stipulates "the whole day" in summer "from Hokeday until after harvest," and "the whole day in winter," but during Lent only "until after none (mid-afternoon)."[14] In some places a work day lasted until none if no food was supplied, and if the lord wanted a longer day, he was obliged to provide dinner. Another determinant of the length of the working day may have been the endurance of the ox (less than that of the horse).[15]

The annual schedule of week-work at Elton divided the year into three parts:

From September 29 (Michaelmas) of one year to August 1 (Gules of August) of the following year, two days' work per week (for a virgater).

From August 1 to September 8 (the Nativity of the Blessed Mary), three days' work per week, with a day and a half of work for the odd three days. This stretch of increased labor on the demesne was the "autumn works."

From September 8 to September 29, five days' work a week, known as the "after autumn works."[16]

Thus the autumn and post-autumn works for the Elton virgater totaled thirty-one and a half days, half of the two critical months of August and September, when he had to harvest, thresh, and winnow his own crop.

The principal form of week-work was plowing. Despite employment of eight full-time plowmen and drivers on the Elton demesne, the customary tenants, with their own plows and animals, were needed to complete the fall and spring plowing and the summer fallowing to keep the weeds down. Default of the plowing obligation brought punishment in the manor court: "Geoffrey of Brington withheld from the lord the plow work of half an acre of land. [Fined] sixpence."[17] "John Page withholds a plowing work of the lord between Easter and Whitsuntide for seven days, to wit each Friday half an acre. Mercy [fine] pardoned because afterwards he paid the plowing work."[18]

By the same token, the main kind of work the villein did on his own land was plowing. Stage by stage through the agricultural year he worked alternately for the lord and for himself.

His plow (not every villein owned one) was iron-shared, equipped with coulter and mouldboard, and probably wheeled, an improvement that allowed the plowman to control the depth of furrow by adjusting the wheels, saving much labor. He might own an all-wooden harrow, made by himself from unfinished tree branches, or possibly a better one fashioned by the carpenter. Only the demesne was likely to own a harrow with iron teeth, jointly fabricated by the smith and the carpenter. The villein's collection of tools might include a spade, a hoe, a fork, a sickle, a scythe, a flail, a knife, and a whetstone. Most virgaters probably owned a few other implements, drawn from a secondary array scattered through the village's toolsheds: mallets, weeding hooks, sieves, querns, mortars and pestles, billhooks, buckets, augers, saws, hammers, chisels, ladders, and wheelbarrows. A number of villagers had two-wheeled carts. Those who owned sheep had broad, flat shears, which were also used for cutting cloth.[19]

Heavy plow, with coulter and mouldboard, drawn by four oxen. British Library, Luttrell Psalter, Ms. Add. 42130, f. 170.

Plows and plow animals were shared to make up plow teams. Agreements for such joint plowing appear in court records. At one time scholars debated the discrepancy between Domesday Book's repeated references to the eight-ox plow team and iconographic evidence insistently showing smaller teams, but a modern consensus agrees that teams varied in size, up to eight animals and occasionally more. The largest teams were required to break new ground, the next largest for first plowing after Michaelmas or in spring. Medieval cattle were smaller than their modern descendants and by the time of spring plowing were probably weakened by poor winter diet.[20] Domesday Book refers to smaller teams in non-demesne plowing: "three freemen" plowing with two oxen; freemen plowing with three oxen; "two freewomen" plowing with two oxen. "The Domesday plow team . . . was quite certainly not always an eight-ox team on the villein lands," says R. Trow-Smith; neither was the post-Domesday team.[21]

Horses and oxen were often harnessed together for village as for demesne plowing, not because Walter of Henley recommended it but because availability dictated. Cows were even pressed into service, though modern experiments indicate a lack of enthusiasm on the part of the cows. Cows were kept mainly to breed oxen. An ox took two years to train to the plow, and averaged only four years in service. Thus a four-ox team required complete replacement every four years without allowing for sickness or accident.[22] When horses and oxen were harnessed jointly, it was done in pairs, the horses together, the oxen together, to accommodate the two quite different styles of harness, horse collar and ox yoke. Such teaming, common in England up to modern times, in itself implies large teams.

The first plowing in spring, to turn under the residue of crop and the weeds and grasses, was done early enough to allow time for decomposition of the organic material.[23] A second, shallower plowing aerated the soil, preparing it for seeding. The plowman began just to one side of the center line of the strip to be plowed, effected the laborious turn at the end, and returned on the other side of the center.[24] Peas and beans were planted in the furrow, grain on the ridge. Spring, or Lenten, sowing was done as soon as the soil was warm and frost no longer a danger.[25] Patterns of ridge-and-furrow from the Middle Ages are still visible in aerial photographs, sometimes with the boundaries between neighboring selions indicated by balks or rows of stones.

Demesne plowing might cease at none or at vespers, but a man working his own land might keep his hand to the plow longer, under pressure of time or weather. The first winter wheat plowing, in April after the spring crops were sown in other fields, was shallow. A second, in June, went deeper, as did a third in midsummer. The field was then harrowed and the last clods crumbled with a mattock or long-handled clodding beetle.[26] Grain seed was sown from a straw basket, two bushels (or more) to the acre.[27] Seed was not sown casually. In 1320 four Elton villagers were fined threepence apiece for carelessness in planting, in one case on the part of a servant who allowed "four or five beans" to fall into a single hole "to the damage of the lord."[28] Besides scarce manure, the peasant cultivator might supply equally scarce marl, a clay containing carbonate of lime.[29]

Walter of Henley warned that spring plowing done too deep too early might make fields muddy at sowing time.[30] Spring crops—barley, oats, peas, beans, vetch—were usually planted

Man and woman breaking up clods, following the plow. British Library, Luttrell Psalter, Ms. Add. 42130, f. 171v.

Man sowing grain, using a seed basket, while one crow raids seed bag and dog drives away another. British Library, Luttrell Psalter, Ms. Add. 42130, f. 170v.

more thickly than winter, about four bushels to the acre.[31] For autumn sowing, Walter recommended small furrows with narrow ridges, and planting early enough to allow the seed to take root before the frost.[32] Heavy rain within a week after sowing, followed by a sharp frost, could destroy a winter wheat crop.

It is probable that Elton villagers had their own meadowland. If so, it was doubtless allocated, in accordance with an ancient tradition, by a lottery among all the holders of arable, both free and unfree.[33] Hay was always in short supply because of the lack of artificial meadow, for want of suitable irrigation, and was precious because it was by far the best winter feed available.

Mowing required care and skill. The grass had to be thoroughly dried (tedded) for storage, and if rained on had to be retedded.[34] Demesne mowing at Elton was assigned entirely to the villeins, among whom it was not notably popular; many fines are recorded for failing to do the job properly. They may well have resented being kept from their own mowing. Some lords sweetened the mowing chore with a bonus in the form of a sheep for the mowers to roast, or as on some Ramsey manors, by the game of "sporting chance." At the end of the haymaking, each man was permitted to carry off as large a bundle of hay as he could lift and keep on his scythe; if the scythe broke or touched the ground, he lost his hay and had to buy an obol's worth of ale for his comrades. In Elton, at least by 1311, mowers were being paid a cash bonus.[35]

After haying, the meadow had to be left alone for three or four weeks to allow the grass to grow; consequently another communal agreement was needed about reopening the meadow for grazing. A good hay crop could take the animals through the winter; a good grain crop could do the same for the human beings. The tension of June, relieved by the drudgery of weeding in July, was redoubled in August and September as the fields reached maturity. First in order of priority came the lord's harvest boon. Not only villeins *ad opus* but free tenants, *censuarii*, cotters, and craftsmen, women and children as well as men, turned out—all save those "so old or so weak [that they] could not work"—reaping, gathering, binding, stacking, carrying, and gleaning.[36] Even a villein rich enough to employ labor was not exempt, though he was usually not asked to wield the scythe himself, only to "hold the rod over his workers," as the custumals phrased it.[37]

The word "boon" or "bene" in "harvest boon" or "boon works" literally meant gift, something freely bestowed, but the usage savored of irony, as the court records indicate: "Geoffrey Gamel . . . made default at the boon works of the autumn. Sixpence."[38] "Richard in Angulo, late in his carrying boon works. Sixpence."[39] On the other hand, a dinner of rare abundance was served in the field to the harvest army. For the 329

Women reaping while man binds. British Library, Luttrell Psalter, Ms. Add. 42130, f. 172v.

persons who turned out for the Elton harvest boon of 1298, the reeve, Alexander atte Cross, listed the victuals consumed: eight rings (thirty-two bushels) of wheat, an almost equal quantity of other grains, a bull, a cow, a calf, eighteen doves, and seven cheeses. The second day's work required only 250 hands, who however ate bread made from eleven rings, along with eight hundred herrings, seven pence worth of salt cod, and five cheeses. A partial third day's boon was exacted from sixty villeins, who were fed on three cheeses and "the residue from the expenses of the [manor] house."[40] Of nineteen recorded harvest boons at Elton, this was the only one to last three days. Seven others lasted two days, eleven only one.

The food supplied at boon-works was an important article of the ancient compact between lord and tenants. Size and composition of the loaves of bread made from the grain were commonly stipulated in writing. At Holywell boons, two men were to share three loaves "such that the quantity of one loaf would suffice for a meal for two men," and the bread was to be of wheat and rye, but mainly wheat.[41] At the Ramsey manor of Broughton in 1291 the tenants actually struck over what they deemed an insufficient quantity of bread supplied them, and only returned to work when appeal to the abbey cartulary proved them mistaken. Reapers liked to wash down their wheat bread with plenty of ale, typically a gallon a day per man, according to one calculation, and "some harvesters consumed twice as much."[42]

Wheat was cut with a sickle, halfway or more up the stalk, and laid on the ground. Binders followed to tie the spears in sheaves and set them in shocks to dry. In demesne harvesting, one binder followed every four reapers, advancing in echelon at a rate of two acres a day.[43] That similar teamwork was applied in village harvesting is a reasonable supposition. Oats and barley were mown with scythes, close to the ground.[44] Harvesting of all three crops left much residue, making gleaning an important function. It was too important, according to Warren Ault, to support a famous assertion by Blackstone in the eighteenth century that "by the common law and custom of England the poor are allowed to enter and glean upon another's ground after

Stacking the sheaves. British Library, Luttrell Psalter, Ms. Add. 42130, f. 173.

the harvest without being guilty of trespass."[45] In the medieval village, gleaning was strictly limited to the old, the infirm, and the very young, less out of charity than to conserve labor, all able-bodied adults of both sexes being needed for the heavier harvest work. Bylaws generally forbade gleaning by anyone offered a fair wage for harvesting, usually meaning "a penny a day and food" or twopence without food (Walter of Henley recommended paying twopence for a man, one penny for a woman).[46] Bylaws welcomed strangers to the village as harvesters while barring them as gleaners.

After cutting, gathering, binding, and stacking their sheaves, the villagers carted them to their barns and sheds to be threshed with the ancient jointed flail and winnowed by tossing in the air from the winnowing cloth or basket, and if necessary supplying breeze with the winnowing fan.

Besides the grain crops, harvest included "pulling the peas," the vegetable crops that matured in late September and whose harvest also required careful policing against theft.

Yields for the villagers could scarcely have exceeded those of the demesne, which enjoyed so many advantages. Three and a half to one was generally a very acceptable figure for wheat, with barley a bit higher and oats lower, and bad crops always threatening. R. H. Hilton has calculated that an average peasant on a manor of the bishop of Worcester might feed a family of three, pay a tithe to the church, and have enough grain left to sell for twelve or thirteen shillings, out of which his rent and other cash

Carting. British Library, Luttrell Psalter, Ms. Add. 42130, f. 173v.

obligations would have to come.[47] If he was required to pay cash in place of his labor obligation, he would need to make up the difference by sale of poultry or wool, or through earnings of wife or sons. As Fernand Braudel observes, "The peasants were slaves to the crops as much as to the nobility."[48]

Harvest time was subject to more bylaws than all the rest of the year together. "The rolls of the manor courts are peppered with fines levied for sheaf stealing in the field, and a close watch had to be kept in the barn as well," says Ault.[49] The small size of the medieval sheaf, twenty to a bushel, contributed to temptation, *Seneschaucie* mentioning as familiar places of secreting stolen grain "bosom, tunic, or boots, or pockets or sacklets hidden near the grange."[50]

Another communal agreement was needed for post-harvest grazing of the stubble. Sometimes a common date was set, such as Michaelmas, for having everybody's harvest in. Bylaws might specify that a man could pasture his animals on his own land as soon as his neighbors' lands were harvested to the depth of an acre. This was easy to do with cows, which could be restrained within a limited space. Sheep and hogs, on the other hand, had to wait until the end of autumn.[51]

The lord's threshing and winnowing were followed by the villagers', with whole families again joining in. Winter was the slack season, at least in a relative sense. Animals still had to be looked after, and harness, plows, and tools mended. Fences, hurdles, hedges, and ditches, both the lord's and those of the villagers, had to be repaired to provide barriers wherever arable land abutted on a road or animal droveway. Houses, byres, pens, and sheds needed maintenance. So did equipment: "The good husbandman made some at least of his own tools and implements."[52]

The true odd-job men of the village were the cotters. They rarely took part in plowing, having neither plows nor plow beasts, but turned to "hand-work" with spade or fork, sheep-shearing, wattle-weaving, bean-planting, ditch-digging, thatching, brewing, even guarding prisoners held for trial. They were commonly hired by wealthier villagers at harvest time, getting paid with an

Threshing, using jointed flail. British Library, Luttrell Psalter, Ms. Add. 42130, f. 74v.

eleventh, a fifteenth, or a twentieth sheaf. Cotters' wives and daughters were in demand for weeding and other chores.[53]

Yet though they occupied the lowest rung on the village ladder, even cotters were capable of asserting their rights, as a remarkable entry in the Elton court rolls of 1300 testifies. Among the few service obligations of the Elton cotters was that of assisting in the demesne haymaking. A score of cotters, including three women, were prosecuted

> because they did not come to load the carts of the lord with hay to be carried from the meadow into the manor as formerly they were wont to do in past times, as is testified by Hugh the claviger. They come and allege that they ought not to perform such a custom save only out of love (amor), at the request of the serjeant or reeve. And they pray that this be inquired into by the free tenants and others. And the inquest [a special panel of the court] comes and says that the abovesaid cotters ought to make the lord's hay into cocks in the meadows and similarly in the courtyard of the lord abbot, but they are not bound to load the carts in the meadows unless it be out of special love at the request of the lord.

That left the lord's hay sitting in haycocks in his meadow and the cotters in the manor courtyard waiting for it to be brought to them. The steward confessed himself unable to resolve the dispute without reference to the rule and precedent given in the register at Ramsey, and so ordered "that the said cotters should have parley and treaty with the lord abbot upon the said demand." The ultimate issue is not recorded.[54]

The pathetic picture in *Piers Plowman* of the peasant husband and wife plowing together, his hand guiding the plow, hers goading the team, their baby and small children nearby, illustrates the fact that the wife of a poor peasant had to turn her hand to every kind of labor in sight.[55] For most of the time, however, in most peasant households, the tasks of men and women were differentiated along the traditional lines of "out-side" and "inside" work. The woman's "inside" jobs were by no means always performed indoors. Besides spinning, weaving, sewing, cheese-making, cooking, and cleaning, women did foraging, gardening, weeding, haymaking, carrying, and animal-tending. They joined in the lord's harvest boon unless excused, and helped bring in the family's own harvest. Often women served as paid labor, receiving at least some of the time wages equal to men's.[56] R. H. Hilton believes that peasant women in general enjoyed more freedom and "a better situation in their own class than was enjoyed by women of the aristocracy, or the bourgeoisie, a better situation perhaps than that of the women of early modern capitalist England."[57] The statement does not mean that peasant women were better off than wealthier women, only that they were less constricted within the confines of their class. "The most important general feature of their existence to bear in mind," Hilton adds, "[is] that they belonged to a working class and participated in manual agricultural labor."[58]

For many village women one of the most important parts of the daily labor was the care of livestock. Poultry was virtually the

Woman milking cow. Bodleian Library, Ms. Bodl. 764, f. 41v.

Woman feeding chickens, holding a distaff under her arm. British Library, Luttrell Psalter, Ms. Add. 42130, f. 166v.

Woman on the left is spinning, using the thirteenth-century invention, the spinning wheel. Woman on the right is carding (combing) wool. British Library, Luttrell Psalter, Ms. Add. 42130, f. 103.

woman's domain, but feeding, milking, washing, and shearing the larger livestock often fell to her also.

The biggest problem with livestock was winter feed, the shortage of which was once thought to have provoked an annual "Michaelmas slaughter." Given the high rate of loss to natural causes, an annual slaughter would have threatened the survival of a small flock or herd.[59] The feed shortage certainly played a role in keeping numbers of animals down, but some successful peasants just as certainly overcame the problem. At Bowerchalk in Wiltshire, twenty-three tenants are known to have owned 885 sheep, or 41 per owner; at Merton, eighty-five tenants owned 2,563 sheep, and one is known to have owned 158.[60] Individual ownership within a combined flock was kept straight by branding or by marking with reddle (red ochre), many purchases of which are recorded.[61]

Among peasants as among lords, sheep were esteemed as the "cash crop" animals. Though worth at best only one or two shillings, compared with two and a half shillings for a pig, they had unique fivefold value: fleece, meat, milk, manure, and skin (whose special character made it a writing material of incomparable durability). Lambing time was in early spring, between winter and spring sowing, so that the lambs, weaned at twelve weeks, could accompany their mothers to graze the harvest stubble of last year's wheatfield.[62] The sheep were sheared in mid-June and the fleeces carted to market, probably, in the case of Elton, to Peterborough, about eight miles away. Medieval fleeces weighed from a pound to two and a half pounds, much below the modern average of four and a half pounds.[63]

Pigs were the best candidates for a Michaelmas slaughter, since their principal value was as food and since their meat

Weeding, using long-handled tools. British Library, Luttrell Psalter, Ms. Add. 42130, f. 17s.

preserved well. A sow farrowed twice a year, and according to *Hosbonderie* was expected to produce seven piglets per litter.[64] Records at Stevenage, Hertfordshire, for the late thirteenth century show sows producing up to nineteen offspring a year, "a good enough figure even by modern standards."[65] They could be eaten "profitably" in their second year, and supplied scarce fat to the medieval diet.[66] Pigs foraged for themselves on the acorns, beechnuts, crab apples, hazelnuts, and leaves of the forest floor. For the privilege, exercised mainly in the autumn, their owners paid the lord pannage, in Elton on a sliding scale of a quarter penny to twopence, depending on the pig's size.[67] Probably pannage was originally a fine for overuse of the limited forest mast, which might deprive the wild boar, favored lordly hunting quarry. Feed for pigs was more of a problem in winter, but might be supplemented by whey, a by-product of the cheese-making process.[68]

Unlike sheep, pigs could take care of themselves against predators and so could be allowed to run free. This led to the problem of their rooting in somebody's garden, especially in winter, leading in turn to numerous bylaws requiring rings—bits of curved wire—in their noses beginning at Michaelmas or another autumn date.[69]

Men knocking acorns from oak trees to feed pigs. British Library, St. Mary's Psalter, Ms. Royal 2B VII, f. 81v.

Cattle were the most expensive animals to keep through the winter but were rarely slaughtered. Cows gave about 120 to 150 gallons of milk a year, far below modern yields, but at a half penny per gallon not a negligible contribution to a peasant income. Calving percentages were high, somewhat contradicting the theory that cows were seriously underfed in winter.[70] Such better-off Elton villagers as John of Elton, Nicholas Blundel, Richard of Barton, and Richer Chapelyn bought grass from the demesne pasture or from the millpond. Other resources included mistletoe and ivy from the forest.[71]

Goats, from the point of view of husbandry a sort of inferior sheep, were seldom kept in the lowlands (though the Ramsey manor of Abbot's Ripton kept a herd), but in mountainous regions could thrive better than any other stock.[72] Nearly all the villagers kept poultry. Geese were a favorite, producing, according to *Hosbonderie*, five goslings apiece per year.[73]

The marketing of animals was done mainly before Christmas, before Lent, and at Whitsuntide.

Villeins, cotters, and free tenants alike, nearly all the villagers spent their days in the fields, manhandling the plow, swinging the scythe or sickle, loading the cart. Not quite all, however. There were also the two bakers at either end of the village, the smith, the carpenter, and the millers and fullers who operated the three mills astride the Nene. Using water power to grind grain was an old story, using it to finish cloth a new one. For centuries fullers, or walkers (whence both English surnames), had done their job with their feet, trampling the rough wool fabric in a trough of water after rubbing it with fuller's earth, an absorbent clay that helped get rid of the grease. The water wheel now drove a set of beaters that took the place of the fullers' feet. After the cloth had been partially dried, it was finished by teasing the nap and shearing it with huge flat shears, preparing it for the final step in the process, dyeing.[74]

For the gristmill, either the same or another mill wheel was geared to rotate the upper of a pair of millstones, which was pierced to allow the grain to be fed in. Millstones were expensive, sometimes imported from abroad. When a mill was farmed, the steward might cause the millstones to be measured before and after the farm, and the farmer charged for the wear.

All three mills were under the supervision of the bailiff, who rendered an annual accounting (in 1297 he recorded the fullers as finishing 22 ells of wool blanket cloth for the abbot).[75] He sold the multure, the flour taken in payment from the grist mills' captive customers, who were kept ever in line by the manor court: "Andrew Saladin [fined] because he keeps a handmill to the lord's damage" and Andrew's handmill confiscated (1331).[76] The customary tenants were permitted to grind their own grain only if the mill was flooded, in which case they were obligated to come and repair it.[77] The millers were responsible for incidental income from the tolls paid by those using the mill as a bridge, from the sale of eels from the millpond, from flax grown on its shores, and from the rental of boats and the sale of grass.[78]

The bakers' monopoly was also guarded by the court. Three villagers were fined in 1300 for "withdrawing themselves from the lord's common oven," and in 1306 eight, one of whom was excused "because she is poor."[79] Later three villagers were fined for going into the baking business: Walter Abbot, Robert son of the chaplain, and Athelina of Nassington were found to be "common bakers" and had to pay twelve pence apiece.[80]

The smith and the carpenter turn up in the Elton accounts

Mill with eel trap in the stream. British Library, Luttrell Psalter, Ms. Add. 42130, f. 181.

in connection with repairs to the mills as well as work on the demesne plows and carts. The smith made horseshoes either from "the lord's iron" or from "his own iron," and also ox shoes, since oxen were often shod (but neither horses nor oxen necessarily on all four feet). The smith fabricated blades, tanged or socketed, to be fitted with wooden knife handles; and also cauldrons, kettles, cups, sickles, billhooks, saws, and fasteners.[81] His shop in the middle of the village was equipped with tools that dated from prehistory: anvil, hammer, and the tongs with which he endlessly returned the workpiece to the fire. He probably also had the more recently invented bellows. Recorded payments to him from the manor ran from a few pence for shoeing horses of the abbot to four shillings sixpence for repairing the demesne plows.[82] Often he collaborated on a job with the carpenter, fashioning a wood-and-iron plow or harrow, wheelbarrow, fork, or spade. The carpenter also appears in the manorial accounts, building a dovecote for the manor house, and repairing the manor's chapel and granary, the porch of the barn, the mill machinery, and the abbey's boats used to transport produce on the Nene.[83]

A product of collaboration of carpenter and smith, the wheelbarrow, here used to transport a crippled beggar. British Library, Luttrell Psalter, Ms. Add. 42130, f. 186v.

Other craftsmen probably served the village on a part-time basis. The cotters, jacks-of-all-trades, doubtless developed specializations. The important trade of tanning was apparently not practiced in Elton, at least not on a full-time basis, but an Elton man, son of Richard Dunning, is known to have gone to Hayham to become John Tanner, "a man of means [who] has many goods."[84] Elton villagers probably did some of their own tanning and harnessmaking at home, along with other craft functions. Among the stream of itinerant tradespeople who passed through the village were slaters, tilers, and thatchers, a tinker ("a man to repair brass jars and brass pans"), carters ("two men with dung carts at mowing time" and "two carters carrying stone"), men to "brand animals" and to "geld suckling pigs," "a woman milking sheep," "three grooms driving animals into the marsh," "a girl drying malt," "a certain excommunicated clerk helping the swineherd in the wood," and "divers other workmen."[85] Plying trades in the abbey village of Ramsey and in Peterborough, Stamford, and other nearby towns were shoemakers, saddlers, chandlers, coopers, glaziers, tanners, tailors, and other merchant craftsmen.

The countryside profited in quality of life from the growth of city crafts. As Henri Pirenne observed, the old manorial workshops, with their serf labor, turned out tools and textiles "not half as well as they were now made by the artisan of the neighboring town."[86] At the same time, the flight of craftsmen tended to restrict the village to the uninspiring toil of plow and sickle. To the variety of life of the town was added the lure of freedom. On the Continent the rule had long been accepted that "free air makes free men" and residence in a town for a year and a day erased serfdom. In England servile disabilities were canceled by similar residence in a borough with a royal charter or on royal demesne land. What a man needed in order to take advantage of the opportunity was a skill, not easy but not impossible to obtain in the village. According to J. A. Raftis, emigration of villeins from the Ramsey estate "was a regular feature of manorial life from the time of the earliest extant court rolls."[87]

One village craft was so widely practiced that it hardly belonged to craftsmen. Every village not only had its brewers, but had them all up and down the street. Many if not most of them were craftswomen (virtually all in Elton). Ale was as necessary to life in an English medieval village as bread, but where flour-grinding and bread-baking were strictly guarded seigneurial monopolies, brewing was everywhere freely permitted and freely practiced. How the lords came to overlook this active branch of industry is a mystery (though they found a way to profit from it by fining the brewers for weak ale or faulty measure). Not only barley (etymologically related to beer) but oats and wheat were used, along with malt, as principal ingredients. The procedure was to make a batch of ale, display a sign, and turn one's house into a temporary tavern. Some equipment was needed, principally a large cauldron, but this did not prevent poor women from brewing. All twenty-three persons indicted by the Elton ale tasters in 1279 were women. Seven were pardoned because they were poor.[88]

Life in a village in the late thirteenth century was not one of abundance for anybody. "Given the productive powers of their soil, their technical knowledge, their capital resources and the burden of their rents and taxes, the numbers of peasants on the land were greater than its produce could support," conclude M. M. Postan and J. Z. Titow, perhaps pessimistically.[89] Certainly ordinary men and women, whether free or unfree, could not escape occasions or degrees of want. What the village offered, at least to its landed tenants, free or unfree, was a measure of relative security in return for a life of unremitting labor. Not surprisingly, many longed for something a little easier and a little better. The fabled land of Cockaigne of popular literature was a place "where the more you sleep the more you earn," and where people "can eat and drink/ All they want without danger."[90]

From the perspective of modern times, the daily drudgery and scant returns of the medieval village appear less the product of the social system than of the state of technology. And even though, like all the social structures that had preceded it, the manorial system was heavily weighted in favor of the ruling class, it was not wholly one-sided. "The manor does not exist for the exclusive use of the lord any more than it exists for the exclusive benefit of the peasantry," concluded Paul Vinogradoff, one of the earliest of its modern historians.[91]

Yet dissatisfaction was inevitable. Protests and minor riots are recorded at numerous places, over labor service, tallage, merchet, the right to buy and sell land, mowing service, and other villein burdens.[92] Similar incidents occurred on the Continent throughout the thirteenth century. For the time being, no large-scale movements developed, but the smoldering potential was there. Piers Plowman endorsed the existing order but insisted that it should be based on justice on the part of the lord, a philosophical solution with only limited practical merit. The villein was bound to resent not only his obligations but his status, and the lord could not forever hold him to either.

8

THE PARISH

BESIDES BEING A VILLAGE AND A MANOR, ELTON was one other thing: a parish, a church district. Like village and manor, village and parish did not always coincide. Some villages had more than one church, usually because they included more than one manor. Some parishes, especially in the north of England, included more than one village, indicating that a large estate, with its church, had been fractioned into several villages and hamlets. By the thirteenth century, however, most villages were geographically coterminous with their parishes, so that the village formed a religious as well as a secular community.[1]

The parish church, like the village, was a medieval invention, the ancient Romans having worshiped at private altars in their own homes. The thousands of Christian churches built in the villages across Europe in the Middle Ages were the product of two different kinds of foundation. Some were planted by the city cathedrals and their subordinate baptisteries, and formed an integral part of the Church establishment. Others were private or "proprietary" churches, built by landowners on their own property, to serve their households and

155

tenants. The landowner might be a wealthy layman, or a monastery, or a bishop. The church was the owner's personal property, to be sold or bequeathed as he pleased. Its revenues went into his pocket. He appointed the priest, had him ordained, and paid him a salary. With the settlement of Northern Europe, these private-enterprise churches spread. In England they followed a similar development, and given the sanction of Saxon and Danish kings, acquired the important right to perform the sacraments of baptism and burial. The church tower became a village landmark, and the parish priest, who usually had enough Latin to witness and guarantee legal documents, became a valued member of village society.[2]

It is likely that when Dacus reluctantly sold Elton to Aetheric in 1017 and it came into the possession of Ramsey Abbey, the property included a church. Seventy years later, Domesday Book states that Elton had "a church and a priest," and in 1178 Pope Alexander III confirmed that "Elton with its church and all pertaining to it" belonged to Ramsey Abbey.[3]

Of the medieval rectors of Elton, only a few scattered names survive. Thuri Priest was rector in 1160, at the time of the earliest manorial survey; Robert of Dunholm in 1209; Henry of Wingham in mid-thirteenth century; and after 1262 Robert of Hale, a member of a local family whose names occur in the manorial court records.

Meanwhile the arrangement had undergone a change. The lord still appointed the rector (*persona* in the extents, hence "parson"), but now he bestowed the parish on him as a "living," from which the appointee received all or most of the revenues. Although he was always a cleric, the rector did not necessarily serve in person, but might live elsewhere, hiring a deputy, usually a vicar, and profiting from the difference between the revenues he collected and the stipend he paid his substitute.[4]

In general, a class difference existed between the rectors who served in person and those who merely collected the revenues. The former were typically local men, sons of free peasants or craftsmen, sometimes of villeins who had paid a fine to license their training and ordination. The absentee was more apt to be a member of the nobility or gentry, a younger son who had been ordained and drew his income from parish churches rather than tenants' rents.

Certain absentee rectors held several livings simultaneously. Some of these "pluralists" held only a few parishes and supervised them conscientiously; others held many and neglected them. A notorious example was Bogo de Clare, younger son of an earl, who in 1291 held twenty-four parishes or parts of parishes plus other church sinecures, netting him a princely income of £2,200 a year. Bogo spent more in a year on ginger than he paid a substitute to serve one of his parishes, in which he took little interest. A monk visiting one of Bogo's livings on Easter Sunday found that in place of the retable (the decorative structure above the high altar), there were only "some dirty old sticks spattered with cow-dung."[5]

The Church did not condone such excesses as that of Bogo, whom Archbishop John Pecham called "a robber rather than a rector."[6] Efforts were made to limit the number of benefices a man could hold, and bishops visited their parishes to check on conditions. In 1172 Pope Alexander III decreed that vicars must have adequate job security and must receive a third of their church's revenues. The Fourth Lateran Council (1215) further denounced the custom whereby "patrons of parish churches, and certain other persons who claim the profits for themselves, leave to the priests deputed to the service of them so small a portion that they cannot be rightly sustained," and pronounced that the rector when not himself residing must see that a vicar was installed, with a guaranteed portion of the revenues.[7]

By the end of the thirteenth century there were about nine thousand parishes in England, perhaps a quarter of them vicarages. Rich parishes tended to attract men in search of income, leading to vicars in many market towns and large villages, and rectors in small ones.[8]

The "poor parson" of the Canterbury Tales was the brother of a plowman who had carted "many a load of dung . . . through the morning dew." This parson "did not set his benefice to hire/ and leave his sheep encumbered in the mire . . ./ He was a shepherd and no mercenary." Despite his peasant background, Chaucer's parson was "a learned man, a clerk/ who truly knew Christ's gospel."[9] His colleagues in the country parishes were not all so well versed. Archbishop Pecham charged priests in general with an "ignorance which casts the people into a ditch of error." Roger Bacon (c. 1214–c. 1294) accused them of reciting "the words of others without knowing in the least what they mean, like parrots and magpies which utter human sounds without understanding what they are saying." The chronicler Gerald of Wales amused his readers with stories about the ignorance of parish priests: one who could not distinguish between Barnabas and Barabbas; another who, confusing St. Jude with Judas Iscariot, advised his congregation to honor only St. Simon at the feast of St. Simon and St. Jude. Still another could not distinguish between the Latin for the obligations of the two debtors in the parable (Luke 7:41–43), one of whom owed five hundred pence and the other fifty. When his examiner pointed out that if the sums were the same, the story had no meaning, the priest replied that the money must be from different mints, in one case Angevin pennies, in the other sterling.[10]

Bishops ordaining candidates for the priesthood, or visiting parishes, often found both candidates and ordained clergy *illiteratus*—unlettered, meaning lacking in Latin and thus ignorant of the Scriptures and the ritual. Laymen were less severe. The dean of Exeter, touring parishes in Devon in 1301, found the parishioners almost universally satisfied with their priests as preachers and teachers.[11]

Facilities for the education of priests were scarce, and many aspiring novices could only apply to another parish priest for a smattering of Latin, the Mass, and the principal rites. The lucky few who were able to attend cathedral schools, monastic schools, and the universities were more likely to become teachers, Church officials, or secretaries in noble households than parish priests. A priest might, however, occasionally obtain a leave of absence to study theology, canon law, and the Bible.[12]

The appearance in the thirteenth century of manuals and treatises for the guidance of parish priests marked a new stage of clerical professionalism. One of the most widely circulated was the *Oculus Sacerdotis* (Eye of the Priest), written by William of Pagula, vicar of Winkfield, Berkshire, in 1314. John Myrc's vernacular, versified *Instructions for Parish Priests*, was a free translation of a portion of William of Pagula's book, intended to inform the reader

How thou shalt thy parish preach
And what thou needest them to teach,
And what thou must thyself be.[13]

Whether the income of the parish church was collected by a resident or an absentee rector, it came from the same sources. Three kinds of revenue were very ancient in England: plow-alms, soul-scot, and church-scot. The first was a charge on each plow-team, payable at Easter; the second was a mortuary gift to the priest, and the third a charge on all free men, paid at Martinmas, always in kind, usually in grain. These were all relatively small charges. The chief support of the church was the tithe or tenth, familiar in the Old Testament, but only becoming obligatory in the Christian Church in the Middle Ages. Gerald of Wales told a story about a peasant who owed ten stone of wool to a creditor in Pembroke at the time of shearing, and when he found that he had only that amount, sent a tithe of it, one stone, to his church, over the protest of his wife, and the remaining nine to his creditor, asking for extra time to make good the deficiency. But when the creditor weighed the wool, it weighed the full ten stone. By this example, Gerald said, "the wool having been miraculously multiplied like the oil of Elisha, many persons . . . are either converted to paying those tithes or encouraged in their readiness to pay."[14]

Tithes were spelled out in detail in a number of the Ramsey Abbey extents: in Holywell, the rector received from the abbot's demesne tithes of sheaves from six acres of a field called Blad-dicas, including two acres of wheat, one of rye, one of barley, and two of oats; and tithes of sheaves from the peasants in Southfield and "in the field west of the barns at Needingworth"; and "in the name of tithes" from the peasants, a penny per year for each chicken, an obol for a calf or a sheep, a quarter-penny for a kid, "and if they have seven sheep or kids, the rector will have one of them and [make up the difference] in silver, according to the value of a tenth part." He received a tenth of the milk every day in the year.[15] At Warboys the rector was also entitled to a tenth of the wool, linen, pigs, geese, and garden products.[16]

Tithes were collected as a kind of income tax from the rector's living. From his spiritual jurisdiction over the villagers he collected voluntary offerings, or oblations, at Mass, on the anniversaries of a parishioner's death, at weddings and funerals, and from penitents after confession. Offerings might be in kind: the bread for communion, wax and candles, eggs at Easter, cheese at Whitsuntide, fowls at Christmas. At Broughton, at the Feast of the Nativity of the Blessed Mary, all the parishioners, free as well as villein, gave as many loaves of bread as they had plow animals, one-third of which went to the church, two-thirds to the paupers of the parish.[17]

Finally, the rector had the income of his "glebe," the land pertaining to the church which he held as a free man, owing no labor services or servile dues, and which he cultivated as a husbandman. Traditionally, the glebe was twice the normal holding of a villein, though in practice it varied. In 1279 the rector of the Elton church held a virgate, probably distributed in the fields, and, adjacent to the church, ten more acres and a farmstead.[18] Surveys of other Ramsey Abbey villages list the rector's lands in more detail. At Warboys, he held two virgates of land, a house and a yard, and common pasture "in the wood, the marsh, and other places."[19] The rector of Holywell held a virgate, "half a meadow which is called Priestsholm," three acres of meadow distributed in "many pieces," a tenth of the villagers' meadow, and shares of a pasture and a marsh.[20] In Abbot's Ripton, the rector had a virgate, a parsonage, three houses with tenants, and "common pasture in Westwood."[21]

The rector of Elton also rented a piece of land called le Brach. The manorial court took unfavorable notice of certain of his activities, the jurors complaining that he "made pits on the common at Broadmoor,"[22] and again that he "dug and made a pit and took away the clay at Gooseholm to the general nuisance."[23] He may have been digging marl for fertilizer or clay to mend his walls. Medieval moralists were occasionally concerned lest the priest's role as husbandman crowd out his spiritual life, and that "all his study [become] granges, sheep, cattle, and rents, and to gather together gold and silver."[24] Perhaps for this reason the glebe was sometimes farmed out to a layman, who paid rent to the rector and made a profit on the sale of the crops.

Nothing is known about the rectory at Elton in the thirteenth century, but some information has survived about other rectories, a handful of which, built in stone, still stand, though usually much altered. In size and characteristics the medieval parsonage evidently fell roughly between a manor house and a decent peasant house. That at Hale, Lincolnshire, was described as a hall house with two small bedchambers, one for residents and one for visitors, and a separate kitchen, bakehouse, and brewhouse.[25] When the monks of Eynsham Abbey built a vicarage in 1268 for a church they had appropriated, they specified construction of oak timbers and a hall twenty-six feet by twenty with a buttery at one end and at the other a chamber and a privy.[26] Like any other farmhouse, the rectory or vicarage included barns, pens, and sheds.

Records mention several persons assisting the rector or vicar in his professional work and daily life—chaplain, curate, clerk, page—without disclosing whether these were full- or part-time aides, or how they were compensated. Not infrequently there was also a wife or concubine. Clerical celibacy was a medieval ideal more often expressed than honored. Although two Lateran councils in the twelfth century prescribed it, a modern canon-law authority comments that in the thirteenth century "everyone who entered the clergy made a vow of chastity but almost none observed it."[27] Gerald of Wales states that "nearly all" English priests were married, though other sources indicate that only a minority were.[28] Concubinage, usually entirely open, was more common. Robert Manning tells the tale of a woman who lived with a "right amorous priest" for many years and bore him four sons, three of whom became priests, the fourth a scholar. After their father died, the four sons urged the mother to repent her "deadly sin." The mother, however, declared that she would never repent "while I have you three priests to pray and chant for me and to bring me to bliss." The mother died "sooner than she willed." For three nights her sons sat by her body at the wake. On the first, at midnight, to their terror, "the bier began to quake." On the second night it quaked again and suddenly a devil appeared, seized the corpse, and dragged it toward the door. The sons sprang up, carried it back, and tied it to the bier. On the third night at midnight a whole host of fiends invaded the house and

> Took the body and the bier
> With loathly cry that all might hear
> And bore it forth none knows where,
> Without end forevermore.

The scholar son then roamed the world advising women not to become "priests' mares," lest they suffer his mother's fate.[29]

The Lanercost Chronicle relates a less cautionary story: a vicar's concubine, learning that the bishop was coming to order her lover to give her up, set out with a basket of cakes, chickens, and eggs, and intercepted the bishop, who asked her where she was going. She replied, "I am taking these gifts to the bishop's mistress who has lately been brought to bed." The bishop, properly mortified, continued on his way to call on the vicar, but never mentioned mistresses or concubines.[30]

The importance of the parish church in the village scheme was permanently underlined by the rebuilding of nearly all of them in stone, a process that began in the late Anglo-Saxon period and was largely completed by the thirteenth century. Many medieval village churches survive today, in whole or, as in the case of Elton's chancel arch, in part. In the smaller villages, the church often remained a single-cell building with one large room. In larger parishes, as at Elton, the church was often two-cell, the nave, where the congregation gathered, linked by an arched doorway to the chancel, where the altar stood and the liturgy was performed. Sometimes lateral chapels flanked the chancel, and side aisles were added to the nave.[31]

In 1287 Bishop Quinel of Exeter listed the minimum furnishing of a church: a silver or silver-gilt chalice; a silver or pewter vessel (ciborium) to hold the bread used in Communion; a little box of silver or ivory (pyx) to hold the remainder of the consecrated bread, and another vessel for unconsecrated bread; a pewter chrismatory for the holy oils; a censer and an incense boat (thurible); an osculatorium (an ornament by which the kiss of peace was given); three cruets; and a holy-water vessel. The church must have at least one stone altar, with cloths, canopy, and frontal (front hanging); a stone font that could be locked to prevent the use of baptismal water for witchcraft; and images of the church's patron saint and of the Virgin Mary. Special candlesticks were provided for Holy Week and Easter, and two great portable crosses served, one for processions and one for visitation of the sick, for which the church also kept a lantern and a hand bell.[32] To these requirements a list dictated by Archbishop Winchelsey in 1305 added the Lenten veil, to hang before the high altar, Rogation Day banners for gang week, "the bells with their cords," and a bier to carry the dead.[33] Conspicuously missing were benches, chairs, or pews; the congregation stood, sat on the floor, or brought stools.

The church was supposed to have a set of vestments for festivals and another for regular use. Bishop Quinel recommended a number of books to help the priest: a manual for baptism, marriage, and burial; an ordinal listing the offices to be recited through the church year; a missal with the words and order of the Mass; a collect book containing prayers; a "legend" with lessons from the Scriptures and passages from the lives of the saints; and music books, including a gradual for Mass, a troper for special services, a venitary for the psalms at matins, an antiphoner for the canonical hours, a psalter, and a hymnal. Books and vestments were stored in a church chest.[34]

The churchyard with its consecrated burial ground was a source of village controversy. In the name of those who lay "awaiting the robe of glory," priests decried its use for such sacrilegious purposes as "dances and vile and dishonorable games which lead to indecency," and court trials, "especially those involving bloodshed." An often-repeated injunction demanded that the churchyard be walled and the walls kept in repair, to ensure that the graves "are not befouled by brute beasts."[35] Robert Manning told the story of a villein of Norfolk who rebuked a knight whose manor "was not far from the church," for allowing his animals to enter the churchyard, since "as oft befalls,/ Broken were the churchyard walls." The peasant addressed the knight:

> "Lord," he said, "your beasts go amiss.
> Your herd does wrong and your knaves
> That let your beasts defile these graves.
> Where men's bones should lie
> Beasts should do no villainy."

The knight's reply was "somewhat vile": Why should one respect "such churls' bones"?

The villein replied:

> "The lord that made of earth earls,
> Of that same earth made he churls . . .
> Earls, churls, all at one,
> Shall none know your from our bones."

The knight, abashed, repaired the churchyard walls "so that no beast might come thereto to eat or defile."[36]

Three services were normally celebrated in the parish church on Sunday: matins, Mass, and evensong. Mass was also said daily, and the priests were supposed to say the canonical hours at three-hour intervals for their own benefit.[37] Sunday Mass was the best-attended service. Robert Manning pictured a man lying abed on Sunday morning and hearing the church bells ring, "to holy church men calling," and preferring to

. . . lie and sweat
And take the merry morning sleep;
Of matins rich men take no keep.

A devil whispers in his ear, urging him to ignore matins:

"Betimes may you rise
When they do the Mass service.
A Mass is enough for you."[38]

Vanity sometimes caused women to be late for Mass, like the
lady of Eynsham described by a fourteenth-century preacher,
"who took so long over adornment of her hair that she barely
arrived at church before the end of Mass." One day the devil
in the form of a giant spider descended on her coiffure. Nothing
would dislodge it, neither prayer, exorcism, nor holy water, until
it was confronted with the Eucharist. The spider then de-
camped, and presumably the lady thenceforth arrived at church
on time.[39]

William of Pagula declared that it was hard to get people to
church at all: "Anon he will make his excuse and say, 'I am old
or sickly, or the weather is cold and I am feeble.' Or else he will
excuse himself and say thus, 'I have a great household,' or else
he has some other occupation to do, but for all these excuses,
if a man would come and hear him and say, 'I will give good
wages [for going to church],' then will they take all manner of
excuses back and come to the divine service according to their
duty."[40]

The Mass was said in Latin, with little participation by the
congregation, and communion was usually administered only at
Easter. Moralists complained that the people chattered, gos-
siped, and flirted at Mass. John Myrc inveighed against casual
worshipers who leaned against a pillar or wall instead of kneel-
ing. When the Gospel was read, they should stand; when it was
finished, they should kneel again. When the bell rang at the
consecration, they should raise their hands and pray.[41]

Sermons were infrequent in the thirteenth century. Instead,
the priest might devote time to a lesson, instructing the congre-

gation about the Articles of the Faith, the seven deadly sins, or the sacraments, or he might read from a collection of sermons in English, though such books were not yet widely distributed.

The art of preaching, however, was undergoing a revival, led by the mendicant friars, the Dominicans and Franciscans. Arriving in England in the 1220s, these roving brothers preached in the parish church with the permission of the rector, or failing that, in the open air, where their sermons offered a lively alternative to the routine of Sunday services. Illustrated with personal experiences, fables, and entertaining stories, they encouraged the participation of the congregation. A preacher might call out, "Stop that babbling," to a woman, who did not hesitate to reply, "What about you? You've been babbling for the last half hour." Such exchanges brought laughter, applause, and more friendly heckling.[42]

When sermons were delivered, either by parish priest or friar, they followed an elaborate formula. The preacher announced his Scriptural text (*thema*), then commenced with the *antethema*, usually a prayer and invocation, or "bidding prayer," like the following (for the day of the Assumption of the Blessed Virgin):

> Almighty God, to whose power and goodness infinite all creatures are subject, at the beseeching of thy glorious mother, gracious lady, and of all thy saints, help our feebleness with thy power, our ignorance with thy wisdom, our frailty with thine sufficient goodness, that we may receive here thine help and grace continual, and finally everlasting bliss. To which bliss thou took this blessed lady this day as to her eternal felicity. Amen.[43]

The theme was then repeated, followed by an introduction which might begin with an "authority," quoted from the Bible or from a Church Father, or a message for the particular occasion or audience, or an attention-getting "exemplum," an illustrative story ("Examples move men more than precepts," advised St. Gregory). The story might be merely "something strange, subtle and curious," or a terrifying tale about devils, death-bed scenes, and the torments of hell. Sources abounded: fable, chronicle, epic, romance. One story that must have had a particular appeal to peasant women began, "I find in the chronicles that there was once a worthy woman who had hated a poor woman more than seven years." When the "worthy woman" went to church on Easter Day, the priest refused to give her communion unless she forgave her enemy. The woman reluctantly gave lip service to the act of forgiveness, "for the shame of the world more than for awe of God," and so that she could have her communion.

> Then, when service was done . . . the neighbors came unto this worthy woman's house with presents to cheer her, and thanked God highly that they were accorded. But then this wretched woman said, "Do you think I forgave this woman her trespass with my heart as I did with my mouth? Nay! Then I pray God that I never take up this rush at my foot." Then she stooped down to take it up, and the devil strangled her even there. Wherefore ye that make any love-days [peace agreements] look that they be made without any feigning, and let the heart and the tongue accord in them.[44]

The body of the sermon was usually divided into three sections: an exposition on three vices, or symbolic meanings of the Trinity, or symbolic features of some familiar object—a castle, a chess game, a flower, the human face.

The sermon ended with a flourish, sometimes a smooth peroration, merely summing up the text and discourse, sometimes, especially if the congregation had dozed, a rousing hellfire diatribe. The priest might compare the agony of a sinner in hell with being rolled a mile in a barrel lined with red-hot nails. Devils were favorite descriptive subjects, with their faces "burned and black." One devil was so horrible that "a man would not for all the world look on him once." Hell rang with the "horrible roaring of devils, and weeping, and gnashing of teeth, and wailing of damned men, crying, 'Woe, woe, woe, how great is this darkness!'" If one of them longed for sweetmeats and drink, he got "no sweetness, nor delicacy, but fire and brimstone . . . If one of them would give a thousand pounds for one drop of water, he gets none. . . . There shall be flies that bite their flesh, and their clothing shall be worms . . . and in short, there are all manner of torments in all the five senses, and above all there is the pain of damnation: pain of privation of the bliss of heaven, which is a pain of all pains. . . . Think on these pains; and I trust to God that they shall steer thee to renounce thy drunken living!"[45]

Sometimes the closing peroration pictured the Last Judgment and the doom that preceded it: fifteen days of terrible portents, tidal waves and the sea turning to blood, earthquakes, fires, tempests, fading stars, yawning graves, men driven mad by fear, followed by the accounting from which no man could escape, by bribes, or influence, or worldly power, "for if thou shall be found in any deadly sin, though Our Lady and all the saints of heaven pray for thee, they shall not be heard."[46]

Or the preacher might close by reminding his congregation of their mortality. "These young people think," cried one preacher, "that they shall never die, especially before they are old! . . . They say, 'I am young yet. When I grow old I will amend.'" Such persons were reminded to "Go to the burials of thy father and mother; and such shalt thou be, be ye ever so fair, ever so wise, ever so strong, ever so gay, ever so light." Death was the inevitable end, and none too far off. Man's earthly being was in fact insignificant and not very comely: "What is man but a stinking slime, and after that a sack full of dung, and at the last, meat for worms?"[47]

Even without sermons, the medieval parishioner was reminded of his fate by the paintings decorating the church walls, only a few of which have survived.* In these murals often over the chancel arch, a symbolic gateway between this world and the next, Christ sat in stern judgment, graves sprang open, and

---

*Such as the Last Judgment discovered in the church at Broughton, currently being restored.

naked sinners tumbled into the gaping mouth of a beast with great pointed fangs, or, chained together, into the claws of demons.

A major function of the parish priest was that of instructing his parishioners. It was up to him to teach the children the Creed, the Lord's Prayer, the *Ave*, and the Ten Commandments. William of Pagula recommended that the priest give not only religious instruction but practical advice: telling mothers to nurse their own children, not to let them smother in bed or tie them in their cradles or leave them unattended; advising against usury and magic arts; giving counsel on sexual morality and marriage. Marriage was a topic well worth discussion, William pointed out: a horse, an ass, an ox, or a dog could be tried out before it was bought, but a wife had to be taken on trust. A poor wife was difficult to support; living with a rich one was misery. Was it better to marry a beautiful wife or an ugly one? On the one hand, it was hard to keep a wife that other men were pursuing, on the other it was irksome to have one that no one else wanted; but on balance an ugly wife brought less misery.[48]

The priest's instruction of adults came largely through confession, in which he not only examined the penitent's morals but his religious knowledge:

Believest thou in Father and Son and Holy Ghost . . .
Three persons in Trinity,
And in God (swear thou to me)?
That God's son mankind took
In maid Mary (as saith the Book),
And of that maid was born:
Believest thou this? . . .
And in Christ's passion
And in His resurrection . . . ?
That He shall come with wounds red
To judge the quick and the dead,

And that we each one . . .
Shall rise at the day of Doom
And be ready when he come . . . ?[49]

The manuals coached the priest to interrogate the penitent about his behavior: "Have you done any sorcery to get women to lie with you?" "Have you ever plighted your troth and broken it?" "Have you spent Sunday in shooting, wrestling, and other play, or going to the ale house?" "Have you stolen anything or been at any robbing?" "Have you found anything and kept it?" "Have you borrowed anything and not returned it?" "Have you ever claimed any good deed of charity that was another man's doing?" "Have you been slow to teach your godchildren Pater Noster and Creed?" "Have you come late to church?" "Have you without devotion heard any sermon?" "Have you been glad in your heart when your neighbor came to harm, and grieved when he had good fortune?" "Have you eaten with such greed that you cast it up again?" "Have you sinned in lechery?" "If your children are shrews, have you taught them good manners?" "Have you destroyed grain or grass or other things that are sown? Are you wont to ride through grain when you could go to one side?"[50]

The penitent must confess his sins completely and without reservation. If he killed a man, he must say who it was, where, and why. If he "sinned in lechery," he must not give the name of his partner, but he should tell whether she was married or single, or a nun, where the sin was committed, and how often, and whether it was on a holy day. The penance should fit the sin, light for a light sin, heavy for a heavy, but never too heavy for the penitent to perform, lest he ignore it and be worse off than if he had not gone to confession. "Better a light penance to send a man to purgatory," wrote John Myrc, "than a too heavy penance to send him to hell." Even more sagely, a woman's penance must be such that her husband would not know about it, lest it cause friction between them.[51]

Above all, the priest must teach by example. His preaching was worth little if he lived an evil life. The sins he was especially warned against indicate those he was most likely to fall into. He should be chaste; he should be true; he should be mild in word and deed. "Drunkenness and gluttony, pride and sloth and envy, all these thou must put away." The priest must forsake taverns, trading, wrestling and shooting, hawking, hunting, and dancing. "Markets and fairs I thee forbid." He must wear "honest clothes," and not knightly "basinet and baldric." His beard and crown must be shaven. He must be hospitable to rich and poor. And finally,

Turn thine eye that thou not see
The cursed world's vanity.
Thus this world thou must despise
And holy virtues have in vise [view].[52]

9

VILLAGE JUSTICE

TWICE OR MORE EACH YEAR THE VILLAGERS
gathered for the hallmote: hall, meaning manor house, and
mote, meeting. The records of this legal body provide unique
insights into the relationship between lord and village community, and at the same time demonstrate the frictions and stresses
of everyday village life.

The hallmote was the lord's manorial court, presided over by
his steward, and transacting primarily the lord's business: collecting merchet, heriot, entry fees, and other manorial dues,
enforcing labor services, electing manorial officers, granting
seisin (legal possession) to heirs and receiving fealty from them,
and providing the lord with substantial profits from its fines and
confiscations.

Yet the principal actors in the hallmote were villagers, who
in effect served as prosecutor, legal authority, witnesses, and
judge. Much of the court's business had nothing to do with the
lord, but was concerned with interaction among the villagers.
Finally, the hallmote's proceedings were ruled not by the lord's
will but by the ancient and powerful body of tradition known
as the custom of the manor.

172

The hallmote, furthermore, was a legislative as well as a judicial body, promulgating the bylaws that governed field, meadow, pasture, and woods from Michaelmas to Michaelmas, sending the men to work and the animals to graze in strict concert, stipulating who should harvest, who should glean, when, and for how long. Surviving Elton court rolls record no bylaw enactments, only references to infractions of existing bylaws, but elsewhere they are recorded as enacted by the "community," the "homage," the "tenants," or the "neighbors." The lord is rarely mentioned in their framing, though the security of his demesne cultivation was a primary object.[1]

A fragmentary document records the itinerary of the Ramsey Abbey steward for the twenty-three manorial courts of early 1294. Holding court first at Ramsey itself on Thursday, January 7, he rode to the nearest manors—Broughton, Wistow, Ripton, Stukeley, and Gidding—reaching Elton on January 16, a Saturday. Thence he proceeded to Weston on Monday the eighteenth, finished off the Huntingdonshire manors, rode south to Therfield in Hertfordshire, then turned back northeast and held court in the Ramsey manors of Cambridgeshire and Bedfordshire, the last session falling on February 19. Nine of the courts required a second day's sitting, the others were all concluded in a day.[2]

A hallmote held in January pretty surely met inside the manor house. In warmer seasons courts often met in the open air, that of St. Albans assembling under an ancient ash tree.[3] The hall must have been crowded and noisy, with all the villeins gathered, reinforced by a few freeholders whose charters stipulated suit, or whose grandfathers had owed it. Though the steward presided, he did not act as judge. Rather, he lent the authority of the abbot to the judgment rendered by the jury. These twelve (sometimes six or nine) *jurati*, sworn men, whose oath extended to periods between court sessions, could be fined substantial sums for "concealment," not bringing cases to court, and for "bad answering and false presentment," as happened to Elton jurors on several occasions.[4] They collected and presented evidence, along with the appropriate law, the custom of the manor and the village bylaws. In modern parlance, it was a grand jury, and in fact was sometimes so called, but the commoner term was jury of presentment. The jury's verdict was recorded as, "It is found by the jurors that . . .", "The jurors say that . . .", or "And they say that . . .", followed by the facts of the case and concluding, "Therefore . . ." and the assessment of fine and damages. The jury's findings received the backing not only of the lord's steward but of the assembled villagers. Their concurrence was usually expressed tacitly, but on certain occasions actively, when plaintiff or defendant or both "put themselves upon the consideration of the whole court." In such a case, the village's assent was inscribed in the court record as *villata dicit* (the village says), or *coram toto halimoto* (in the presence of the whole hallmote), or *per totum halimotum* (by the whole hallmote). In either case, the endorsement of the jury's findings by the assembly at large was of utmost importance.[5]

Sometimes either a plaintiff or a defendant or both asked for an inquest by a special panel, paying for the privilege. Whatever nuances of favor or knowledgeability a litigant hoped to get from one group or the other of his fellow villagers, his fate was nearly always, for better or for worse, in the hands of people who knew him, knew his adversary, knew the circumstances of the case, knew the relevant law and custom, and had talked it over among themselves.

The court's record was kept by the steward's clerk, on a long strip of parchment about eight inches wide, its segments stitched end to end. At its top he inscribed the place and date: "Aylingtone, on the day of St. Clement the Pope in the 12th year of W[illiam] the Abbot"—in other words, Elton, November 23, 1279. Less accomplished than the clerk of the accounts, he left a record in not very elegant Latin, with many errors in syntax and employing numerous abbreviations. In the left margin he noted the category of case, the judgment, and the amount of the fine. At the end of the record of each court he totaled the fines, exactly as the clerk of the accounts did at the end of the reeve's demesne account. Whatever else the court was, it was part of the lord's business enterprise. By the late thirteenth century, the court records were carefully preserved and often consulted for precedents.[6]

The court's appearance, whether indoors or out, was informal, the crowd of villagers standing before the seated steward and clerk, but court procedure was formal and order strictly enforced. At St. Albans in 1253 a man was fined for cursing the twelve jurors, and many cases are recorded of punishment meted out for false accusations against officials and jurors, for abuse of opposing litigants, and for making a disturbance: *"Fecerunt strepitum, in curia garrulando"* ("they made a racket, talking much in court").[7] In Elton in 1307, John son of John Abovebrook, haled into court for a debt of 32 pence owed to Robert of Teyngton, failed to make good his promise to pay, and the following year was again cited, but "immediately in contempt of the court withdrew without finding pledges." The court ordered that the 32 pence be levied from him, and that he be fined a stiff 40 pence for his behavior. "And afterwards he came and made fine for 40 pence . . . and . . . he will be obedient henceforth to the lord and to his neighbors."[8]

A fourteenth-century manual for the instruction of novice stewards called *The Court Baron* (another name for the manorial court) prescribes a formality of procedure amounting to ritual. It pictures the clerk commencing by reading aloud a model presentment, a charge of battery done by a villager against an outsider:

> Sir steward, Henry of Combe, who is here [pointing], complains of Stephen Carpenter, who is there [pointing], that as he was going his way in the peace of God and in the peace of the lord through this vill which is within the surety of your franchise, at such an hour on such a day in the last year, there came this Stephen Carpenter and encountered him in such a place [naming it], and assailed him with evil words which were undeserved, insomuch that he called him thief and lawless man and whatever other names seemed good to him except only his right name, and told him that he was spying from house to

house the secrets of the good folk of the vill in order that
he might come another time by night with his fellows to
break [into] their houses and carry off their goods
larcenously as a felon; whereupon this Henry answered
him civilly and said that he was good and lawful in all
things and that [Stephen] was talking at random;
whereupon the said Stephen was enraged and snatched his
staff of holly out of his hand and gave it to him about his
head and across his shoulders and his loins and elsewhere
all over his body as he thought fit and then went off. This
trespass did the said Stephen wrongfully and against
reason and against the peace of the lord and of you, who
are charged to guard and maintain the peace, to his
damage 20 shillings and shame a half-mark.[9]

The accused then answered the charge with as nice a regard
for the proper formula as the clerk had shown, taking each
accusation in order:

Tort and force and all that is against the peace of God
and the peace of the lord and of you, who are charged to
guard and maintain the peace, and his [Henry's] damages
of 20 shillings and shame of a half-mark and every penny
of it, Stephen defends, who is here, and all manner of evil
words against Henry of Combe, who is there, and against
his suit and all that he surmises against him, that never he
called him thief nor gave him evil word, nor surmised evil
slander against him, nor with staff of holly nor other staff
beat him across the head or shoulders or loins or any part
of his body as he surmises; and that this is true, he is
ready to acquit himself in all such wise as this court shall
award that acquit himself he ought.[10]

It may be doubted that hallmotes insisted on such exquisite
perfection of jargon, but it is known that defendants and litigants in serious cases were often alert to slips of language by
which technical flaws could be imputed and judgment perhaps
evaded.[11]

The steward in *The Court Baron* next addresses the accused: "Fair friend Stephen, this court awards that you be at your law six-handed at the next court to acquit yourself," to which the defendant replies, "Willingly, sir."[12] "Be at your law six-handed" meant that Stephen was to bring with him five men who would join him in swearing either that his account of the case was true or that he was himself a trustworthy person. In cases of more serious character or when there was reason to doubt the accused, he might be called on to "be at your law twelve-handed," requiring him to find eleven "oath helpers." Oath helping, or compurgation, was by 1300 a basic element of medieval jurisprudence. The sense of it was that several men who attested the truth of their statements on the holy relics would be unlikely to swear their souls away simultaneously.[13]

At this point a uniquely medieval step in the court's procedure took place: both plaintiff and defendant were ordered to "find pledges," persons to act as sureties to guarantee their appearance in court. Such personal pledging was also used to guarantee fulfillment of a promised obligation, or even that the pledge's subject would behave himself. Pledges were held accountable by the court and were liable to fine: "John Page and John Fraunceys were pledges of Henry Smith for the payment of two shillings to John son of Alexander in the Lane . . . and nothing is paid. Therefore both of them in mercy [fined] . . . Better pledges are William of Barnwell and Reginald son of Benedict."[14] Those needing pledges sought them among the better class of fellow villagers, those with substantial holdings, who served in village offices. Reeves and beadles were especially in demand. Pledges' fines were usually three pence, half the standard fine for most offenses. Husbands commonly acted as pledges for wives, but otherwise most pledging was extra-familial.[15]

The Court Baron stipulated a particular order in which cases should be heard. In real life the hallmote heard cases by category, but the categories followed no discernible order. The invariably lengthy list of fines for the ale brewers sometimes led off the Elton calendar, sometimes concluded it, and sometimes came in the middle. In 1279, twenty-three violations of the assize of ale were recorded at the end of the court record, just before the selection of new ale tasters. Prior to the brewing violations, thirty-four cases were presented. Ten dealt with defaults of harvest or plow work, three with chevage, the rest with a variety of offenses, from the diversion of a watercourse by a neighboring village to a theft of furrows by a villager.[16] The dispatch with which cases were handled compared with that of a modern traffic court. Yet "the law's delay" was already an established judicial feature. Most defendants were permitted three summonses, three distraints (for failing to appear), and three essoins (excuses for non-appearance), making nine successive postponements.[17]

Litigations between villagers began with a complaint: "John Juvet complains of John Hering." "Robert Maynard complains of Gilbert de Raundes." "Thomas Clerk complains of Nicholas son of Richard Smith." The complainant brought suit—in other words, he brought men with him to vouch for the truth of his complaint. Both he and the defendant were then ordered to find pledges.

Once the suit was initiated, if the complainant did not carry it through, he and his pledge were fined. "From Ralph Hert and Isolda his wife and their pledge, namely Reginald Child, for their non-suit against Richard Reeve and John Abovebrook, six pence."[18] The defendant might wage his law, as John of Elton did "sufficiently" in 1294 against Emma Prudhomme, who had made accusations against him, and who was herself consequently fined.[19] Or the case might be postponed. The delay might result in settlement, either through the defendant's offering to pay a fine or through the two litigants reaching an out-of-court agreement. Such compacts were encouraged by the judicial device of the "love-day" (dies amoris), on which the parties to a dispute were directed to try to reconcile their differences.[20] An out-of-court settlement, however, could not be allowed to become an out-of-pocket settlement for the lord. The parties still owed a fee, in this case recorded under the title of "license to agree": "From John son of John of Elton for license to agree with

John of Langetoft and Alice his wife sixpence." "From Nicholas le Rous for license to agree with Henry Daysterre and Emma his wife four pence."[21] Part of the agreement was the determination of which of the two parties would pay the fine.

Yet the court was lenient toward the destitute, or realistic about the difficulty of getting blood out of turnips. "In mercy, but [fined] nothing because [he or she is] poor," recurs many times in the records.

At least once a year, usually in late winter or spring, a form of manorial court known as the view (review) of frankpledge was held. A uniquely English institution, frankpledge antedates the Conquest.[22] All the village's male residents under the age of twelve belonged to units of ten or a dozen called frankpledges or tithings, each of which was collectively responsible for the behavior of its members, and whose interests it defended. If a man was accused by a neighbor, the members of his tithing were responsible for his appearance in court. At the head of each tithing was a leader called a chief pledge, an important man in the village: "It was commanded to Hugh Achard and his tithing at the last view to have [a certain man] at this court and he had him not. Therefore he and his tithing in mercy."[23]

The tithing was not kinship-based, though in some ways it served the purpose of the old clan or supra-family group. Originally it was a cell in the royal administration, and its review in some places was still performed by the king's sheriff (shire-reeve, chief officer of the shire), but usually the local lord had acquired frankpledge along with manorial justice. Carried out by the steward, the view of frankpledge assured the integrity of the village's tithings, making certain that every boy turning twelve years of age and every male newcomer to the village acquired membership. By the end of the thirteenth century, the tithing system and personal pledging were showing signs of decadence as the royal courts developed more modern juridical techniques, such as prison and bail.[24]

In theory, and perhaps at one time in fact, there was some

distinction in procedure and type of case between the regular hallmote and the view of frankpledge, but by the late thirteenth century it had virtually disappeared. *The Court Baron's* list of offenses typically heard by the view of frankpledge—shedding of blood, rape, theft of grain or poultry, placing a dung-heap in the high street, building a fence on a neighbor's land or on the king's highway—are very much the same things heard in ordinary hallmotes.[25] However, where the hallmote, usually held in the autumn, elected the reeve, beadle, and wardens of autumn, the view of frankpledge chose the village ale tasters.[26]

Killers, professional robbers, and other hardened felons, regular defendants in the royal courts, were rarely seen in the hallmote, which was nevertheless no stranger to violent crime. It was reported in several different forms: "Agnes daughter of Philip Saladin raised the hue-and-cry upon Thomas of Morburn who wanted to have sex with her."[27] "Matilda Prudhomme justly raised the hue-and-cry against John Blaccalf because he drew blood from Hugh the man of the said Matilda."[28] "The wife of Matfrid and her daughter justly raised the hue-and-cry upon Henry Marshal because he beat them."[29] "It was found by neighboring jurors that John ate Lane maliciously assaulted Alice his stepmother in her own house . . . and beat, ill-treated, and maimed the said Alice with a stick, breaking her right hand."[30]

The last category of assault, in the victim's own home, was considered a graver offense than similar violence on neutral ground, and was usually designated hamsoken: "Matilda Saladin justly raised the hue-and-cry upon five men of Sir Gilbert de Lyndsey who were committing hamsoken upon Philip Saladin and beat and badly treated him."[31] Similarly, drawing blood was regarded as especially serious.

The hue-and-cry raised by the victim, or by a relative, neighbor, friend, or passerby, obligated everyone within earshot to drop what he was doing and come to the rescue. Failure to do so brought a collective penalty: "And they say that Alexander Prudhomme badly beat Henry son of Henry Smith [who] justly raised the hue-and-cry upon him. Not prosecuted, *villata* fined two shillings [and] commanded to distrain Alexander to answer."[32]

Blood did not have to be actually shed, or even a blow struck, to justify the hue-and-cry. Richard son of Richard Reeve gave clear indication of a desire to beat Richard Blakeman, who "by reason of terror and fear" was justified in the jurors' eyes in raising the hue-and-cry.[33]

On the other hand, the hue was not to be raised lightly or wrongfully: "The jurors say that Adam Fot committed hamsoken upon Andrew son of Alkusa and nonetheless the wife of the said Adam unjustly raised the hue-and-cry upon the same Andrew. Fine sixpence."[34] Anyone raising the hue was obliged immediately to find a personal pledge to support his claim of raising it justly.

Sometimes two parties to an altercation raised the hue against each other, in which case the court decided which was justified: "Henry Abovebrook justly raised the hue-and-cry upon Richard Sabyn. Richard fined sixpence. . . . And they say that Richard Sabyn unjustly raised the hue-and-cry upon Henry Abovebrook. Richard fined [an additional] sixpence."[35]

When the hue-and-cry posse collared its quarry, he was turned over to the bailiff, the reeve, or the beadle. In Elton in 1312 the beadle was fined three pence "because he did not arrest John son of Matfrid, a bondman, to answer concerning the hue-and-cry."[36]

Serious injury in an assault case brought damages along with the fine: "It is found by the jurors that Robert Sabyn assaulted Nicholas Miller and beat him to his damage of sixpence. Fine sixpence."[37] The three men who assaulted Gilbert son of Reginald le Wyse in 1279 were directed to "satisfy him for damages" as well as pay a sixpence fine.[38] Similarly in cases of property damage: for the malicious injury to the house of Richard son of Elias done by Thomas of Chausey in 1308, Thomas was directed to pay sixpence damages along with the usual sixpence fine.[39]

Only rarely do the Elton records reveal a punishment imposed other than a fine. In the case in 1292 in which John ate

Lane was convicted of maliciously assaulting his stepmother and breaking her hand, the account concludes, "Therefore the said John is put in the stocks."[40]

Moral transgression was a precinct of the law in which the superior competence of the Church courts was conceded, and in which canon law had developed an extensive literature. Adultery was the most conspicuous of moral offenses, and drew the Church's most severe penalties, typically a whipping for peasants, a heavy fine for their betters. The Church also ruled on the validity of marriage contracts (an active legal issue in the absence of state licensing or requirement of witnesses), separations, and prescribed penances for such delinquencies as departing from the traditional posture in intercourse.[41]

Nevertheless, the lord took an interest in sex mores, at least a financial interest, focusing on men and women previously haled into Church court for adultery, and young women detected indulging in premarital sex. The jurors were relied on to report cases of leirwite, or of matrimony without the lord's license, and were fined for failing to do so.

A village woman, however, ran a much greater risk of being fined for her brewing than for her dallying. "[Allota] is a common brewer at a penny and sometimes at a halfpenny, and sold before the tasting [by the village ale tasters] and sometimes made [the ale] weak. Therefore [she is] in mercy two shillings."[42] "Alice wife of Blythe [sold] three times at a halfpenny and at a penny and sold before the tasting, did not bring her measures [to be checked]. Twelve pence." "Matilda Abovebrook at a halfpenny and a penny, sometimes weak ale, she sells before the tasting, did not bring her measures. Sixpence."[43] Sometimes the lengthy list of women (only six men ever appear among Elton brewers) is simply put down in the court record with the fine noted. The unfailing frequency of the ale fines has led to a conjecture that the assize of ale was a sort of back-door license fee collected by the lord in lieu of the monopoly he had failed to obtain in this important branch of village business.[44] At the same time, the very number of home brewers makes credible a need for government regulation, while the fines varied and the charges differed: the ale is "weak," "not of full value," "not worth the money," the measures are not sealed, the price is too high. Enforcement of standards for price and quality was of value to consumers, and the insistence on checking brewers' measures indicates serious purpose.

In Elton as everywhere that open field agriculture prevailed, a large proportion of the manor court's business consisted of enforcement of the bylaws and customs governing crops and pasture. Reeve and bailiff were mainly responsible for bringing to book defaulters on work obligations, but for surveillance of the army of harvest workers they had the help of the two "wardens of autumn." "The wardens of autumn present that Master Stephen made default at one boon-work. . . . Therefore let him be distrained to answer [be arrested and brought to court]." "Of Reginald Child for the same at another boon-work of the autumn of one man [as] above. Pledge Richard the beadle." "Of John Heryng for the same of one man three pence. Pledge Roger Gamel." "Of Robert Chapman for the same of one man sixpence. Pledge John Page."[45] Failure to appear, tardiness, or simply performing the service badly brought sure, if moderate, penalties.

"I do not advise you to plead against your lord," warned a satiric poem ascribed to a canon of Leicester Abbey. "Peasant, you will be vanquished. . . . You must endure what the custom of the earth has given you."[46] Modern scholar George C. Homans, however, has written: "The striking fact is that many such disputes [between lord and tenant] were settled in the hallmote just as they would have been if the parties had both been simple villagers." Homans cites a case involving tenants of the Bishop of Chichester in 1315, in which an inquest of three hallmotes backed the tenants in their refusal to cart dung for the lord. "The lord's arbitrary will was bounded, or rather he allowed it to be bounded, by custom as found by the tenants."[47]

A number of cases in Elton pitted villagers against the lord, his steward, or his lesser officials. In 1312 "John Troune entered a plea contrary to the lord's statutes" and was fined sixpence for contempt.[48] Two men who pleaded "in opposition to the steward" in the court of 1331 were fined three pence and sixpence, respectively.[49] Thus an individual peasant, as the canon of Leicester warned, appears to have been at a substantial disadvantage in pleading against his betters. But in three other cases, though no final outcome is recorded, the villagers' side of the argument is unmistakably accorded a respectful hearing. One difference in these cases is that the other party was not the lord or his steward, but a lesser official or officials. Another difference, highly significant in the light of later history, is that the village viewpoint was maintained not by an individual tenant but by a large group of villagers, or even the whole village united.

All three cases were heard in 1300. In the first the villagers accused the bailiff and his assistants of having dug a ditch to enclose "a certain place which is called Gooseholm where they planted willows, which place is a common pasture for all the men of the whole village." In the second case, they accused the bailiffs of encroaching on a furlong called Michelgrove by taking away from all the lands abutting on it "to the breadth of four feet."[50] Presumably the officials were doing their encroaching in the interests of the lord's demesne, though there is no indication that they were acting under instructions.

The third case involved an exchange of complaints between the villagers and Hugh Prest, the claviger. First the jurors reported that "the bailiffs of the lord unjustly hinder the community of the vill of Elton from driving by the way which is called the Greenway all their draught-beasts and other animals, whereas they ought to have it for the common of their pasture." In turn, Hugh Prest cited nine villagers, most of them virgaters, "because they drove their beasts by the way which is called Greenway when the furlongs of the lord abbot abutting thereupon were sown." The jurors protested strongly: "And they say that they and all men of the vill of Elton ought by right to have the said droveway at all times of the year, inasmuch as all strangers passing by the same way can have a free droveway with their animals of all kinds without challenge or hindrance."

Hugh Prest replied that although strangers were permitted to use the droveway, in the past "the said customary tenants and their partners have sometimes contributed four shillings to the use of the lord for having their droveway when the furlongs of the lord there had been sown." The anger and indignation of the villagers is unmistakable in the reply recorded in the court rolls: "And the aforesaid customary tenants and all others of the vill, free tenants as well as others, and also the twelve jurors whose names are contained at the beginning of the roll, say and swear that if any money has been contributed by the customary tenants of the vill to have their droveway there, the said claviger has taken that money at his will by distraint and extortion and has levied it from them unjustly." The steward, clearly embarrassed at "seeing the dissension and discord between the claviger demanding and the said men gainsaying him, was unwilling to pronounce judgment against the claviger"—as the united villagers clearly insisted. Instead he "left this judgment wholly to the disposition of the lord abbot, that the same lord, having scrutinized the register concerning the custom in the matter of this demand, should do and ordain as he should see ought to be done according to the will of God."[51]

Although no further record of the case has survived, it seems unlikely that the abbot provoked further resentment by the villagers over a problem that touched his interests only lightly and vexed them so much. Homans perhaps exaggerates in claiming that "The lord, in his own court and in a case in which his interest was involved, was treated much like any other villager."[52] Nevertheless, the steward's conciliatory attitude toward the angry Elton tenants is noteworthy. One peasant breaking a rule was easy to deal with; a whole village up in arms over what it deemed an infringement of village rights was something else.

The fact that few decisions in the hallmote went against the lord was less owing to pressure on the court exerted by his officials than to the basic relationship between lord and village.

His rights, privileges, and monopolies made it unlikely for him to infringe legally on the villagers while making it easy for them to infringe on him.

In the endless small fines levied for default of work obligations, it may even be possible to discern the same rationale as that suggested for the fines for violation of the ale regulations. Edward Britton, reviewing the evidence from Broughton, suggests that the moderation of the fines makes them amount to a standard fee which a villager could pay if he wished to skip a day's work on the demesne.[53]

Not all the infractions by villagers were against the lord. Villagers also infringed on each other: "It is found that Robert of Teygnton carried away the fittings of the plow of John Above-brook, in consequence whereof the same John lost his plowing during one day to his damage of one halfpenny, which he will pay him," plus a three-penny fine.[54] John Allot was convicted of carrying away the hay of Reginald of Brington "to the value of four pence which he will pay to the same Reginald before the next court, fine pardoned."[55]

Nor did all the cases originate in the fields: "John Ivet has not repaired the house of Richard Crane satisfactorily, as agreed between them, to the damage of Richard sixpence, which John will pay. For trespass, fine three pence."[56] Some court cases were family matters, as when Robert Smith "unjustly detained in his smithy the horse of Sarah his mother against her will," and was fined sixpence.[57]

Debts were a frequent subject of villager-versus-villager suits: "Richard Blythe acknowledges himself to be bound to Andrew Noppe for one ring of barley, which he will pay him. Unjust detention, fine three pence."[58] "John Roger unjustly detains from Richard Baxter one quarter of barley to his damage of two pence, which he will pay him. Sixpence fine."[59] In one case the debt was between two men, both of whom had died: "Sarah widow of Henry Smith, and John and Robert her sons, executors of the testament of Henry, bound to John Hering and Joan widow of Robert Hering for one quarter of barley which Henry borrowed from Robert in their lifetime. Will satisfy them concerning the grain, sixpence fine."[60] The creditor was sometimes an outsider: in 1294 two Elton villagers, Geoffrey in Angulo and Philip Noppe, owed grain to Richard Abraham of Haddon, and were instructed to pay but were excused the court's fine because they were poor.[61]

The Elton records contain no outright references to money-lending, though some of the cases of debt may have been loans disguised as purchases. Other sources show it to have been a common feature of rural life, often leading to court judgment and seizure of property. The loan was often in the form of a pawn. Interest rates were always high and frequently condemned by the Church as usurious, without stemming the flow of loans, in which churchmen themselves engaged. Debtors often took refuge in flight, leading down the path of vagabondage to crime.[62]

One frequently heard suit of villager against villager was for slander. In 1279 Andrew Reeve accused Gilbert Gamel of malingering and working in his own barn and yard instead of performing his labor services. The accusation was public enough so that it "came to the ears of the bailiffs." The jurors cleared Gilbert and fined Andrew twelve pence.[63] Slander could also bring damages. John Page was fined sixpence, and paid Richard Benyt twelve pence damages for "defaming" him.[64] Sarah Wagge "unjustly defamed" Nicholas son of Elias, accusing him of having stolen two of her hens and "eating them to her damage of sixpence"; Sarah was fined sixpence and had to pay Nicholas damages of sixpence, the price of the hens she claimed he had stolen.[65] Another villager "defamed Adam son of Hubert by calling him false and faithless," and was fined three pence.[66] In one case in 1300, Allota of Langetoft accused Robert Harpe of defaming her "by calling her a thief"; the jury found Robert innocent and fined Allota sixpence for false claim.[67]

In the hallmote, a decision might be appealed to the documents, especially the "register of customs" (meaning in all probability the Ramsey Abbey cartulary), as in the case of the Greenway dispute of 1300. The cartulary contained information about tenure, customary obligations, and servile status. When it failed to resolve a question, an appeal could be made to the lord, who might be an impartial arbiter if his own interest was not involved, or perhaps a fair or reasonable one if it was.

There is also evidence of a more modern system of appeal. This was one made from the hallmote to the honor court, the court of the whole estate (honor), which for Ramsey Abbey met at Broughton, with suit owed by the free tenants of Elton and the other manors. A case of 1259 involved a dispute among the villagers about repairs to the millpond after flooding. The twelve jurors of the Elton hallmote, all villeins, accused five free tenants—Reginald Benyt, Ralph Blaccalf, Andrew L'Hermite, Henry Miller, and Henry Fraunceys—of refusing to help, the accused claiming that they were not obligated because of their free status.[68] The case may have been referred to the court at Broughton because of the defendants' allegiance to that court, but in other instances Broughton seems to have acted as a true court of appeal, with villeins summoned thither from their hallmotes. The principal function of the Broughton honor court, however, was not judicial but administrative, the arrangement of the military service owed by the abbey.[69] Elsewhere, the central court of an estate is known to have acted at times as an appeals court. The court of St. Albans, assembled under its famous ash tree, regularly heard cases forwarded to it by the other St. Albans manors, returning its interpretation to the local courts.[70]

For the typical villein tenant, nearly any offense he might commit, from default of his work obligations to hamsoken against his neighbor, brought him to the hallmote, attended by his fellow villagers acting as his judges. Members of his tithing supported his appearance in court. Twelve villagers examined and discussed his case, made accusation against him, and found him guilty or not guilty. If he was required to corroborate his defense or his claim, he called on friends and neighbors to give him oath-help so that he could "be at his law six-handed." When he was fined he appealed to a fellow villager to act as his pledge and guarantee his payment. Rarely was he subjected to either imprisonment or corporal punishment, though aggravated assault might land him in the stocks on the village green.

Fundamental to the system of justice was the inequality between lord and villager. If the villager missed an autumn boonwork, neglected his demesne plowing, or defaulted on any of his other obligations, he was certain of being fined. The system was onerous and exploitative, yet it apparently felt less oppressive to those who lived under it than it appears to modern eyes. The villager knew the rules and could rely on them. If they were not equal for everybody, they were the same for all villeins, a fact which doubtless contributed to the success with which they were applied—"neighbors" who turned out for the harvest boon would feel little sympathy for one who did not.

The hallmote's emphasis on the united voice of the community in judgment reflected the need of a weakly policed society for acceptance of its judicial decisions by all parties. No single individual or small group could be blamed by a losing party in court when his fate had been pronounced *per totum halimotum*.

The apparatus of the law was certainly the more readily accepted because it was operated by the villagers themselves. As Paul Vinogradoff says, in the hallmote, "customs are declared by [the villagers] and not [by the lord]; inquests and juries are empaneled from among them; the agrarian business of the customary court is entirely of their making."[71]

The hallmote was the sole court with which most villeins ever had contact. It belonged to one of the three great medieval systems of justice, the manorial, or seigneurial, courts, the other two systems being the Church courts and the royal courts. Though the three overlapped in some degree, each had its own clientele and its own law. Church courts dispensed canon law in cases either involving clergy or dealing with moral and marital problems of the laity. In England the royal courts dispensed the "common law," created by William the Conqueror out of Saxon, Danish, and Norman precedents and made common to the whole kingdom. Royal courts sat in the shires and hundreds, the political divisions of the kingdom, and royal *eyres* (circuit courts) visited the districts at intervals.

As the clergy formed the main clientele of the Church courts, the free men of the kingdom formed that of the royal courts, and the villeins, subject to the "customary law" of their own manors, that of the manorial courts. But the royal courts also held a monopoly on felony, sometimes known as "high justice," and defined as homicide, rape, larceny, burglary, arson, and petty treason (a crime by a servant or apprentice against a master).[72] Trespass, the other major category of crime, which included assault, breaking and entering, theft of goods worth less than twelve pence, issuing threats, abduction, extortion, false weights and measures, and other petty offenses, was left to the manorial courts in cases involving villeins, and was awarded to the royal courts in those involving free men.[73] Rape was also sometimes dealt with in the manorial court.

The division of function was never as neat as theory suggested. Many lords enjoyed "high justice" as a result of some past concession by the monarch. The abbot of Ramsey held what amounted to exclusive judicial power within his banlieu, a radius of one league (three miles) from the high altar of the abbey church. Lords often held rights to special kinds of crimes, such as "infangenethef," the thief caught in the act within the manor, whose belongings could be confiscated when he was hanged.

Thus any villager who committed homicide or any other felony and was apprehended by the hue-and-cry was subject to the jurisdiction of the royal courts. The case was likely to be given a preliminary investigation by the coroner's court, which held an inquest whenever a death was either accidental, sudden, or in suspicious circumstances. The coroner was a knight or a substantial freeholder, elected in the county court by other knights and freeholders. His jury was made up of twelve free-holders of the hundred where the death had occurred.[74] The coroner examined the body for signs of violence, and questioned neighbors and witnesses, with particular attention to the person or persons who discovered the body. In cases of accidental death, the object that had caused the accident was adjudged the "deodand" (gift to God) and was sold and the price given to the king—a Norman adaptation of an old Anglo-Saxon custom of selling the deodand to buy prayers for the soul of the victim. The deodand might be a horse that threw its rider, the timber of a wall that collapsed, a cart that ran over a man, or a vat of boiling water that overturned.[75]

In cases of murder, the coroner's jury appraised the chattels of the accused, with a view to later confiscation by the king. Sometimes it reported that "nothing could be discovered about his chattels," or that "he had no chattels," but often they were listed in detail: animals, household goods, grain, and tools, with their monetary value. Sometimes only the value was recorded. One such list turns up in the Elton records because the hanged man's forfeited property had disappeared. The villagers (villata) were "commanded to answer for the chattels of Richard son of Thomas Frelond of Pappele who was hanged at Peterborough," said chattels consisting of boots, harness, knife, belt, dog collar with silver fittings, gloves, wooden chest, and slippers—total 18 pence 2 farthings.[76]

The prisoner was turned over either to the itinerant justices of the royal eyre, or to the shire or hundred courts, where trial was usually by jury. Jury trial was not, however, perceived as especially protective. Early in the thirteenth century, a prisoner could be tried by jury only with his consent, but the principle was annulled by Edward I in the First Statute of Westminster (1275) mandating jury trial in criminal cases in the interest of more reliable prosecution.

Trial by combat was by now archaic, as was trial by ordeal (immersion in water or exposure to fire), condemned by the Church in 1215. The sense of participation by Providence in the judicial process which combat and ordeal had invoked was retained in the more civilized method of compurgation, or joint oath-swearing on the sacred relics.

In 1285 Edward I issued the Second Statute of Westminster, holding the men of the village and hundred collectively responsible for arresting and holding malefactors—in effect, making the hue-and-cry royal as well as manorial law. Not very surprisingly, large numbers of wrongdoers continued to escape capture. Bands of thieves flourished, terrorizing whole districts. Sometimes they were abetted by wealthy sponsors known as "receivers" or "maintainers." As John Bellamy observes, "There was . . . less of a gulf between honest men and criminals than in modern society," a situation that also made corruption of officials easier.[77]

Of those tried by royal justice sitting in cases where the accused was actually detained, only some 10 to 30 percent of the defendants were convicted. One popular technique for evading punishment was the claim of "benefit of clergy," meaning that the accused was a cleric and could only be tried in Church court where capital punishment was not used. Felons not only took the tonsure (clerical haircut) in prison but even learned to read. Benefit of clergy was of limited value to habitual criminals, however, since it could only be claimed once.[78]

The same limitation applied to another Church-related evasion of justice, the sanctuary. All consecrated buildings and land, including every parish church and churchyard, were sanctuary, on a one-time basis, but not for everyone. Excluded were notorious offenders, traitors, heretics, sorcerers, clerics, perpetrators of felonies in church, criminals caught red-handed, and minor offenders in no danger of loss of life or limb. The fugitive had to confess his misdeeds, surrender his weapons, attend Mass, and ring the church bells. In a parish church, where he could remain for forty days, he had to beg food from the priest. The royal coroner came, heard his oath to abjure the realm forever, assigned him a port or border town by which to depart, and saw him branded on the thumb with an A (for abjuror). He was obliged to keep to the highway, to avoid footpaths, to take the first ship available, and until one appeared, to walk into the sea up to his knees each day in sign of his renewed intention. Very often, however, the abjuror never reached his assigned port, but went into hiding as an outlaw.[79]

Prison as punishment was virtually unknown to the Middle Ages. The Church courts dealt in penances and pilgrimages, the manor court in fines, and the royal court in death penalties, abjuration, and outlawry. The outlaw could be captured or slain by anyone, and his goods appropriated. Outlaws, however, often had powerful protectors and sometimes popular sympathy. The prototype of Robin Hood probably flourished in the late thirteenth or early fourteenth century rather than in the twelfth century of Richard Lionheart favored by Walter Scott.[80]

Capital punishment was generally by hanging, with the chief alternative, reserved for better-class offenders, the headsman's axe. Since hanging was by strangulation, the axe was normally less cruel. By a custom that was a relic of ancient Germanic law, the felon's principal accuser, usually the victim or a relative, was often obliged to find a hangman or perform the office himself. Lack of professionalism may account for recorded cases of the hanged man's surviving.

Deliberately cruel executions were limited to extraordinary crimes: heresy, treason, witchcraft. Mutilation, a common form of punishment in the earlier Middle Ages, was rare by the thirteenth century, but a thief might still lose an ear or thumb, a rapist be castrated, or a vicious assailant blinded. The stocks sometimes caused loss of limb. Torture was a rarity, except when the defendant stood mute, or on the part of some jailers or coroners practicing extortion.[81]

A condemned prisoner in a royal court had a single avenue of appeal, that of royal pardon. His hope of getting one depended on one of two aids: a powerful protector with influence at court, or an ongoing war. In the late thirteenth and early fourteenth centuries, the king's expeditions against the Scots saved many English felons from the scaffold.[82]

*   *   *

Historically, medieval justice stood somewhere between the ancient system of family-and-clan justice by which an offender was punished or protected by his kin, and the modern system of state-organized police and prosecution. Perhaps it resembled other systems in the discrepancy in outcomes between serious felonies, so often unpunished, and minor offenses against the custom of the manor, so frequently pursued and penalized, though rarely beyond a fine of sixpence.

10

THE PASSING
OF THE
MEDIEVAL VILLAGE

ARLY IN THE FOURTEENTH CENTURY THE POPU-
lation of England probably surpassed four million, as compared with the Domesday figure of a million and a half to two
million.[1] By far the greater part of the increase came from the
villages, "the primary seedbeds of population."[2] The Europe-
wide demographic surge was halted by a series of calamities that
began with the floods and famine of 1315–1317. Two cata-
strophic harvests in succession, possibly related to a long-term
climatic change, sent grain prices to levels "unparalleled in English history," and, accompanied by typhoid, hit poor families
especially hard.[3] The lords added to the misery by cutting down
their alms-giving, reducing staff, and halting livery of grain to
their *famuli*, like latter-day governments and business firms re-
sponding to business depression by laying off workers and reducing purchases. Severe murrain and cattle disease added to the

calamity. Thefts of food and livestock rose sharply, and bodies of paupers were found in the streets. Dogs and cats disappeared, and cannibalism was rumored.[4]

By the time the next, even worse disaster struck, three long-term changes in agriculture and rural life were already evident: a discernible shift from crop farming toward sheep grazing; a general return by lords to farming out their demesnes; and a growth in the proportion of peasant cultivation as opposed to demesne cultivation.[5] The lord was slipping from his role as producer-consumer to being merely a consumer, a "rentier," albeit one with a large appetite.

In Elton in the agricultural year of 1349–1350, three different villeins held the office of reeve, for which there was suddenly little enthusiasm.[6] The Black Death, sweeping through England in the summer of 1349 via the rats that infested houses, barns, and sheds, left so many holdings vacant that it was impossible to collect rents or enforce services. The manorial accounts read like a dirge: "Twenty-three virgates in the hand of the lord [vacant]."[7] "Rent lacking from eleven cottages . . . by reason of the mortality in the preceding year." "Of the rent of . . . Robert Amys . . . nothing here for the cause abovesaid. Of the rent of John Suteer . . . and William Abbot . . . nothing here for the cause aforesaid. And [the reeve answers for] two shillings six-pence from Robert Beadle for twelve acres of demesne land formerly of Hugh Prest lately deceased."[8] "From the fulling mill nothing because it is broken and useless."[9] "Of divers rents of tenements which are in the hand of the lord owing to the death of the tenants . . ."[10] "Three capons and no more this year because those liable to chevage are dead."[11]

The following year things were no better: "Of the farm of one common oven . . . nothing this year because it is ruinous. Second common oven . . . nothing for the same cause." "And for sixpence from the smithy this year because it fell down after All Saints and from then on was empty."[12] "Of chevage nothing because all the chevagers are dead."[13]

Expenses were up because of the shortage of villeins doing labor service: "In divers workmen hired by the day to mow and lift the lord's hay, seventeen shillings five pence by tally."[14] The harvest was costly: "Expenses of forty workmen coming at the bailiff's request to one repast and of divers other workmen hired by the day. . . . And in the expenses of forty workmen coming . . . to reap and bind the lord's grain during one day . . . one young bullock. And in the expenses of two boon-works of the autumn, on each occasion of ninety workmen, each of whom take three loaves whereof eight are made from one bushel . . . and in divers workmen hired to reap and bind the lord's grain for lack of customary tenants . . ."[15]

Grain production on Ramsey manors was reduced by one half.[16] In desperation, stewards and bailiffs strictly enforced work services on the surviving tenants, and sought to hold down the cost of hired labor with the help of a royal Statute of Laborers (1351), backed by a threat of the stocks. The main result they achieved was to stir resentment among both tenants and hired laborers. With depopulation, land inevitably fell in value and labor inevitably rose in price.

The Hundred Years War added heavy taxation to peasant burdens. For many years, "lay subsidies" (to distinguish them from taxes on the clergy) had been occasionally levied at the rate of a tenth or a twentieth on all movable goods above a certain figure. In the long reign of Henry III (1216–1272), the lay subsidy was collected only five times. In those of Edward I (1272–1307) and Edward II (1307–1327), marked by wars with Scotland, the royal tax collectors appeared in the villages a total of sixteen times.

Edward III imposed the tax three times in the first seven years of his lengthy reign, then as the war in France escalated, he needed it no fewer than twenty-four times (1334–1377).[17] To facilitate collection, he changed the mechanics of taxation, putting the burden of it on the villagers themselves and charging the royal administration with the task of seeing that every village met its quota. The new method made it possible for the better-off peasants who filled the village offices to arrange distribution of the tax in their favor.[18] Besides the lay subsidy, the village was afflicted with conscription, which itself was apparently a light burden—volunteers were found, and a village might perceive the army a good place to get rid of its bad characters—but each community had to pay for its own recruits' equipment. Finally, in 1377, amid a succession of defeats in France, a poll tax was introduced: four pence per head on everyone over fourteen years of age, with only genuine beggars exempt. In 1379 a second poll tax was piled on top of a double subsidy, and in 1381 a third on top of a subsidy and a half. Wealthy taxpayers were rather piously requested to help pay the share of poor taxpayers.[19]

The accumulation of tax levies, the Statute of Laborers, and the other burdens, afflictions, and irritants resulted in the Peasant Rebellion of 1381. Sometimes known as Wat Tyler's Rebellion, from the name of one of its several leaders, the English revolt was part of a larger pattern. "A chain of peasant uprisings clearly directed against taxation exploded all over Europe," says Georges Duby.[20] If they were discernibly triggered by taxation, the risings had a broader content, both substantive and ideological. Another leader of the English rebels, the Kentish priest John Ball, preached that "things cannot go right in England . . . until goods are held in common and there are no more villeins and gentlefolk, but we are all one and the same." Unsympathetic Froissart, chronicler of the nobility, may not be recording Ball's words with reportorial exactness, but there is little doubt that the gist is accurate: "[The lords] are clad in velvet and camlet lined with squirrel and ermine, while we go dressed in coarse cloth. They have the wines, the spices, and the good bread: we have the rye, the husks, and the straw, and we drink water. They have shelter and ease in their fine manors, and we have hardship and toil, the wind and the rain in the fields. And from us must come, from our labour, the things which keep them in luxury." And the fiery preacher's auditors, "out in the fields, or walking together from one village to another, or in their homes, whispered and repeated among themselves, 'That's what John Ball says, and he's right!' "[21] One chronicler credits Ball with the phrase, "All men are created equal," and with a declaration that villein servitude is "against the will of God."[22] One of several priests who took part in the rising, Ball was certainly on the far Left of his age, but there is no doubt that the aims of the mainstream of rebellion included the abolition of villeinage. The demand was put forward in the rebels' negotiations and dramatized by the destruction of manorial records "from Norfolk to Kent," not to mention the number of lawyers killed.[23] The Continental revolts showed the same revolutionary tendencies.

A feature especially noted by modern historians is the participation, even domination, by the better-off peasants. "Peasant revolts . . . were wont to spring up, not in the regions where the serf was in deepest oppression, but in those in which he was comparatively well off, where he was strong enough to aspire to greater liberty and to dream of getting it by force," says Sir Charles Oman.[24]

All the risings were suppressed, naturally, by the united upper class—monarchy, nobility, upper clergy, and wealthy townsmen—but all nevertheless left their mark. In England the poll tax was abandoned, and the Statute of Laborers left unenforced. Everywhere, the process by which serfdom was withering was accelerated. In England the villein class rid itself of its disabilities mainly through "copyhold tenure," which amounted to a reversal of the law's point of view: instead of the manorial records' proving the legality of a villein's obligations, they were now taken to prove the sanctity of his claim to his holding, since the succession within the family was registered (copied down) in the court rolls. Over the course of the fifteenth century, the villeins bought their way free of, or simply refused to pay, merchet, heriot, gersum, chevage, wardpenny, woolsilver, and all the rest of the vicious or petty exactions of the long past. On Ramsey manors, customary payments and labor services were "relaxed" in 1413. The last fines for default on boon-works were recorded at Elton in 1429. Quietly and unobtrusively, an era in social relations was closed.[25]

Closed, but not altogether forgotten. A century after the Peasant Rebellion, it was still possible to pour scorn on a family of the gentry, such as the Pastons of Norfolk, by pointing triumphantly to their alleged bondman ancestor, while to this day the

English language retains the word *villein*, slightly altered, as a pejorative, and its synonyms *boor* and *churl*, now mainly in adjective form, to convey a connotation of base manners.

The fifteenth century witnessed a return of prosperity—uneven, checkered, with plenty of setbacks and slowdowns, but nevertheless a recovery for Europe and its villages. In the wake of depopulation, individual holdings grew, the shrinkage of arable provided more pasture and stimulated increase of livestock, and the manure probably helped improve crop yields. Wealthy townsmen joined with the newly freed villagers in sharecropping arrangements. "The conduct of village economy passed decisively into the hands of peasants backed by townsmen's money," says Georges Duby.[26]

The era was one of extensive rebuilding. Peasant houses began to be constructed with masonry foundations and stronger frames, and many added rooms or even a second floor, with fireplace and chimney. Manor houses were enlarged. Parish churches were rebuilt in the new Perpendicular style, the vertical lines of the building emphasized with elaborate tracery and fan vaulting. The Elton church was extensively remodeled, the great square tower built, the aisles extended on either side, a south porch added, and the nave lighted by a clerestory.[27]

Not all villages shared in the prosperity, or even survived it. From about 1450, as grass became the favored land use in England, some villages, such as Wharram Percy, saw fields that had grown cereal crops for centuries turned exclusively into pastures for sheep. The smaller and less prosperous villages were especially vulnerable, as were those with few free tenants, who were much harder to displace than villeins. Vulnerable also were villages whose landlords, whether old feudatories or new men of wealth, had connections in the wool trade, or merely intelligently acquisitive appetites.[28] Where enclosure struck, families packed up their belongings, drove their animals ahead of them, and departed the village. Behind them their wattle-and-daub houses tumbled into ruins, the ditches that marked their crofts were filled in by erosion, the fences tottered, and the lanes and footpaths tramped by the feet of so many men and animals disappeared in weeds. The manor house often survived, with the shepherds sleeping in the bailiff's old quarters.

In maps showing the two phenomena, a clear correlation between the belt of open field agriculture and the distribution of the deserted villages can be seen, and a further correlation becomes apparent in comparing the two with a map showing enclosures of the fifteenth and sixteenth centuries.[29]

"Within a century and a half of the Black Death, ten percent of the settlements of rural England had been erased from the landscape," says one historian, possibly with exaggeration.[30] By the year 1600 over thirty villages in Huntingdonshire had been deserted, leaving behind sometimes the ruin of a church, sometimes the site of a manor house, sometimes nothing but plow marks discernible from the air.[31]

The old feudal landlord class was dealt a devastating blow from an unexpected source with Henry VIII's famous "Dissolution" of the monastic orders beginning in 1536. The king, embroiled with the Church over his divorce problems—and, like so many kings, needing money—violently suppressed all the great monasteries and seized their manors, which he then sold off at an ultimate profit of a million and a half pounds. Among the suppressed monasteries was Ramsey Abbey. A Huntingdonshire chronicler, Edmund Gibson, observed, "Most of the County being Abbey-land . . . many new purchasers planted themselves therein."[32] The new purchasers were entrepreneurs out to make money, and not surprisingly many of them saw the merits of sheep farming.

The enclosure movement appeared on the Continent too, but nowhere on the same scale as in England, where petty incidents of resistance multiplied without slowing the progress of the sheep, who, it was said, now devoured men instead of the men devouring sheep. The process "produced much controversy, many pamphlets, a number of government inquiries, some ineffective acts of Parliament, and a revolt in the Midlands in 1607," summarizes Alan R. H. Baker.[33] Yet many of the old villages

Relics of the Dissolution: ruins of Glastonbury Abbey (above) and Whitby Abbey. Of Ramsey Abbey, nothing medieval survives.

survived, some even gaining new population and character as numbers of craftsmen quit the cities, in part to escape guild regulation, and took their weaving, dyeing, tanning, and other skills to the now freer village environment. Some villages became primarily industrial. The village of Birmingham in the sixteenth century became a burgeoning town of 1,500, specializing in tanning and clothmaking.[34]

At the same time cereal crop agriculture made belated progress. Yields improved, if slowly, in the seventeenth century, reaching a general average in England of seven to one.[35] Famine became largely a threat of the past. "Starvation . . . cannot be shown to have been an omnipresent menace to the poor in Stuart times," says Peter Laslett.[36]

In 1610 a Herefordshire husbandman named Rowland Vaughan solved the problem of meadow and hay shortage that had vexed medieval lord and villager by devising an irrigation technique.[37] This and other improvements in agricultural technology made possible the servicing of a rapidly expanding market for English produce in Britain, on the Continent, and in English colonies overseas. The market gave scope for the ambitious, the industrious, the competent, and the fortunate, creating new, deeper divisions of rich and poor among the villagers. Individual enterprise moved to the center of the economic stage, as those who could afford it took advantage of the land market to buy up and consolidate holdings, forming compact plots that could be enclosed by fences or hedges and set free from communal regulation. At the other end of the scale, the number of landless laborers multiplied. In some places the old open field arrangements, with their cooperative plowing, common grazing, and bylaws, hung on amid a changing world. In 1545 the hallmote of Newton Longville, Buckinghamshire, ordained "that no one shall pasture his beasts in the sown fields except on his own lands from the Feast of Pentecost next-to-come until the rye and wheat have been taken away under penalty of four pence . . ."[38] But the future of individualism was already assured. "The undermining of the common fields, the declining effectiveness of the village's internal government, and the development of a distinct group of wealthy tenants [spelled the] triumph of individualism over the interests of the community," in the words of Christopher Dyer.[39]

Among the last guardians of the old communal tradition were

the English colonists who settled in New England, laid out their villages with churchyard and green (but no manor house), divided their fields into strips apportioned in accordance with wealth, plowed them cooperatively with large ox teams, and in their town meetings elected officials and enacted bylaws on cropping, pasturing, and fencing.[40] But in land-rich North America the open field village was out of place, and it soon became apparent that the American continent was destined for exploitation by the individual homestead farm. (It may be worth noting, however, that even technology-oriented American agriculture proved resistant to radical change; until the introduction of the tractor, one to two acres was considered an ample day's work for two men and a plow team.)

The village of Elton survived famine, Black Death, the Dissolution, and the enclosure movement. It even gained an architectural ornament with the building of Elton Hall, an imposing structure surrounded by a moat, begun by Sir Richard Sapcote about 1470 and expanded in the following centuries along with many other new peasant houses and old manor houses that reflected the general prosperity. Richard Cromwell, a nephew by marriage of Henry VIII's minister Thomas Cromwell, acquired Ramsey Abbey and became landlord of the dependent manors. Elton, however, went to another proprietor, through whom it gained a little guidebook distinction. The king bestowed it on his latest queen, Katherine Howard, as part of her jointure, the property settlement made on noble wives. On Katherine's execution for adultery Henry took back the jointure and presently bestowed Elton in 1546 on his last wife, Katherine Parr, under whose regime Elton Hall was given extensive repairs. On her death in 1548 Elton reverted to the crown, now held by the infant Edward VI, from whom it passed to Queen Elizabeth and James I, who disposed of it to Sir James Fullerton and Francis Maxwell, from whom it passed through still other hands to Sir Thomas Cotton, who held what must have been one of the last views of frankpledge in the manor court in 1633. Sir Thomas's daughter Frances and her husband Sir Thomas Proby inherited Elton; from them it passed to a collateral branch, raised to the peerage as earls of Carysfort, and in 1909 went to a nephew who took the name of Proby, and whose descendants remain in residence in Elton Hall.[41]

Enclosures, slow to penetrate Huntingdonshire, finally replaced the old arable strips and furlongs with rectangular hedged fields; one drives down a long straight road to arrive in a village whose irregular lanes and closes still carry a hint of the Middle Ages.

Though it had many ancestors in the form of hamlets, encampments, and other tiny, temporary, or semipermanent settlements, and though its modern descendants range from market towns to metropolitan suburbs, the open field village of the Middle Ages was a distinctive community, something new under the sun and not repeated since. Its intricate combination of social, economic, and legal arrangements, invented over a long period of time to meet a succession of pressing needs, imparted to its completed form an image, a personality, and a character. The traces of its open fields that aerial photographs reveal, with their faded parallel furrows clustered in plots oddly angled to each other, contain elements of both discipline and freedom.

Simultaneously haphazard and systematic, the medieval village is unthinkable without its lord. So much of its endless round of toil went to cultivate his crops, while its rents, court fines, and all the other charges with the curious archaic names went to supply his personal wants and the needs of his monastic or baronial household. Yet at the same time the village enjoyed a high degree of autonomy, regulating its own cultivation, settling its own quarrels, and living its life with little interference.

The legal division of the villagers into "free" and "unfree" had genuine meaning, but went much less deep than the words imply. The unfree villeins had to work for the lord and pay many fees that the free tenants escaped, yet the division into prosperous and poor was more meaningful. Looking at the men of the Middle Ages, Marc Bloch asked, "In social life, is there any more elusive notion than the free will of a small man?"[42]

Village life for men and women alike was busy, strenuous, unrelenting, much of it lived outdoors, with an element of danger that especially threatened children. Diet was poor, dress simple, housing primitive, sanitary arrangements derisory. Yet there were love, sex, courtship, and marriage, holidays, games and sports, and plenty of ale. Neighbors quarreled and fought, sued and countersued, suspected and slandered, but also knew each other thoroughly and depended on each other, to help with the plowing and harvesting, to act as pledges, to bear witness, to respond when danger threatened.

The most arresting characteristic of the medieval open field village is certainly its system of cooperation: cultivation in concert of individually held land, and pasturing in common of individually owned animals. It was a system that suited an age of low productivity and scarcity of markets, and one that hardly fostered the spirit of innovation. The lords were content to leave things as they were, the villeins had little power to change them. When change came, it came largely from outside, from the pressure of the market and the enterprise of new landlords. Yet change builds on an existing structure. The open field village helped create the populous—and in comparison with the past, prosperous—Europe of the high Middle Ages, the Europe from which so much of the modern world emerged.

In the shift toward that world, many villagers lost their homes, many of their villages disappeared. Argument, protest, and violence accompanied change, which only historical perspective makes clearly inevitable.

Was something larger lost? A sense of community, of closeness, of mutual solidarity? Perhaps it was, but the clearest message about the people of Elton and other villages of the late thirteenth century that their records give us seems to be that they were people much like ourselves. Not brutes or dolts, but men and women, living out their lives in a more difficult world, one underequipped with technology, devoid of science, nearly devoid of medicine, and saddled with an exploitative social system. Sometimes they protested, sometimes they even rose in rebellion, mostly they adapted to circumstance. In making their system work, they helped lay the foundation of the future.

NOTES

PROLOGUE: ELTON

1. *Chronicon abbatiae Rameseiensis,* ed. by W. Duncan Macray, London, 1886, p. 135.

2. Maurice Beresford and John G. Hurst, eds., *Deserted Medieval Villages,* London, 1971; Maurice Beresford, *The Lost Villages of the Middle Ages,* London, 1954; John G. Hurst, "The Changing Medieval Village," in J. A. Raftis, ed., *Pathways to Medieval Peasants,* Toronto, 1981; Trevor Rowley and John Wood, *Deserted Villages,* Aylesbury, England, 1982.

CHAPTER 1. THE VILLAGE EMERGES

1. Edward Miller and John Hatcher, *Medieval England: Rural Society and Economic Change, 1086–1348,* London, 1978, pp. 85–87.

2. Rowley and Wood, *Deserted Villages,* pp. 6–8.

3. Jean Chapelot and Robert Fossier, *The Village and House in the Middle Ages,* trans. by Henry Cleere, Berkeley, 1985, p. 327.

4. P. J. Fowler, "Later Prehistory," in H. P. R. Finberg, gen. ed., *The Agrarian History of England and Wales,* vol. 1, pt. 1, *Prehistory,* ed. by Stuart Piggott, Cambridge, 1981, pp. 157–158.

5. Butser Ancient Farm Project Publications: *The Celtic Experience; Celtic Fields; Evolution of Wheat; Bees and Honey; Quern Stones; Hoes, Ards, and Yokes; Natural Dyes.*

6. Tacitus, *De Vita Iulii Agricola and De Germania,* ed. by Alfred Gudeman, Boston, 1928, pp. 36–37, 40–41.

7. Chapelot and Fossier, *Village and House,* pp. 27–30.

8. S. Applebaum, "Roman Britain," in H. P. R. Finberg, ed., *The Agrarian History of England and Wales,* vol. 1, pt. 2, A.D. *43–1042,* Cambridge, 1972, p. 117.

9. Ibid., pp. 73–82.

10. Ibid., pp. 186, 208.

11. Chapelot and Fossier, *Village and House*, pp. 61, 100–103.

12. Ibid., p. 26.

13. Ibid., p. 15.

14. Ibid., pp. 144–150.

15. Joan Thirsk, "The Common Fields" and "The Origin of the Common Fields," and J. Z. Titow, "Medieval England and the Open-Field System," in *Peasants, Knights, and Heretics: Studies in Medieval English Social History,* ed. by R. H. Hilton, Cambridge, 1981, pp. 10–56; Bruce Campbell, "Commonfield Origins—the Regional Dimension," in Trevor Rowley, ed., *Origins of Open-Field Agriculture,* London, 1981, p. 127; Trevor Rowley, "Medieval Field Systems," in Leonard Cantor, ed., *The English Medieval Landscape,* Philadelphia, 1982; H. L. Gray, *English Field Systems,* Cambridge, Mass., 1915; C. S. and C. S. Orwin, *The Open Fields,* Oxford, 1954.

16. Joseph and Frances Gies, *Life in a Medieval Castle,* New York, 1974, p. 148.

17. George C. Homans, *English Villagers in the Thirteenth Century,* New York, 1975, pp. 12–28.

18. Grenville Astill and Annie Grant, eds., *The Countryside of Medieval England,* Oxford, 1988, pp. 88, 94.

19. Georges Duby, *Rural Economy and Country Life in the Medieval West,* Columbia, S.C., 1968, pp. 109–111.

20. Joan Thirsk, "Farming Techniques," in *Agrarian History of England and Wales,* vol. 4, *1500–1640,* ed. by Joan Thirsk, Cambridge, 1967, p. 164.

21. R. H. Hilton, *The Transition from Feudalism to Capitalism,* London, 1984, pp. 15–16.

22. W. G. Hoskins, *The Midland Peasant: The Economic and Social History of a Leicestershire Village,* London, 1957, p. 79; Homans, *English Villagers,* p. 368.

CHAPTER 2. THE ENGLISH VILLAGE: ELTON

1. For Huntingdonshire: Peter Bigmore, *The Bedfordshire and Huntingdonshire Landscape,* London, 1979. For England in general: H. C. Darby, *A New Historical Geography of England Before 1600,* Cambridge, 1976; Cantor, ed., *The English Medieval Landscape;* W. G. Hoskins, *The Making of the English Landscape,* London, 1955.

2. Applebaum, "Roman Britain," in *The Agrarian History of England and Wales,* vol. 1, pt. 2, p. 53.

3. Bigmore, *Bedfordshire and Huntingdonshire Landscape,* pp. 37–42.

4. Frank M. Stenton, *Anglo-Saxon England,* Oxford, 1971, p. 25.

5. H. C. Darby, "The Anglo-Scandinavian Foundations," in Darby, ed., *New Historical Geography,* pp. 13–14.

6. Ibid., p. 15.

7. H. P. R. Finberg, "Anglo-Saxon England to 1042," in *The Agrarian History of England and Wales,* vol. 1, pt. 2, p. 422.

8. *The Anglo-Saxon Chronicles,* trans. by Anne Savage, London, 1983, pp. 90–92, 96.

9. J. A. Raftis, *The Estates of Ramsey Abbey: A Study of Economic Growth and Organization,* Toronto, 1957, pp. 6–9.

10. A. Mawer and F. M. Stenton, *The Place-Names of Bedfordshire and Huntingdonshire,* London, 1926, pp. 183–184; James B. Johnston, *The Place Names of England and Wales,* London, 1915, p. 258; Eilert Ekwall, *The Concise Oxford Dictionary of English Place Names,* Oxford, 1947, p. 158.

11. *Chronicon abbatiae Rameseiensis,* pp. 112–113.

12. Ibid., pp. 135–140.

13. E. A. Kosminsky, *Studies in the Agrarian History of England in the Thirteenth Century,* Oxford, 1956, p. 73.

14. *Cartularium monasterii de Rameseia,* ed. by William Hart, London, 1884–1893, vol. 1, p. 234. (Henceforth referred to as *Cart. Rames.*)

15. Barbara Dodwell, "Holdings and Inheritance in East Anglia," *Economic History Review* 2nd ser. 20 (1967), p. 55.

16. Raftis, *Estates of Ramsey Abbey,* pp. 26–34.

17. Susan B. Edgington, "Ramsey Abbey vs. Pagan Peverel, St. Ives, 1107," *Records of Huntingdonshire* 2 (1985), pp. 2–5; Edgington, "Pagan Peverel: An Anglo-Norman Crusader," in *Crusade and Settlement,* ed. by P. Edbury, Cardiff, 1985, pp. 90–93.

18. H. C. Darby, "Domesday England," in Darby, ed., *New Historical Geography,* p. 39.

19. W. Page and G. Proby, eds., *Victoria History of the Counties of England: Huntingdonshire,* vol. 1, London, 1926, p. 344. (Henceforth referred to as *V.C.H. Hunts.*)

20. *Rotuli Hundredorum temp. Hen. III et Edw. I in Turri Lond' et in curia receptae scaccarii Westm. asservati,* London, 1818, vol. 2, p. 656. (Henceforth referred to as *Rot. Hund.*)

21. Beresford, *Lost Villages,* p. 55.

22. G. R. Owst, *Literature and Pulpit in Medieval England,* Oxford, 1961, pp. 27–28, 37.

23. R. H. Hilton, *A Medieval Society: The West Midlands and the End of the Thirteenth Century,* New York, 1966, p. 95; Hoskins, *The Midland Peasant,* p. 284; Chapelot and Fossier, *Village and House,* pp. 253–254, 296–302; Margaret Wood, *The English Mediaeval House,* London, 1965, pp. 215–216; Maurice W. Barley, *The English Farmhouse and Cottage,* London, 1961, pp. 22–25; H. M. Colvin, "Domestic Architecture and Town-Planning," in A. Lane Poole, ed., *Medieval England,* London, 1958, vol. 1, pp. 82–88.

24. Wood, *English Mediaeval House*, p. 293.

25. Chapelot and Fossier, *Village and House*, pp. 313–315; Sarah M. McKinnon, "The Peasant House: The Evidence of Manuscript Illuminations," in Raftis, ed., *Pathways to Medieval Peasants*, p. 304; Colvin, "Domestic Architecture," p. 87.

26. Hurst, "The Changing Medieval Village," pp. 42–43; Beresford and Hurst, *Deserted Medieval Villages*, pp. 104–105; Hilton, *A Medieval Society*, p. 97.

27. *Bedfordshire Coroners' Rolls*, ed. by R. F. Hunnisett, Streatley, England, 1969, pp. 8, 35, 45, 83, 92, 112–113.

28. *Elton Manorial Records, 1279–1351*, ed. by S. C. Ratcliff, trans. by D. M. Gregory, Cambridge, 1946, p. 152. (Henceforth referred to as *E.M.R.*)

29. Ibid., pp. 392, 393.

30. Hilton, *A Medieval Society*, p. 95.

31. Beresford and Hurst, *Deserted Medieval Villages*, p. 116.

32. *E.M.R.*, pp. 196, 300, 316; Grenville Astill, "Rural Settlement, the Toft and the Croft," in Astill and Grant, eds., *Countryside of Medieval England*, pp. 36–61.

33. *E.M.R.*, p. 52.

34. Ibid., pp. 52, 370.

35. Ibid., p. 52.

36. Ibid., pp. 50, 82, 110.

37. *Rot. Hund.*, p. 656; Leslie E. Webster and John Cherry, "Medieval Britain in 1977," *Medieval Archaeology* 22 (1978), pp. 142, 178.

38. *E.M.R.*, pp. 22, 66, 275.

39. Ibid., pp. 13, 79, 214.

40. Ibid., pp. 137, 138, 169, 275, 322, 323, 336.

41. Ibid., p. 213.

42. Ibid., pp. 21, 64, 138, 169, 170, 215, 386.

43. Ibid., pp. 65, 66, 80, 169, 174, 176, 185, 322, 323.

44. Ibid., pp. 14, 22, 137, 386.

45. Ibid., pp. 14, 137, 138, 139, 323.

46. Ibid., pp. 137, 138, 168, 214, 371.

47. Ibid., p. 169.

48. Ibid., pp. 137, 213, 214, 272, 288.

49. Ibid., pp. 52, 77–78.

50. Ibid., p. 112.

51. Ibid., pp. 10, 19, 57, 126, 158, 203, 266–267.

52. Ibid., p. li.

53. Brian K. Roberts, *The Making of the English Village, a Study in Historical Geography*, Harlow, England, 1987, pp. 21–29; Chapelot and Fossier, *Village and House*, p. 184.

54. Hilton, *A Medieval Society*, pp. 93–95.

55. *E.M.R.*, p. 69.

56. *Rot. Hund.*, pp. 656–658.

57. Hilton, *A Medieval Society*, p. 92.

58. *E.M.R.*, p. 97.

59. *Rot. Hund.*, p. 657.

CHAPTER 3. THE LORD

1. *The Estate Book of Henry de Bray, Northamptonshire, c. 1289–1340*, ed. by D. Willis, Camden Society 3rd ser. 27 (1916).

2. Miller and Hatcher, *Medieval England*, p. 17.

3. R. H. Hilton, *The English Peasantry in the Later Middle Ages*, Oxford, 1975, pp. 132–133.

4. Homans, *English Villagers*, pp. 330–331.

5. Raftis, *Estates of Ramsey Abbey*, p. 77; R. Lennard, *Rural England, 1086–1135, a Study of Society and Agrarian Conditions*, Oxford, 1959, p. 199.

6. Christopher Dyer, *Lords and Peasants in a Changing Society: The Estates of the Bishopric of Worcester, 680–1548*, Cambridge, 1980, p. 55; Duby, *Rural Economy and Country Life*, p. 35.

7. Kosminsky, *Studies in Agrarian History*, Table 3, p. 100; *Cart. Rames.*, vol. 1, pp. 294, 306.

8. Raftis, *Estates of Ramsey Abbey*, pp. 68–69.

9. *E.M.R.*, p. 117.

10. Ibid., pp. 193, 299.

11. Ibid., p. 45.

12. Ibid., p. 46.

13. Ellen W. Moore, *The Fairs of Medieval England: An Introductory Study*, Toronto, 1985.

14. *Cart. Rames.*, vol. 2, p. 342.

15. George Homans, "The Rural Sociology of Medieval England," *Past and Present* 4 (1953), p. 39.

16. Ibid., p. 40.

17. *Walter of Henley's Husbandry, Together with an Anonymous Husbandry, Seneschaucie, etc.*, ed. by E. Lamond, Oxford, 1890, p. 35.

18. Ibid. *(Rules of St. Robert)*, p. 125.

19. Ibid. *(Seneschaucie)*, pp. 88–89; Frances Davenport, *The Economic Development of a Norfolk Manor, 1086–1565*, Cambridge, 1906, pp. 22–23.

20. *Walter of Henley (Seneschaucie),* p. 105.

21. *E.M.R.,* p. xviii.

22. *E.M.R.,* p. 173; Davenport, *Economic Development of a Norfolk Manor,* p. 23.

23. Miller and Hatcher, *Medieval England,* pp. 192–193.

24. *Walter of Henley,* p. 11.

25. *E.M.R.,* pp. xxxvii–xxxviii.

26. Ibid., pp. 2, 4, 138, 272, 275, 386.

27. Ibid., pp. 67–68, 140–141, 276–277.

28. Ibid., pp. 13, 67.

29. Ibid., p. 63.

30. *Walter of Henley (Seneschaucie),* p. 99.

31. Homans, *English Villagers,* pp. 297–305; Duby, *Rural Economy and Country Life,* p. 233; Raftis, *Estates of Ramsey Abbey,* pp. 125–127; Miller and Hatcher, *Medieval England,* pp. 193–197.

32. *Walter of Henley (Seneschaucie),* pp. 100–102.

33. *E.M.R.,* pp. 56–85.

34. Ibid., p. 15.

35. Ibid., p. 24.

36. Ibid., p. 68.

37. Raftis, *Estates of Ramsey Abbey,* p. 95.

38. Nigel Saul, *Scenes from Provincial Life, Knightly Families in Sussex, 1280–1400,* Oxford, 1987, p. 127.

39. Geoffrey Chaucer, *The Canterbury Tales,* in *The Complete Works of Geoffrey Chaucer,* ed. by F. N. Robinson, Boston, 1933, p. 25 (lines 593–594).

40. *Walter of Henley,* pp. 17–18.

41. J. S. Drew, "Manorial Accounts of St. Swithun's Priory, Winchester," in E. M. Carus-Wilson, ed., *Essays in Economic History,* London, 1962, pp. 27–30.

42. *Walter of Henley,* p. 11.

43. Homans, *English Villagers,* p. 293.

44. *E.M.R.,* pp. 70, 79, 278, 373.

45. *Walter of Henley (Rules of St. Robert),* p. 145.

46. *Cart. Rames.,* vol. 3, pp. 168–169, 230–232.

47. Paul Vinogradoff, *The Growth of the Manor,* London, 1911; Dyer, *Lords and Peasants,* p. 67.

48. M. M. Postan, "The Famulus: The Estate Labourer in the Twelfth and Thirteenth Centuries," *Economic History Review,* supplement no. 2, Cambridge, 1954, p. 3.

49. *E.M.R.*, pp. 16, 173, 218.

50. Ibid., pp. 24, 48, 172–173, 217–218.

51. Postan, "The Famulus," p. 21; *Cart. Rames.*, vol. 3, pp. 236–241; vol. 1, pp. 319, 330, 340, 351, 363.

52. Postan, "The Famulus," p. 21.

53. *Walter of Henley (Seneschaucie)*, p. 110; *Walter of Henley*, pp. 11–13; David L. Farmer, "Prices and Wages," in H. E. Hallam, ed., *The Agrarian History of England and Wales*, vol. 2, *1042–1350*, Cambridge, 1988, p. 748; Annie Grant, "Animal Resources," in Astill and Grant, eds., *Countryside of Medieval England*, p. 174.

54. *E.M.R.*, pp. 25–26; J. A. Raftis, "Farming Techniques (East Midlands)," in *The Agrarian History of England and Wales*, vol. 2, pp. 336–337.

55. *E.M.R.*, p. 173.

56. Raftis, *Estates of Ramsey Abbey*, p. 206.

57. *E.M.R.*, pp. lii–liii.

58. Raftis, *Estates of Ramsey Abbey*, p. 167.

59. Warren O. Ault, *Open-Field Farming in Medieval England: A Study of Village By-Laws*, London, 1972, p. 31.

60. Farmer, "Prices and Wages," in *The Agrarian History of England and Wales*, vol. 2, p. 734.

61. *Walter of Henley (Seneschaucie)*, p. 113.

62. *Walter of Henley*, p. 25.

63. Robert Trow-Smith, *History of British Livestock Husbandry*, London, 1957–1959, vol. 1, p. 156.

64. Ibid., p. 153.

65. *E.M.R.*, pp. liii–liv.

66. Trow-Smith, *British Livestock Husbandry*, vol. 1, p. 149.

67. *Walter of Henley (Seneschaucie)*, pp. 117–118.

68. *E.M.R.*, p. lv.

69. Miller and Hatcher, *Medieval England*, p. 77.

70. *Walter of Henley (Rules of St. Robert)*, p. 141.

71. E. A. Kosminsky, "Services and Money Rents in the Thirteenth Century," in Carus-Wilson, ed., *Essays in Economic History*, pp. 31–48.

72. *The Estate Book of Henry de Bray*, pp. xxiv–xxvii.

73. Beresford and Hurst, *Deserted Medieval Villages*, p. 127.

74. *Walter of Henley*, p. 19.

75. Ibid., p. 29.

76. *E.M.R.*, pp. 17, 25.

77. *Walter of Henley (Seneschaucie)*, p. 113.

78. Trow-Smith, *British Livestock Husbandry*, p. 112.

79. Ibid., p. 161; Farmer, "Prices and Wages," in *The Agrarian History of England and Wales*, vol. 2, p. 757; *E.M.R.*, p. liii.

80. Miller and Hatcher, *Medieval England*, p. 215.

81. Thirsk, "Farming Techniques," in *The Agrarian History of England and Wales*, vol. 4, p. 163.

82. Trow-Smith, *British Livestock Husbandry*, p. 169.

CHAPTER 4. THE VILLAGERS: WHO THEY WERE

1. Miller and Hatcher, *Medieval England*, p. 20.

2. Ibid., p. 113.

3. Frederic William Maitland, *The Domesday Book and Beyond*, New York, 1966 (first pub. in 1897), p. 31.

4. R. H. Hilton, "Freedom and Villeinage in England," in Hilton, ed., *Peasants, Knights, and Heretics*, pp. 174–191.

5. F. Pollock and F. W. Maitland, *The History of English Law Before the Time of Edward I*, Cambridge, 1968, vol. 1, p. 419. On the subject of freedom versus serfdom: R. H. Hilton, *The Decline of Serfdom in Medieval England*, London, 1969; Miller and Hatcher, *Medieval England*, pp. 111–133; M. M. Postan, "Legal Status and Economic Condition in Medieval Villages," in M. M. Postan, *Essays on Medieval Agriculture and General Problems of the Medieval Economy*, Cambridge, 1968, pp. 278–289.

6. Miller and Hatcher, *Medieval England*, pp. 111–112.

7. Ibid., p. 112.

8. Duby, *Rural Economy and Country Life*, p. 282.

9. *Cart. Rames.*, vol. 3, pp. 257–260.

10. J. A. Raftis, *Warboys: Two Hundred Years in the Life of an English Medieval Village*, Toronto, 1974, pp. 67–68.

11. Kosminsky, *Studies in the Agrarian History of England*, pp. 230–237.

12. *Rot. Hund.*, pp. 656–658.

13. *V.C.H. Hunts.*, p. 161.

14. *Rot. Hund.*, pp. 656–658.

15. *Cart. Rames.*, vol. 1, pp. 299–300, 310, 324, 336, 345, 350, 357, 361, 365, 393–394, 460–461, 475, 483; vol. 2, pp. 45–46.

16. *E.M.R.*, p. 128.

17. Ibid., p. 268.

18. Ibid., p. 10.

19. Raftis, *Estates of Ramsey Abbey*, pp. 224–227.

20. *E.M.R.*, pp. 5–6.

21. Ibid., pp. 28, 78, 181, 227, 287–288, 334.

22. *Rot. Hund.*, p. 657.

23. *E.M.R.*, pp. 93, 150.

24. Ibid., pp. 147, 151.

25. Ibid., pp. 147, 201, 255.

26. Ibid., p. 10. See also Postan, "The Famulus," pp. 7–14.

27. *E.M.R.*, p. 93.

28. Ibid., p. 261.

29. Ibid., p. 249.

30. Ibid., p. 44.

31. Chaucer, *Canterbury Tales*, p. 32.

32. *E.M.R.*, p. 43.

33. Ibid., p. 44.

34. Ibid., p. 10.

35. Ibid., p. 126.

36. Ibid., p. 43.

37. Ibid., p. 43.

38. Ibid., p. 43.

39. Ibid., p. 196.

40. Ibid., p. 115.

41. *Bedfordshire Coroners' Rolls*, p. 114.

42. *E.M.R.*, p. 34.

43. Ibid., p. 89.

44. Ibid., p. 190.

45. Ibid., p. 254.

46. Ibid., p. 261.

47. Ibid., p. 257.

48. Ibid., p. 261.

49. Ibid., p. 293.

50. Anne De Windt, "A Peasant Land Market and Its Participants: King's Ripton 1280–1400," *Midland History* 4 (1978), pp. 142–149.

51. M. M. Postan, "Village Livestock in the Thirteenth Century," *Economic History Review* 2nd ser. 15 (1962), pp. 219–249.

52. Trow-Smith, *British Livestock Husbandry*, vol. 1, p. 103.

53. *E.M.R.*, p. 200.

54. *Bedfordshire Coroners' Rolls*, p. 87.

55. Ibid., p. 82.

56. Edmund Britton, *The Community of the Vill: A Study in the History of the Family and Village Life in Fourteenth-Century England*, Toronto, 1977.

57. Edwin De Windt, *Land and People in Holywell-cum-Needingworth: Structures of Tenure and Patterns of Social Organization in an East Midlands Village, 1253–1453*, Toronto, 1972.

58. *E.M.R.*, p. 3.

59. Ibid., p. 44.

60. Ibid., pp. 120–121.

61. Ibid., p. 122.

62. Ibid., p. 146.

63. Ibid., p. 200.

64. Ibid., p. 234.

65. Ibid., p. 2.

66. Ibid., p. 30.

67. Ibid., p. 46.

68. Ibid., p. 34.

69. Ibid., p. 116.

70. Ibid., p. 120.

71. Ibid., p. 95.

72. Ibid., p. 261.

73. Emmanuel Le Roy Ladurie, *Montaillou, the Promised Land of Error*, trans. by Barbara Bray, New York, 1978.

74. *E.M.R.*, pp. 5–6.

CHAPTER 5. THE VILLAGERS: HOW THEY LIVED

1. Beresford and Hurst, *Deserted Medieval Villages*, p. 122; Cantor, "Villages and Towns," in Cantor, ed., *The English Medieval Landscape*, pp. 173–174; Chapelot and Fossier, *Village and House*, pp. 204–205; Hurst, "The Changing Medieval Village," p. 44.

2. R. K. Field, "Worcestershire Peasant Buildings, Household Goods and Farming Equipment in the Later Middle Ages," *Medieval Archaeology* 9 (1965), pp. 105–145.

3. *E.M.R.*, p. 115.

4. Ibid., p. 151.

5. Ibid., p. 300.

6. Beresford and Hurst, *Deserted Medieval Villages*, p. 104; Hilton, *A Medieval Society*, pp. 96–97; Trow-Smith, *British Livestock Husbandry*, vol. 1, p. 114.

7. Wood, *English Mediaeval House*, pp. 300–302; Chapelot and Fossier, *Village and House*, pp. 284–314; Colvin, *English Farmhouse*, pp. 21–36.

8. Beresford and Hurst, *Deserted Medieval Villages*, p. 105.

9. *E.M.R.*, p. 170.

10. Beresford and Hurst, *Deserted Medieval Villages*, pp. 98, 100; Wood, *English Mediaeval House*, pp. 257–260.

11. *Hali Meidenhod*, ed. by O. Cockayne, London, 1922, p. 53.

12. Owst, *Literature and Pulpit*, pp. 27, 35–36.

13. Barbara Hanawalt, *The Ties That Bound: Peasant Families in Medieval England*, New York, 1986, pp. 45–49; Hoskins, *The Midland Peasant*, pp. 295–296; Hilton, *A Medieval Society*, pp. 100–101; Field, "Worcestershire Peasant Buildings," pp. 121–123.

14. Wood, *Mediaeval English House*, pp. 368–374.

15. *E.M.R.*, pp. 12, 62, 78, 133, 209.

16. Duby, *Rural Economy and Country Life*, p. 65.

17. Miller and Hatcher, *Medieval England*, p. 164.

18. H. E. Hallam, "The Life of the People," in *Agrarian History of England and Wales*, vol. 2, pp. 830, 838.

19. Cecily Howell, *Land, Family, and Inheritance in Transition*, Cambridge, 1983, pp. 164–165; Grenville Astill, "Fields," in Astill and Grant, eds., *Countryside of Medieval England*, p. 118.

20. Kosminsky, *Studies in the Agrarian History of England*, p. 240.

21. Miller and Hatcher, *Medieval England*, pp. 147–148; H. S. Bennett, *Life on the English Manor, A Study of Peasant Conditions, 1150–1400*, Cambridge, 1960 (first pub. in 1937), p. 95; Hallam, "Life of the People," in *The Agrarian History of England and Wales*, vol. 2, p. 824; J. Z. Titow, *English Rural Society, 1200–1350*, London, 1969, p. 79; Howell, *Land, Family, and Inheritance*, p. 159.

22. Michel Mollat, *The Poor in the Middle Ages, an Essay in Social History*, trans. by Arthur Goldhammer, New Haven, 1986, pp. 194–195.

23. Anear MacConglinne, "The Vision of Viands," in *The Portable Medieval Reader*, ed. by James Bruce Ross and Mary Martin McLaughlin, New York, 1966, pp. 497–499.

24. John Gower, *Miroir de l'Omme*, II, lines 450–460, in *Complete Works of John Gower*, ed. by G. C. Macaulay, Oxford, 1899–1902, vol. 1, p. 293.

25. *E.M.R.*, p. 47.

26. William Langland, *Piers Plowman's Crede*, ed. by W. W. Skeat, London, 1867, pp. 16–17.

27. John Stow, *Survey of London*, London, 1603, p. 92, translating William Fitzstephen's description of twelfth-century London, cited in Bennett, *Life on the English Manor*, p. 261.

28. Homans, *English Villagers,* p. 358.

29. Bennett, *Life on the English Manor,* p. 262.

30. *E.M.R.,* p. 172.

31. Homans, *English Villagers,* p. 362.

32. Ibid., p. 365.

33. Ibid., pp. 368, 370.

34. *E.M.R.,* p. 69.

35. Homans, *English Villagers,* p. 372.

36. *E.M.R.,* p. 172.

37. Robert Manning, *Handlyng Synne,* ed. by Idelle Sullens, Binghamton, New York, 1983, p. 224.

38. Owst, *Literature and Pulpit,* p. 362.

39. *Bedfordshire Coroners' Rolls,* pp. 97–98.

40. Hanawalt, *Ties That Bound,* pp. 44, 60.

41. *Bedfordshire Coroners' Rolls,* pp. 2–3.

42. Ibid., pp. 55–57.

43. Ibid., p. 108.

44. Ibid., p. 51.

45. Ibid., pp. 71–72.

46. Ibid., p. xxiii.

47. Ibid., p. 7.

48. Ibid., pp. 12–13.

49. Ibid., p. 116.

CHAPTER 6. MARRIAGE AND THE FAMILY

1. Frances and Joseph Gies, *Marriage and the Family in the Middle Ages,* New York, 1987, pp. 157–177.

2. Miller and Hatcher, *Medieval England,* p. 138.

3. P. D. A. Harvey, *A Medieval Oxfordshire Village: Cuxham, 1240 to 1400,* Oxford, 1965, p. 124.

4. Rosamond Jane Faith, "Peasant Families and Inheritance Customs in Medieval England," *Agricultural History Review* 4 (1966), p. 91.

5. Ibid., pp. 86–87.

6. *E.M.R.,* p. 208.

7. *Court Roll of Chalgrave Manor,* ed. by Marian K. Dale, *Bedfordshire Historical Record Society* 28 (1950), p. 10.

8. *E.M.R.,* pp. 56, 68, 70.

9. Ibid., p. 392.

10. Ibid., p. 313.

11. Ibid., pp. 84–85, 264, 317.

12. Ibid., p. 313.

13. *Cart. Rames.*, vol. 1, p. 416.

14. Ibid., vol. 1, pp. 294, 306, 320, 330, 352.

15. Ibid., vol. 1, pp. 359, 384.

16. *Court Roll of Chalgrave Manor*, p. 9.

17. Trow-Smith, *British Livestock Husbandry*, pp. 100–101.

18. Britton, *Community of the Vill*, pp. 59–64.

19. Anne De Windt, "Peasant Land Market," pp. 151–153.

20. Duby, *Rural Economy and Country Life*, p. 284.

21. *E.M.R.*, p. 96.

22. Ibid., p. 261.

23. Ibid., p. 5.

24. Eleanor Searle, "Seigneurial Control of Women's Marriage: The Antecedents and Function of Merchet in England," *Past and Present* 82 (1979), pp. 3–43; also Searle, "Freedom and Marriage in Medieval England: An Alternative Hypothesis," *Economic History Review* 2nd ser. 29 (1976).

25. *E.M.R.*, p. 28.

26. Ibid., p. 132.

27. Judith M. Bennett, "Medieval Peasant Marriage: An Examination of the Marriage License Fines in *Liber Gersumarum*," in Raftis, ed., *Pathways to Medieval Peasants*, p. 195.

28. Ibid., p. 197.

29. Ibid., pp. 205–209, 213–214.

30. Ibid., pp. 208–209.

31. *Cart. Rames.*, vol. 1, p. 432.

32. Bennett, "Medieval Peasant Marriage," pp. 200–204.

33. *E.M.R.*, pp. 61, 132, 208–209.

34. Gies, *Marriage and the Family*, pp. 135–141.

35. William Langland, *The Vision of Piers Plowman*, ed. by A. V. C. Schmidt, London, 1984, passus ix, lines 162–165, p. 97.

36. Manning, *Handlyng Synne*, p. 279.

37. Ibid., p. 277.

38. G. R. Owst, *Preaching in Medieval England*, London, 1926, p. 269.

39. Ibid., p. 269.

40. *Cart. Rames.*, vol. 1, p. 312.

41. Gies, *Marriage and the Family*, pp. 242–245, 299–300.

42. Manning, *Handlyng Synne,* p. 211.

43. *E.M.R.,* p. 3.

44. Ibid., pp. 132, 146.

45. Ibid., p. 200.

46. G. G. Coulton, *Medieval Village, Manor, and Monastery,* New York, 1960 (first pub. in 1925), pp. 477–478.

47. J. A. Raftis, in correspondence with the authors.

48. Britton, *Community of the Vill,* pp. 34–37.

49. Hanawalt, *Ties That Bound,* p. 216.

50. John Myrc, *Instructions for Parish Priests,* ed. by E. Peacock, London, 1868, pp. 18–19.

51. Manning, *Handlyng Synne,* pp. 240–241.

52. Myrc, *Instructions for Parish Priests,* pp. 4–5.

53. Hanawalt, *Ties That Bound,* pp. 172–173.

54. Ibid., pp. 175–179.

55. *Bedfordshire Coroners' Rolls,* p. 1.

56. Ibid., p. 51.

57. Ibid., pp. 59–60.

58. Ibid., p. 98.

59. Barbara Hanawalt, "Childbearing Among the Lower Classes of Late Medieval England," *Journal of Interdisciplinary History* 8 (1977), pp. 20–21.

60. Owst, *Literature and Pulpit,* pp. 34–35.

61. Ibid., pp. 33–34.

62. Ibid., p. 34.

63. Hanawalt, *Ties That Bound,* pp. 166–167.

64. *Cart. Rames.,* pp. 300–301.

65. M. M. Postan and J. Titow, "Heriots and Prices on Winchester Manors," *Economic History Review* 2nd ser. 11 (1959), pp. 392–410; Hanawalt, *Ties That Bound,* pp. 228–229; Miller and Hatcher, *Medieval England,* pp. viii–ix.

66. *E.M.R.,* p. 311.

67. Elaine Clark, "Some Aspects of Social Security in Medieval England," *Journal of Family History* 7 (1982), pp. 307–320.

68. Manning, *Handlyng Synne,* pp. 30–32.

69. J. A. Raftis, *Tenure and Mobility: Studies in the Social History of the Mediaeval English Village,* Toronto, 1964, pp. 43–44.

70. Ibid., pp. 44–45.

71. Homans, *English Villagers,* p. 146.

72. Clark, "Some Aspects of Social Security," p. 313.

73. Ibid., pp. 312–313.

74. Raftis, *Tenure and Mobility*, p. 45.

75. Ibid., p. 44.

76. Clark, "Some Aspects of Social Security," pp. 310–311.

77. Howard Morris Stuckert, *Corrodies in English Monasteries: A Study in English Social History of the Middle Ages*, Philadelphia, 1923; Hilton, *A Medieval Society*, pp. 111–113.

78. Hilton, *A Medieval Society*, p. 163.

79. *Bedfordshire Coroners' Rolls*, p. 4.

80. Ibid., p. 89.

81. Manning, *Handlyng Synne*, pp. 280–281.

82. Myrc, *Instructions for Parish Priests*, pp. 53–59.

83. *Roberti Grosseteste Epistolae episcopi quondam Lincolniensis*, ed. by H. R. Luard, London, 1861, p. 74, cited in Homans, *English Villagers*, p. 392.

84. Homans, *English Villagers*, p. 392.

85. Cited in Owst, *Preaching in Medieval England*, p. 268.

CHAPTER 7. THE VILLAGE AT WORK

1. E.M.R., p. 90; Raftis, "Farming Techniques," in *The Agrarian History of England and Wales*, vol. 2, p. 329.

2. Ault, *Open-Field Farming*, pp. 22–23.

3. Gray, *English Field Systems*, especially pp. 39–49 and 71–82; Gray expresses the change from two-field to three-field as bringing "under tillage one-sixth more of the [total] arable" (p. 76); Homans, *English Villagers*, p. 57; Duby, *Rural Economy and Country Life*, pp. 22–23, 92–96; Miller and Hatcher, *Medieval England*, pp. 88–97.

4. Miller and Hatcher, *Medieval England*, pp. 89–97 for a general discussion of field systems; Homans, *English Villagers*, p. 54; Trevor Rowley, "Medieval Field Systems," in Cantor, ed., *The English Medieval Landscape*, pp. 36–38.

5. Maurice Beresford, *Studies in Leicestershire Agrarian History*, London, 1949, p. 93, cited in Ault, *Open-Field Farming*, p. 52.

6. E.M.R., p. 4.

7. Ibid., p. 34.

8. Ibid., p. 30.

9. Ibid., p. 3.

10. Miller and Hatcher, *Medieval England*, p. 99.

11. Ibid., p. 123.

12. E.M.R., p. xxx.

13. V.C.H. Hunts., vol. 1, p. 75; Rot. Hund., p. 657.

14. *Cart. Rames.,* vol. 1, pp. 323–324.

15. Raftis, *Estates of Ramsey Abbey,* pp. 194–195; Robert R. Reynolds, *Europe Emerges: Transition Toward an Industrial World-Wide Society, 600–1750,* Madison, 1967, p. 132.

16. *E.M.R.,* p. xxx.

17. Ibid., p. 4.

18. Ibid., p. 5.

19. John Langdon, "Agricultural Equipment," in Astill and Grant, eds., *Countryside of Medieval England,* p. 96; Orwin and Orwin, *The Open Fields,* p. 12; Field, "Worcestershire Peasant Buildings," pp. 123–125.

20. Ault, *Open-Field Farming,* p. 20; Miller and Hatcher, *Medieval England,* pp. 154–155.

21. Trow-Smith, *British Livestock Husbandry,* pp. 69–70.

22. Butser Hill Ancient Farm Project; M. L. Ryder, "Livestock," in *The Agrarian History of England and Wales,* vol. 1, pt. 1, p. 349; *E.M.R.,* p. lix; Trow-Smith, *British Livestock Husbandry,* vol. 1, p. 123.

23. Ault, *Open-Field Farming,* p. 20.

24. Ibid., p. 22; Orwin and Orwin, *The Open Fields,* pp. 33–35; Homans, *English Villagers,* pp. 44–45.

25. Ault, *Open-Field Farming,* p. 23.

26. Thirsk, "Farming Techniques," in *The Agrarian History of England and Wales,* vol. 4, p. 166; *Walter of Henley,* p. 19.

27. Ibid., p. 19; J. A. Raftis, "Farming Techniques: the East Midlands," in *The Agrarian History of England and Wales,* vol. 2, p. 327.

28. *E.M.R.,* p. 249; Christopher Dyer, "Farming Techniques: the West Midlands," in *The Agrarian History of England and Wales,* vol. 2, p. 378.

29. Homans, *English Villagers,* p. 40.

30. *Walter of Henley,* p. 13; Raftis, "Farming Techniques: the East Midlands," in *The Agrarian History of England and Wales,* vol. 2, p. 327.

31. Dyer, *Lords and Peasants,* p. 69.

32. *Walter of Henley,* p. 15.

33. Maitland, *Domesday Book and Beyond,* p. 348.

34. Ault, *Open-Field Farming,* pp. 26–27.

35. *Cart. Rames.,* vol. 1, p. 311; *E.M.R.,* p. 173; Homans, *English Villagers,* pp. 269–270.

36. *Cart. Rames.,* vol. 1, p. 311.

37. Ibid., vol. 1, pp. 311, 336.

38. *E.M.R.,* p. 30.

39. Ibid., p. 3.

40. Ibid., p. 69.

41. *Cart. Rames.*, vol. 1, p. 300.

42. Britton, *Community of the Vill*, pp. 170–171; H. E. Hallam, "The Life of the People," in *The Agrarian History of England and Wales*, vol. 2, p. 838.

43. *Walter of Henley (Hosbonderie)*, p. 69.

44. Ault, *Open-Field Farming*, p. 28.

45. Cited in Ault, *Open-Field Farming*, p. 31 (*Commentary on the Laws of England*, vol. 3, p. 212, 1772).

46. *Walter of Henley*, p. 69; Homans, *English Villagers*, p. 103.

47. Hilton, *A Medieval Society*, p. 123.

48. Fernand Braudel, *Civilization and Capitalism 15th–18th Century*, vol. 1, *The Structures of Everyday Life: The Limits of the Possible*, New York, 1981, p. 124.

49. Ault, *Open-Field Farming*, p. 29.

50. *Walter of Henley (Seneschaucie)*, p. 99.

51. Ault, *Open-Field Farming*, pp. 42–43.

52. Langdon, "Agricultural Equipment," in Astill and Grant, eds., *Countryside of Medieval England*, p. 103.

53. Duby, *Rural Economy and Country Life*, p. 270; F. R. H. DuBoulay, *The Lordship of Canterbury*, London, 1966, p. 12.

54. *E.M.R.*, p. 92.

55. Langland, *Piers Plowman's Crede*, pp. 16–17.

56. Hilton, *The English Peasantry in the Later Middle Ages*, pp. 102–103.

57. Ibid., p. 105.

58. Ibid., p. 97.

59. Trow-Smith, *British Livestock Husbandry*, p. 129.

60. Ibid., p. 147.

61. Ibid., p. 159.

62. Thirsk, "Farming Techniques," in *The Agrarian History of England and Wales*, vol. 4, p. 187.

63. Miller and Hatcher, *Medieval England*, p. 217.

64. *Walter of Henley (Hosbonderie)*, pp. 76–77.

65. Trow-Smith, *British Livestock Husbandry*, p. 128.

66. Ault, *Open-Field Farming*, pp. 48–49.

67. *V.C.H. Hunts.*, p. 78.

68. Joan Thirsk, "Farming Techniques," in *The Agrarian History of England and Wales*, vol. 4, pp. 192–193.

69. Ault, *Open-Field Farming*, p. 50.

70. Trow-Smith, *British Livestock Husbandry*, pp. 117, 121; Miller and Hatcher, *Medieval England*, p. 217.

71. James Greig, "Plant Resources," in Astill and Grant, eds., *Countryside of Medieval England,* p. 121; *E.M.R.,* p. 60.

72. Raftis, "Farming Techniques," in *The Agrarian History of England and Wales,* vol. 2, p. 338; Thirsk, "Farming Techniques," in *The Agrarian History of England and Wales,* vol. 4, p. 195.

73. *Walter of Henley (Hosbonderie),* p. 77.

74. Joseph and Frances Gies, *Life in a Medieval City,* New York, 1969, pp. 102–103.

75. *E.M.R.,* p. 81.

76. Ibid., p. 303.

77. *Cart. Rames.,* vol. 1, pp. 489–490.

78. *E.M.R.,* p. 52.

79. Ibid., pp. 96, 117.

80. Ibid., p. 260.

81. Ibid., pp. 64, 111–112, 211.

82. Ibid., pp. 13, 64.

83. Ibid., p. lvii.

84. Ibid., pp. 5, 45.

85. Ibid., pp. 66, 67, 138, 141, 171, 172.

86. Henri Pirenne, *Economic and Social History of Medieval Europe,* New York, 1937, p. 88.

87. Homans, *English Villagers,* p. 236; Raftis, *Tenure and Mobility,* p. 139.

88. *E.M.R.,* pp. 6–7.

89. Postan and Titow, "Heriots and Prices on Winchester Manors."

90. Mollat, *The Poor in the Middle Ages,* p. 178.

91. Vinogradoff, *Growth of the Manor,* p. 307.

92. Hallam, "The Life of the People," in *The Agrarian History of England and Wales,* vol. 2, p. 846.

CHAPTER 8. THE PARISH

1. Miller and Hatcher, *Medieval England,* pp. 106–107.

2. John Godfrey, *The English Parish, 600–1300,* London, 1969; J. R. H. Moorman, *Church Life in England in the Thirteenth Century,* Cambridge, 1945, pp. 2–9.

3. *Cart. Rames.,* vol. 2, p. 136.

4. Moorman, *Church Life in England,* pp. 24–37; A. Hamilton Thompson, *The English Clergy and Their Organization in the Later Middle Ages,* Oxford, 1947, pp. 101–131.

5. Moorman, *Church Life in England,* pp. 26–28.

6. *Chronicon de Lanercost*, Edinburgh, 1839, p. 158, cited in Moorman, *Church Life in England*, p. 27n.

7. Moorman, *Church Life in England*, pp. 28–31; Godfrey, *The English Parish*, pp. 74–75.

8. Ibid., pp. 76–77.

9. Chaucer, *Canterbury Tales*, pp. 30–31.

10. Moorman, *Church Life in England*, pp. 90–91.

11. Ibid., pp. 92–94.

12. Ibid., pp. 95–98.

13. Myrc, *Instructions for Parish Priests*, p. 1; W. A. Pantin, *The English Church in the Fourteenth Century*, Cambridge, 1955, pp. 195–243.

14. *The Autobiography of Giraldus Cambrensis*, ed. and trans. by H. E. Williams, London, 1937, p. 40.

15. *Cart. Rames.*, vol. 1, pp. 293–294.

16. Ibid., vol. 1, p. 306.

17. Ibid., vol. 1, p. 331.

18. *Rot. Hund.*, p. 658.

19. *Cart. Rames.*, vol. 1, pp. 305–306.

20. Ibid., vol. 1, p. 293.

21. Ibid., vol. 1, p. 320.

22. *E.M.R.*, p. 196.

23. Ibid., p. 300.

24. Owst, *Preaching in Medieval England*, p. 31.

25. Moorman, *Church Life in Medieval England*, p. 59.

26. Colin Platt, *The Parish Churches of Medieval England*, London, 1981, p. 58.

27. Adhémar Esmein, *Le Mariage en droit canonique*, ed. by R. Génestal, Paris, 1929–35, vol. 1, p. 131.

28. Moorman, *Church Life in England*, pp. 64–65.

29. Manning, *Handlyng Synne*, pp. 201–203.

30. *Chronicon de Lanercost*, pp. 2–3, cited in Moorman, *Church Life in England*, p. 64.

31. Platt, *Parish Churches*, pp. 13–26.

32. Ibid., pp. 27–28.

33. P. H. Ditchfield, *Old Village Life*, London, 1920, pp. 104–105.

34. Platt, *Parish Churches*, pp. 28–29.

35. W. O. Hassall, *How They Lived: An Anthology of Original Accounts Written Before 1485*, New York, 1960, p. 344.

36. Manning, *Handlyng Synne*, pp. 217–218.

37. Moorman, *Church Life in England*, pp. 68–70.

38. Manning, *Handlyng Synne*, pp. 108–109.

39. Owst, *Preaching in Medieval England*, p. 170.

40. Ibid., p. 172.

41. Myrc, *Instructions for Parish Priests*, p. 9.

42. Moorman, *Church Life in England*, pp. 79–80.

43. Owst, *Preaching in Medieval England*, p. 319.

44. Owst, *Literature and Pulpit*, p. 156.

45. Owst, *Preaching in Medieval England*, pp. 336–337.

46. Ibid., p. 339.

47. Ibid., pp. 341–342.

48. Pantin, *English Church in the Fourteenth Century*, pp. 199–200.

49. Myrc, *Instructions for Parish Priests*, p. 26.

50. Ibid., pp. 29–43.

51. Ibid., pp. 43–48.

52. Ibid., pp. 1–3.

CHAPTER 9. VILLAGE JUSTICE

1. Homans, *English Villagers*, pp. 309–327.

2. *E.M.R.*, pp. 37–38.

3. A. E. Levett, *Studies in Manorial History*, Oxford, 1938, p. 111.

4. Homans, *English Villagers*, p. 312; *E.M.R.*, pp. 7, 34, 47, 105.

5. Levett, *Studies in Manorial History*, p. 149.

6. *E.M.R.*, p. 1.

7. Levett, *Studies in Manorial History*, p. 151.

8. *E.M.R.*, p. 153.

9. *The Court Baron*, ed. by F. W. Maitland and W. P. Baildon, London, 1891, p. 27.

10. Ibid., p. 28.

11. Homans, *English Villagers*, pp. 315–316.

12. *The Court Baron*, p. 28.

13. Homans, *English Villagers*, pp. 314–315.

14. *E.M.R.*, p. 2.

15. Martin Pimsler, "Solidarity in the Medieval Village? The Evidence of Personal Pledging at Elton, Huntingdonshire," *Journal of British Studies* 17 (1977), pp. 1–11; Britton, *Community of the Vill*, p. 104.

16. *E.M.R.*, pp. 2–7.

17. Homans, *English Villagers*, p. 315.

18. *E.M.R.*, p. 89.

19. Ibid., p. 46.

20. Homans, *English Villagers*, p. 315.

21. *E.M.R.*, pp. 30, 89.

22. Marc Bloch, *Feudal Society*, trans. by L. A. Manyon, Chicago, 1964, vol. 1, p. 271.

23. *E.M.R.*, p. 5.

24. Homans, *English Villagers*, pp. 324–325; John G. Bellamy, *Crime and Public Order in the Later Middle Ages*, London, 1973, pp. 90–91.

25. *The Court Baron*, pp. 93–94.

26. *V.C.H. Hunts.*, vol. 1, p. 159.

27. *E.M.R.*, p. 3.

28. Ibid., p. 44.

29. Ibid., p. 94.

30. Ibid., p. 31.

31. Ibid., p. 94.

32. Ibid., p. 120.

33. Ibid., p. 197.

34. Ibid., p. 102.

35. Ibid., p. 94.

36. Ibid., p. 189.

37. Ibid., p. 152.

38. Ibid., p. 3.

39. Ibid., p. 152.

40. Ibid., p. 31.

41. Gies, *Marriage and the Family*, p. 63; Jean-Louis Flandrin, "Sex in Married Life in the Early Middle Ages," in Philippe Ariès and André Béjin, *Western Sexuality*, London, 1985, pp. 140–157.

42. *E.M.R.*, pp. 31–32.

43. Ibid., p. 39.

44. Homans, *English Villagers*, pp. 312–313.

45. *E.M.R.*, p. 42.

46. Mollat, *The Poor in the Middle Ages*, p. 172.

47. Homans, *English Villagers*, p. 320.

48. *E.M.R.*, p. 200.

49. Ibid., p. 299.

50. Ibid., p. 94.

51. Ibid., p. 98.

52. Homans, *English Villagers*, p. 323.

53. Britton, *Community of the Vill,* pp. 170–171.

54. *E.M.R.,* p. 153.

55. Ibid., p. 44.

56. Ibid., p. 191.

57. Ibid., p. 146.

58. Ibid., p. 154.

59. Ibid., p. 257.

60. Ibid., p. 154.

61. Ibid., p. 42.

62. Mollat, *The Poor in the Middle Ages,* p. 171; Duby, *Rural Economy and Country Life,* pp. 253–254.

63. *E.M.R.,* p. 3.

64. Ibid., p. 30.

65. Ibid., p. 247.

66. Ibid., p. 247.

67. Ibid., p. 90.

68. W. O. Ault, *The Court Rolls of Ramsey Abbey and the Honour of Clare,* New Haven, 1928, p. xx.

69. Britton, *Community of the Vill,* pp. 174–175.

70. Levett, *Studies in Manorial History,* p. 140.

71. Vinogradoff, *Growth of the Manor,* p. 364.

72. Bellamy, *Crime and Public Order,* pp. 32–33.

73. Ibid., p. 33.

74. *Bedfordshire Coroners' Rolls,* pp. v–ix.

75. Ibid., pp. 58, 74, 76–77, 89–90.

76. Ibid., *passim.; E.M.R.,* p. 238.

77. Bellamy, *Crime and Public Order,* p. 30.

78. Ibid., p. 160.

79. Ibid., p. 113.

80. Ibid., p. 87.

81. Ibid., p. 188.

82. *Bedfordshire Coroners' Rolls,* p. 107.

CHAPTER 10. THE PASSING OF THE MEDIEVAL VILLAGE

1. H. C. Darby, "Domesday England," and R. E. Glasscock, "England Circa 1334," both in Darby, ed., *A New Historical Geography,* pp. 45–47, 143–145; Hallam, "Population Movements in England, 1086–1350," in *The Agrarian History of England and Wales,* vol. 2, p. 536, gives higher estimates.

2. J. C. Russell, "Late Medieval Population Patterns," *Speculum* 20 (1945), p. 164.

3. Ian Kershaw, "The Great Famine and Agrarian Crisis in England, 1315–1322," in Hilton, ed., *Peasants, Knights, and Heretics*, p. 95.

4. Ibid., pp. 93–94, 102–104.

5. Alan H. R. Baker, "Changes in the Later Middle Ages," in Darby, ed., *A New Historical Geography*, pp. 291–318.

6. *E.M.R.*, p. 337.

7. Ibid., p. 342.

8. Ibid., p. 351.

9. Ibid., p. 359.

10. Ibid., p. 361.

11. Ibid., p. 342.

12. Ibid., p. 364.

13. Ibid., p. 383.

14. Ibid., p. 373.

15. Ibid., p. 373.

16. Raftis, *Estates of Ramsey Abbey*, p. 253.

17. R. H. Hilton, *Bondmen Made Free: Medieval Peasant Movements and the English Rising of 1381*, New York, 1973, p. 147.

18. Ibid., p. 148.

19. Ibid., pp. 160–162.

20. Duby, *Rural Economy and Country Life*, p. 334.

21. Froissart, *Chronicles*, trans. by Geoffrey Brereton, Harmondsworth, England, 1968, p. 212.

22. Thomas Walsingham, *Historia Anglicana*, cited in R. B. Dobson, *The Peasants' Revolt of 1381*, London, 1970, pp. 373–375.

23. Hilton, *Bondmen Made Free*, p. 227.

24. Cited in Maurice Ashley, *Great Britain to 1688*, Ann Arbor, 1961, p. 147.

25. Hilton, *Transition from Feudalism to Capitalism*, p. 25; Dyer, *Lords and Peasants*, pp. 285–286; *V.C.H. Hunts.*, vol. 1, p. 84.

26. Duby, *Rural Economy and Country Life*, p. 357.

27. *V.C.H. Hunts.*, p. 162.

28. Beresford, *Lost Villages*, p. 166.

29. R. A. Donkin, "Changes in the Early Middle Ages," and Baker, "Changes in the Later Middle Ages," both in Darby, ed., *A New Historical Geography*, pp. 82, 208, 212.

30. Bigmore, *Bedfordshire and Huntingdonshire Landscape*, p. 132.

31. Ibid., pp. 126–127.

32. Cited in Bigmore, *Bedfordshire and Huntingdonshire Landscape,* p. 136.

33. Baker, "Changes in the Later Middle Ages," in Darby, ed., *A New Historical Geography,* p. 211.

34. Ibid., p. 242.

35. Braudel, *Civilization and Capitalism,* vol. 1, p. 123.

36. Peter Laslett, *The World We Have Lost: England in the Industrial Age,* New York, 1971, p. 35.

37. Joan Thirsk, "Farming Techniques," in *The Agrarian History of England and Wales,* vol. 4, pp. 180–181.

38. Ault, *Open-Field Farming,* p. 143.

39. Dyer, *Lords and Peasants,* p. 372.

40. Ault, *Open-Field Farming,* p. 78.

41. *V.C.H. Hunts.,* p. 160.

42. Marc Bloch in *The Cambridge Economic History of Europe,* vol. 1, *The Agrarian Life of the Middle Ages,* ed. by M. M. Postan, Cambridge, 1966, p. 61.

BIBLIOGRAPHY

The Agrarian History of England and Wales. H. P. R. Finberg, general editor. Vol. 1, Pt. 1, *Prehistory,* edited by Stuart Piggott, Cambridge, 1981. Vol. 1, Pt. 2, *A.D. 43–1042,* edited by H. P. R. Finberg, Cambridge, 1972. Vol. 2, *1042–1350,* edited by H. E. Hallam, Cambridge, 1988. Vol. 4, *1500–1640,* edited by Joan Thirsk, Cambridge, 1967.

Alcock, N. W. "The Medieval Cottages of Bishops Clyst, Devon." *Medieval Archaeology* 9 (1965): 146–153.

The Anglo-Saxon Chronicles. Translated by Anne Savage. London, 1983.

Ariès, Philippe, and André Béjin, eds. *Western Sexuality: Practice and Precept in Past and Present Times.* London, 1985.

Astill, Grenville, and Annie Grant, eds. *The Countryside of Medieval England.* Oxford, 1988.

Ault, Warren O. *Open-Field Farming in Medieval England: A Study of Village By-Laws.* New York, 1972.

———. *Open-Field Husbandry and the Village Community: A Study of Agrarian By-Laws in Medieval England.* Philadelphia, 1965.

The Autobiography of Giraldus Cambrensis. Edited and translated by H. E. Williams. London, 1937.

Barley, M. W. *The English Farmhouse and Cottage.* London, 1961.

Bedfordshire Coroners' Rolls. Translated by R. F. Hunnisett. *Bedfordshire Historical Record Society* 41 (1961).

Bellamy, John G. *Crime and Public Order in the Later Middle Ages.* London, 1973.

Bennett, H. S. *Life on the English Manor, A Study of Peasant Conditions, 1150–1400.* Cambridge, 1960 (first published in 1937).

Beresford, Maurice. *Studies in Leicestershire Agrarian History.* London, 1949.

Beresford, Maurice, and John G. Hurst, eds. *Deserted Medieval Villages.* London, 1971.

Bigmore, Peter. *The Bedfordshire and Huntingdonshire Landscape.* London, 1979.

Blair, Peter Hunter. *An Introduction to Anglo-Saxon England.* Cambridge, 1966.

Bloch, Marc. *Feudal Society.* Translated by L. A. Manyon. 2 vols. Chicago, 1964.

————. *Slavery and Serfdom in the Middle Ages.* Translated by William R. Beer. Berkeley, 1975.

Braudel, Fernand. *Civilization and Capitalism 15th–18th Century.* Vol. 1, *The Structures of Everyday Life: The Limits of the Possible.* New York, 1981.

Britton, Edward. *The Community of the Vill: A Study in the History of the Family and Village Life in Fourteenth-Century England.* Toronto, 1977.

————. "The Peasant Family in Fourteenth-Century England." *Peasant Studies* 5 (1976): 2–7.

Cam, Helen. *Liberties and Communities in Medieval England: Collected Studies in Local Administration and Topography.* Cambridge, 1933.

Cantor, Leonard, ed. *The English Medieval Landscape.* Philadelphia, 1982.

Cartularium monasterii de Ramesia. Edited by William H. Hart. 3 vols. London, 1884–1893.

Carus-Wilson, E. M. *Essays in Economic History.* London, 1962.

Chapelot, Jean, and Robert Fossier. *The Village and House in the Middle Ages.* Translated by Henry Cleere. Berkeley, 1985.

Chaucer, Geoffrey. *The Canterbury Tales.* Translated by Nevill Coghill. Baltimore, 1960.

Chertsey Abbey Court Rolls Abstracts. Edited by E. Toms. *Surrey Record Society* 38 (1937) and 48 (1954).

Chronicon abbatiae Rameseiensis. Edited by W. Dunn Macray. London, 1886.

Chronicon de Lanercost. Edited by J. Stevenson. Edinburgh, 1839.

Clark, Elaine. "Some Aspects of Social Security in Medieval England." *Journal of Family History* 7 (1982): 307–320.

Colman, F. S. *A History of the Parish of Barwick-in-Elmet, in the County of York.* Thoresby Society 17 (1908).

Colvin, H. M. "Domestic Architecture and Town Planning," in A. Lane Poole, ed., *Medieval England,* vol. 1: 77–97. London, 1958.

Coulton, G. G. *Medieval Village, Manor, and Monastery.* New York, 1969 (first published in 1925).

The Court Baron. Edited by F. W. Maitland and W. P. Baildon. London, 1891.

Court Roll of Chalgrave Manor. Edited by Marian K. Dale. *Bedfordshire Historical Record Society* 28 (1950).

Court Rolls of the Abbey of Ramsey and the Honour of Clare. Edited by Warren O. Ault. New Haven, 1928.

Court Rolls of the Manor of Carshalton from the Reign of Edward III to That of Henry VII. Translated by D. L. Powell. *Surrey Record Society* 2 (1916).

Court Rolls of the Wiltshire Manors of Adam de Stratton. Edited by R. B. Pugh. *Wiltshire Archaeological Society Record Series* 24 (1970).

Custumals of the Manors of Laughton, Willingdon, and Goring. Edited by A. E. Wilson. *Sussex Record Society* 60 (1961).

Custumals of the Sussex Manors of the Archbishop of Canterbury. Edited by B. C. Redwood and A. E. Wilson. *Sussex Record Society* 57 (1958).

Cutts, E. L. *Parish Priests and Their People in the Middle Ages in England.* London, 1898.

Darby, H. C. *A New Historical Geography of England Before 1600.* Cambridge, 1973.

Davenport, Frances G. *The Economic Development of a Norfolk Manor, 1086–1565.* Cambridge, 1906.

Denholm-Young, N. *Collected Papers on Medieval Subjects.* Oxford, 1946.

De Windt, Anne. "A Peasant Land Market and Its Participants, King's Ripton (1280–1400)." *Midland History* 4 (1978): 142–159.

De Windt, Edwin. *Land and People in Holywell-cum-Needingworth: Structures of Tenure and Patterns of Social Organization in an East Midlands Village, 1253–1457.* Toronto, 1972.

Ditchfield, P. H. *Old Village Life.* London, 1920.

Dobson, R. B., ed. *The Peasants' Revolt of 1381.* London, 1970.

Dodwell, Barbara. "Holdings and Inheritance in East Anglia." *Economic History Review,* 2nd ser., 20 (1967): 53–66.

Du Boulay, F. R. H. *The Lordship of Canterbury.* London, 1966.

Duby, Georges. *Rural Economy and Country Life in the Medieval West.* Translated by Cynthia Postan. Columbia, S.C. 1968.

Dyer, Christopher. "Families and Land in the West Midlands," in R. M. Smith, ed., *Land, Kinship, and Life Cycle.* Cambridge, 1986: 305–311.

————. *Lords and Peasants in a Changing Society: The Estates of the Bishopric of Worcester, 680–1540.* Cambridge, 1980.

Edgington, Susan B. "Pagan Peverel: An Anglo-Norman Crusader." In P. Edbury, ed., *Crusade and Settlement.* Cardiff, 1985.

————. "Ramsey Abbey vs. Pagan Peverel, St. Ives, 1107." *Records of Huntingdonshire* 2 (1985).

Ekwall, Eilert. *Concise Oxford Dictionary of English Place Names.* Oxford, 1947.

Elton Manorial Records, 1279–1352. Edited by S. C. Ratcliff, translated by D. M. Gregory. Cambridge, 1946 (privately printed for the Roxburghe Club).

English, Barbara. *A Study in Feudal Society: The Lords of Holderness, 1086–1260.* Oxford, 1979.

Esmein, Adhémar. *Le Mariage en droit canonique.* Edited by R. Génestal. 2 vols. Paris, 1929–1935.

The Estate Book of Henry de Bray, Northamptonshire c. 1289–1340. Edited by D. Willis. *Camden Society*, 3rd ser., 27 (1916).

Faith, Rosamond J. "Peasant Families and Inheritance Customs in Medieval England." *Agricultural History Review* 4 (1966): 77–95.

Field, John. *English Field-Names, a Dictionary.* Newton Abbot, 1972.

Field, R. K. "Worcestershire Peasant Buildings, Household Goods, and Farming Equipment in the Later Middle Ages." *Medieval Archaeology* 9 (1965): 105–145.

Finberg, H. P. R. *Tavistock Abbey: A Study in the Social and Economic History of Devon.* Cambridge, 1951.

Froissart, Jean. *Chronicles.* Translated by Geoffrey Brereton. Harmondsworth, England, 1968.

Gasquet, F. A. *Parish Life in Medieval England.* London, 1929.

Gies, Joseph and Frances. *Life in a Medieval Castle.* New York, 1974.

————. *Life in a Medieval City.* New York, 1969.

————. *Marriage and the Family in the Middle Ages.* New York, 1987.

Godfrey, John. *The English Parish, 600–1300.* London, 1969.

Gower, John. *Le Miroir de l'Omme.* In *Complete Works of John Gower.* Edited by G. C. Macaulay. 4 vols. Oxford, 1899–1902.

Gray, Howard L. *English Field Systems.* Cambridge, Mass., 1915.

Hali Meidenhod. Edited by Oswald Cockayne. London, 1922.

Hanawalt, Barbara. "Childrearing Among the Lower Classes of Medieval England." *Journal of Interdisciplinary History* 8 (1972): 1–22.

————. "Community, Conflict, and Social Control: Crime in the Ramsey Abbey Villages." *Mediaeval Studies* 39 (1977): 402–423.

————. *Crime and Conflict in English Communities, 1300–1348.* Cambridge, Mass., 1979.

————. *The Ties That Bound: Peasant Families in Medieval England.* New York, 1986.

Harvey, P. D. A. *A Medieval Oxfordshire Village: Cuxham, 1240 to 1400.* Oxford, 1965.

Hassall, W. O. *How They Lived: An Anthology of Original Accounts Written Before 1485.* New York, 1962.

Hilton, Rodney H. *Bond Men Made Free, Medieval Peasant Movements and the English Rising of 1381.* New York, 1973.

————. "The Content and Sources of English Agrarian History Before 1500." *Agricultural History Review* 3 (1955): 3–19.

————. *The Decline of Serfdom in Medieval England.* London, 1969.

———. *The English Peasantry in the Later Middle Ages.* Oxford, 1975.

———. "Medieval Agrarian History," in *The Victoria County History of Leicestershire* 2 (1954): 145–198.

———. *A Medieval Society: The West Midlands at the End of the Thirteenth Century.* New York, 1966.

———, ed. *Peasants, Knights, and Heretics: Studies in Medieval English Social History.* Cambridge, 1981.

———, ed. *The Transition from Feudalism to Capitalism.* London, 1984.

Homans, George C. *English Villagers of the Thirteenth Century.* New York, 1975 (first published in 1941).

———. "The Rural Sociology of Medieval England." *Past and Present* 4 (1953): 32–43.

Hoskins, W. G. *The Making of the English Landscape.* London, 1955.

———. *The Midland Peasant: The Economic and Social History of a Leicestershire Village.* London, 1957.

Howell, Cecily. *Land, Family, and Inheritance in Transition, Kibworth Harcourt 1288–1709.* Cambridge, 1983.

———. "Peasant Inheritance Customs in the Midlands, 1280–1700," in Jack Goody, ed., *Rural Society in Western Europe.* Cambridge, 1976: 112–155.

Johnston, James B. *The Place Names of England and Wales.* London, 1915.

Jones, Andrew. "Harvest Customs and Labourers' Perquisites in Southern England, 1150–1350." *Agricultural History Review* 25 (1977): 14–22, 98–107.

Kerridge, E. "A Reconsideration of Some Former Husbandry Practices." *Agricultural History Review* 3 (1955): 27–38.

Kosminsky, E. A. *Studies in the Agrarian History of England in the Thirteenth Century.* Oxford, 1956.

Langland, William. *The Vision and Creed of Piers Plowman.* Edited by Thomas Wright. London, 1887.

———. *The Vision of Piers Plowman.* Edited by A. V. C. Schmidt. London, 1984.

Laslett, Peter. *The World We Have Lost: England Before the Industrial Age.* New York, 1971.

Lennard, R. *Rural England 1086–1135: A Study of Social and Agrarian Conditions.* Oxford, 1959.

Le Roy Ladurie, Emmanuel. *Montaillou, the Promised Land of Error.* Translated by Barbara Bray. New York, 1978.

Levett, A. E. *Studies in Manorial History.* Oxford, 1938.

Maitland, Frederic William. *Domesday Book and Beyond, Three Essays in the Early History of England.* New York, 1966 (first published in 1897).

Manning, Robert. *Handlyng Synne.* Edited by Idelle Sullens. Binghamton, New York, 1983.

Mawer, A., and F. M. Stenton. *The Place-Names of Bedfordshire and Huntingdonshire.* London, 1926.

Medieval Customs of the Manors of Taunton and Bradford-on-Tone. Edited by T. J. Hunt. *Somerset Record Society* 66 (1962).

Miller, Edward, and John Hatcher. *Medieval England: Rural Society and Economic Change, 1086–1348.* London, 1978.

Mollat, Michel. *The Poor in the Middle Ages, an Essay in Social History.* Translated by Arthur Goldhammer. New Haven, 1986.

Moore, Ellen W. *The Fairs of Medieval England: An Introductory Study.* Toronto, 1985.

Moorman, J. R. H. *Church Life in England in the Thirteenth Century.* Cambridge, 1945.

Myrc, John. *Instructions for Parish Priests.* Edited by E. Peacock. London, 1868.

Orwin, C. S., and C. S. Orwin. *The Open Fields.* Oxford, 1967.

Owst, G. R. *Literature and Pulpit in Medieval England.* Oxford, 1961.

————. *Preaching in Medieval England.* Oxford, 1926.

Page, F. M. *The Estates of Crowland Abbey: A Study in Manorial Organization.* Cambridge, 1934.

Pantin, W. A. *The English Church in the Fourteenth Century.* Cambridge, 1955.

Peckham, W. D., ed. "Thirteen Custumals of the Sussex Manors of the Bishop of Chichester." *Sussex Record Society Publications* 31 (1925).

Pfander, Homer G. *The Popular Sermon of the Medieval Friar in England.* New York, 1937.

Phythian-Adams, C. *Continuity, Fields, and Fission: The Making of a Midland Parish.* Leicester University, Department of English Local History, Occasional Papers, 3rd ser., 4 (1978).

Pimsler, Martin. "Solidarity in the Medieval Village? The Evidence of Personal Pledging at Elton, Huntingdonshire." *Journal of British Studies* 17 (1977): 1–11.

Pirenne, Henri. *Economic and Social History of Medieval Europe.* Translated by I. E. Clegg. New York, 1937.

Platt, Colin. *The Parish Churches of Medieval England.* London, 1981.

Platts, Graham. *Land and People in Medieval Lincolnshire.* Lincoln, England, 1985.

Pollock, F., and F. W. Maitland. *The History of English Law Before the Time of Edward I.* Cambridge, 1968.

Postan, M. M. *Essays on Medieval Agriculture and General Problems of the Medieval Economy.* Cambridge, 1968.

————. "The Famulus: The Estate Labourer in the Twelfth and Thirteenth Centuries." *Economic History Review Supplement No. 2.* Cambridge, 1954.

———. *The Medieval Economy and Society: An Economic History of Britain, 1100–1500.* Berkeley, 1972.

———. "Village Livestock in the Thirteenth Century." *Economic History Review,* 2nd ser., 15 (1962): 219–249.

Postan, M. M., and J. Z. Titow. "Heriots and Prices on Winchester Manors." *Economic History Review,* 2nd ser., 11 (1959): 392–413.

Raftis, J. A. *The Estates of Ramsey Abbey: A Study of Economic Growth and Organization.* Toronto, 1957.

———, ed. *Pathways to Medieval Peasants.* Toronto, 1981.

———. "Social Structures in Five East Midland Villages: A Study of Possibilities in the Use of Court Roll Data." *Economic History Review,* 2nd. ser., 18 (1965): 83–100.

———. *Tenure and Mobility: Studies in the Social History of the Mediaeval English Village.* Toronto, 1964.

———. *Warboys: Two Hundred Years in the Life of an English Mediaeval Village.* Toronto, 1974.

Razi, Zvi. *Life, Death, and Marriage in a Medieval Parish: Economy, Society, and Demography in Halesowen, 1270–1400.* Cambridge, 1980.

Reynolds, Robert R. *Europe Emerges: Transition Toward an Industrial World-Wide Society, 600–1750.* Madison, 1967.

Richardson, H. G. "The Parish Clergy of the Thirteenth and Fourteenth Centuries." *Transactions of the Royal Historical Society,* 3rd ser., 6 (1912): 89–128.

Roberti Grosseteste epistolae episcopi quondam Lincolniensis. Edited by H. R. Luard. London, 1861.

Roberts, Brian K. *The Making of the English Village, a Study in Historical Geography.* London, 1987.

———. "Village Plans in County Durham: A Preliminary Statement." *Medieval Archaeology* 16 (1972): 33–56.

Rotuli hundredorum tempore Hen. III & Edw. I in Turr' Lond' et in curia receptae scaccarii Westm. asservati. 2 vols. London, 1812, 1818.

Rowley, Trevor, ed. *The Origins of Open-Field Agriculture.* London, 1981.

Rowley, Trevor, and John Wood. *Deserted Villages.* Aylesbury, England, 1982.

Russell, J. C. "Late Medieval Population Patterns." *Speculum* 20 (1945).

Saul, Nigel. *Scenes from Provincial Life, Knightly Families in Sussex, 1280–1400.* Oxford, 1987.

Sawyer, P. H., ed. *Medieval Settlement: Continuity and Change.* London, 1976.

Scammell, Jean. "Freedom and Marriage in Medieval England." *Economic History Review* 27 (1974): 523–537.

————. "Wife-Rents and Merchet." *Economic History Review,* 2nd ser., 29 (1976): 487–490.

Schumer, Beryl. *The Evolution of Wychwood to 1400: Pioneers, Frontiers, and Forests.* Leicester University, Department of English Local History, Occasional Papers, 3rd ser., 6 (1984).

Searle, Eleanor. "Freedom and Marriage in Medieval England: An Alternative Hypothesis." *Economic History Review,* 2nd ser., 29 (1970): 482–490.

————. *Lordship and Community: Battle Abbey and Its Banlieu.* Toronto, 1974.

————. "Seigneurial Control of Women's Marriage: The Antecedents and Function of Merchet in England." *Past and Present* 82 (1979): 3–43.

Seebohm, F. *The English Village Community: An Essay on Economic History.* London, 1883.

Select Cases from the Coroners' Rolls. Edited by G. J. Turner. London, 1896.

Select Cases from the Ecclesiastical Courts of the Province of Canterbury, c. 1200–1301. Edited by Norma Adams and Charles Donahue. London, 1981.

Select Civil Pleas, A.D. 1200–1203. Edited by William Paley Baildon. London, 1896.

Select Pleas in Manorial and Other Seignorial Courts, Hen. III–Edw. I. Edited by F. W. Maitland. London, 1889.

Spufford, M. *A Cambridgeshire Community: Chippenham from Settlement to Enclosure.* Leicester University, Department of English Local History, Occasional Papers 20 (1964).

Stenton, Frank M. *Anglo-Saxon England.* Oxford, 1971.

Stow, John. *Survey of London.* Edited by H. B. Wheatley. London, 1956.

Stuckert, Howard M. *Corrodies in the English Monasteries: A Study in English Social History of the Middle Ages.* Philadelphia, 1923.

Tacitus. *De vita Iulii Agricola and De Germania.* Edited by Alfred Gudeman. Boston, 1928.

Taylor, C. C. "Polyfocal Settlement and the English Village." *Medieval Archaeology* 21 (1977): 189–193.

Thirsk, Joan. *The Rural Economy of England, Collected Essays.* London, 1984.

Thompson, A. Hamilton. *The English Clergy and Their Organization in the Later Middle Ages.* Oxford, 1947.

Titow, J. Z. *English Rural Society, 1200–1350.* London, 1969.

————. *Winchester Yields: A Study in Medieval Agricultural Productivity.* Cambridge, 1972.

Trow-Smith, Robert. *History of British Livestock Husbandry.* 2 vols. London, 1957–1959.

Victoria History of the Counties of England: Huntingdonshire. Edited by W. Page and G. Proby. 3 vols. London, 1926, 1932, 1936.

Vinogradoff, Paul. *The Growth of the Manor.* London, 1911.

Walter of Henley's Husbandry, Together with an Anonymous Husbandry, Seneschaucie, etc. Edited by E. Lamond. London, 1890.

West, Stanley. "The Anglo-Saxon Village of West Stow: An Interim Report of the Excavations, 1965–1968." *Medieval Archaeology* 13 (1969): 1–20.

White, Lynn, Jr. *Medieval Technology and Social Change.* Oxford, 1978 (first published in 1962).

Wood, Margaret. *The English Mediaeval House.* London, 1965.

GLOSSARY

AD CENSUM Status of villeins who pay a cash rent in lieu of labor services.

AD OPUS Status of villeins owing labor services.

AMERCEMENT Fine.

ASSART Tract of wasteland cleared or drained to be added to village arable.

ASSIZE OF BREAD AND ALE Royal law fixing prices and standards.

BAILIFF The lord's chief official on the manor.

BALK Turf left unplowed to provide separation between strips.

BEADLE Manorial official, usually assistant to reeve.

BONDMAN Serf, q.v., villein.

BOON-WORK Obligation of tenants for special work services, notably the lord's harvest.

BYLAWS Rules made by open-field villagers governing cultivation and grazing.

CELLARER Official of a monastery responsible for food supplies.

CENSUARIUS Tenant *ad censum.*

CHARTER Official document, usually deed or grant of privilege.

CHEVAGE Payment, typically in kind, owed annually by villein living outside the manor.

CORRODY Old age pension, usually purchasable from a monastery, consisting of lodging, food, and incidentals.

COTTER Tenant of a cottage, usually holding little or no land.

CROFT Garden plot of a village house.

CURIA Courtyard.

CUSTUMAL Document listing obligations and rights of tenants.

DEMESNE Part of the manor cultivated directly by the lord.

DISTRAINT Summons or arrest.

ESSOIN Excuse for non-attendance in court, or delay permitted a defendant.

EXTENT Document enumerating lands, services, and rents of a manor.

EYRE Royal circuit court ("justices in eyre").

FARM Lease.

FEE, FIEF Land granted by a lord in return for services.

FEUDALISM Medieval social and political system by which the lord-vassal relationship was defined.

FRANKPLEDGE Police system by which every member of a tithing was responsible for the conduct of every other member.

FURLONG Plot of arable land, subdivision of a field.

GERSUM Entry fee for taking possession of a tenancy.

GLEBE Land assigned to support the parish church.

GORE Wedge of arable land created by irregularity of terrain and plowing in strips.

HALLMOTE Manorial court.

HAMSOKEN Assault in the victim's own house.

HAYWARD OR MESSOR Lesser manorial official; assistant to reeve.

HEADLAND Segment of land left at end of plow strips for turning plow around.

HERIOT Death duty, usually "best beast" or other chattel, paid to lord.

HEUSHIRE House rent.

HIDE Tax assessment unit of land area, varying in size, theoretically 120 acres.

HUE-AND-CRY Criminal apprehension system by which all within earshot were required to give chase to the malefactor.

HUNDRED Administrative division of English shire (county).

INFANGENETHEF Right to prosecute thieves caught in the act within a territory and to confiscate their goods.

LEIRWITE Fine levied against an unmarried woman for sexual misconduct.

LOVE-DAY *(DIES AMORIS)* Opportunity given litigants to reconcile differences.

MANOR Estate consisting of lord's demesne and tenants' holdings.

MERCHET Fee paid by villein for a daughter's marriage.

MESSUAGE House and yard.

MORTUARY Death duty paid by villein to parish church, usually second-best beast or chattel.

MULTURE Portion of meal or flour kept by the miller in payment for his services.

PANNAGE Fee to allow pigs to feed on forest mast.

PINFOLD OR PUNFOLD The lord's pound for stray animals.

PLEDGING Legal institution by which one villager served as guaranty for another's court appearance, veracity, good conduct, payment of a debt, etc.

QUARTER Unit of volume, eight bushels.

REEVE Principal manorial official under the bailiff, always a villein.

RING Unit of volume, four bushels.

SEISIN Legal possession of a property.

SELION Plow strip.

SERF Peasant burdened with week-work, merchet, tallage, and other obligations; bondman, villein.

STEWARD OR SENESCHAL Chief official of an estate, supervisor of the lord's manors.

SUIT Attendance.

TALLAGE Annual tax levied by lord on villeins.

TALLY, TALLY-STICK Reeve's method of accounting for manor's production, deliveries, receipts, and expenditures; notched stick on which it was kept.

TITHE Payment to church consisting of a tenth of produce.

TITHING Unit of ten or twelve village men mutually responsible for each other's conduct.

TOFT Yard of a village house.

VILLEIN English term for serf.

VIRGATE Land unit theoretically sufficient to support a peasant family, varying between 18 and 32 acres (in Elton, 24).

WARDENS OF AUTUMN Officials appointed by the villagers to help supervise harvest work.

WARDSHIP Right of guardianship exercised by a lord over a minor.

WEEK-WORK Principal labor obligation of a villein, comprising plowing and other work every week throughout the year.

WOODWARD Manorial official in charge of the lord's woodland.

INDEX

COPYRIGHT ACKNOWLEDGMENTS